Learning to Teach ICT in the Secondary School

This book is designed specifically for students training to teach ICT as a curriculum subject at secondary level. It develops the key ideas of teaching and learning in ICT in a structured, accessible way, and provides a wealth of ideas and inspiration for the learning teacher. Key areas covered are:

- The place and nature of ICT as curriculum subject
- Analysing and developing your own subject knowledge
- Planning schemes of work, individual lessons, activities and resources
- Monitoring, assessment and exams
- ICT across the curriculum
- Differentiation and Special Education Needs
- Professional development

Throughout the book there are useful tasks and activities to help you analyse your own teaching and explore the knowledge and skills needed to become a successful teacher of ICT. Rooted in best practice and up-to-the minute research, this book is also the ideal refresher for more experienced ICT teachers.

Steve Kennewell teaches on the Secondary PGCE course in ICT at the University of Wales Swansea. **Howard Tanner** teaches on the PGCE Mathematics course and **John Parkinson** teaches on the PGCE Science course, also at the University of Wales Swansea.

Related titles

Learning to Teach Subjects in the Secondary School Series

Series Editors
Susan Capel, Canterbury Christ Church College; Marilyn Leask, De Montfort University, Bedford; and Tony Turner, Institute of Education, University of London.

Designed for all students learning to teach in secondary schools, and particularly those on school-based initial teacher training courses, the books in this series complement *Learning to Teach in the Secondary School* and its companion, *Starting to Teach in the Secondary School*. Each book in the series applies underpinning theory and addresses practical issues to support students in school and in the training institution in learning how to teach a particular subject.

Learning to Teach English in the Secondary School
Jon Davison and Jane Dowson

Learning to Teach Modern Foreign Languages in the Secondary School, second edition
Norbert Pachler and Kit Field

Learning to Teach History in the Secondary School, second edition
Terry Haydn, James Arthur and Martin Hunt

Learning to Teach Physical Education in the Secondary School
Edited by Susan Capel

Learning to Teach Science in the Secondary School
Tony Turner and Wendy DiMarco

Learning to Teach Mathematics in the Secondary School
Edited by Sue Johnston-Wilder, Peter Johnston-Wilder, David Pimm and John Westwell

Learning to Teach Religious Education in the Secondary School
Edited by Andrew Wright and Ann-Marie Brandom

Learning to Teach Art and Design in the Secondary School
Edited by Nicholas Addison and Lesley Burgess

Learning to Teach Geography in the Secondary School
David Lambert and David Balderstone

Learning to Teach Design and Technology in the Secondary School
Edited by Gwyneth Owen-Jackson

Learning to Teach Music in the Secondary School
Edited by Chris Philpott

Learning to Teach in the Secondary School, third edition
Edited by Susan Capel, Marilyn Leask and Tony Turner

Learning to Teach ICT in the Secondary School
Edited by Steve Kennewell, John Parkinson and Howard Tanner

Learning to Teach ICT in the Secondary School

A Companion to School Experience

Edited by
Steve Kennewell, John Parkinson and
Howard Tanner

RoutledgeFalmer
Taylor & Francis Group

LONDON AND NEW YORK

First published 2003 by RoutledgeFalmer
11 New Fetter Lane, London EC4P 4EE

Simultaneously published in the USA and Canada
by RoutledgeFalmer
29 West 35th Street, New York, NY 10001

Reprinted 2003

RoutledgeFalmer is an imprint of the Taylor & Francis Group

© 2003 Selection and editorial matter: Steve Kennewell, John Parkinson and Howard Tanner;
Individual chapters: the contributors

Typeset in 10.5/12pt Mono Bembo by Graphicraft Limited, Hong Kong
Printed and bound in Great Britain by TJ International Ltd, Padstow, Cornwall

British Library Cataloguing in Publication Data
A catalogue record for this book is available from the British Library

Library of Congress Cataloging in Publication Data
A catalog record has been requested.

ISBN 0-415-27669-1

Contents

Illustrations

TABLES

FIGURES

TASKS

Contributors

Dave Hendley is Lecturer in Education, specialising in Design and Technology, at the University of Wales Swansea. He leads the Secondary PGCE Design and Technology course and his research interests include pupils' attitudes to and perceptions of D&T, and learning skills through CAD/CAM.

Ian Hughes is head of ICT at Bishop Gore Comprehensive School, Swansea. He teaches on the IT PGCE course at the University of Wales Swansea as an associate tutor, and is researching the impact of effective ICT teaching on pupils' learning across the curriculum.

Chris Jones is Senior Lecturer in Education at the University of Sunderland. He specialises in information technology as a subject and leads initial teacher education programmes in IT.

Dr Steve Kennewell leads the Secondary PGCE course for IT specialists at the University of Wales Swansea, as well as directing the department's graduate studies courses. His research interests cover most aspects of ICT in education, with a particular specialism in teaching and learning ICT as a subject. He is co-author of *Computer Studies through Applications* (with Chris Mitton, Ian Selwood and Peter Fox, 1989) and *Developing the ICT-capable School* (with John Parkinson and Howard Tanner, 2000).

Dr John Parkinson teaches on the PGCE Science course at the University of Wales Swansea and leads Masters' courses on school improvement. His research interests include the use of ICT to promote pupils' learning. He is the author of *The Effective Teaching of Secondary Science* (1994) and *Reflective Practice in Science 11–18* (2002) and co-author of *Developing the ICT-capable School* (with Steve Kennewell and Howard Tanner, 2000).

Neil Stanley is Senior Lecturer in Educational Information Technology at Liverpool John Moores University. He leads the IT teacher education programmes and his research interests include assessment and issues in the area of information skills.

Dr Howard Tanner teaches on the Secondary PGCE course at the University of Wales Swansea, commended by HMI for its quality, particularly its effective use of ICT. His research interests include evaluating the impact of ICT on thinking and learning in the secondary school. He is co-author of *Developing the ICT-capable School* (with Steve Kennewell and John Parkinson, 2000), *Becoming a Successful Teacher of Mathematics* (with Sonia Jones, 2000) and *Developing Numeracy in the Secondary School* (with Sonia Jones and A. Davies, 2002).

Acknowledgements

Thanks to Lillian Potter at Park High School, Birkenhead, for the sample documents in Chapter 7 and to Teresa Farran of Liverpool John Moores University for the subject knowledge audit on which the appendix is based.

Introduction

This book is intended primarily for people who are training to become specialist teachers of Information and Communication Technology (ICT), or have recently qualified as ICT teachers, or who are teaching ICT without the benefit of specialist training for the subject. As the first book which addresses learning how to teach ICT specifically it will also be of value to more experienced ICT teachers, who can use it to help them reflect on their own practice and incorporate new ideas. Finally, it will be a helpful resource for tutors of ICT specialist student teachers.

ICT has regularly been highlighted by the school inspection bodies in England and Wales as the National Curriculum subject that is least well taught (Estyn, 2002), and achievement in the subject is still unsatisfactory for a large number of pupils (Ofsted, 2002). The inspectors acknowledge that there is much good practice in teaching ICT as a subject to be found, but we feel that there has been little effort to date to develop and disseminate knowledge concerning effective teaching strategies. Furthermore, much teaching of ICT has been carried out by non-specialists: teachers with some ICT skills have often been expected to teach the subject without specialist training. This book contributes to the improvement of ICT teaching by setting out systematically many of the issues which need to be considered and the strategies we have found to be effective. The text is structured in order to induct new and non-specialist teachers into an ICT teaching community within which they can continue to share ideas and develop their skills beyond the initial period of preparation and teaching practice.

Part I orients you to the nature of ICT in secondary schools and helps you to understand the cultural norms associated with it. It should stimulate reflection on your personal ICT knowledge, and promote further learning within a framework of application in teaching rather than information systems for commerce and industry.

Part II structures the essential basic matters in which the new ICT teacher must quickly gain confidence during early classroom experience. It promotes the development of skill and understanding in the planning of lessons, the preparation of resources, the selection and implementation of teaching strategies, the management of the classroom and the monitoring of progress. Emphasis is placed on factors for which we have evidence of their impact on attainment in other subjects, such as whole class interaction, reflective discussion, cooperative group work, challenging activities and high expectations.

Part III expands on particular aspects of teaching and learning ICT – assessment, examination courses and special educational needs – and Part IV on wider issues concerning the improvement of ICT teaching in secondary schools – cross-curricular ICT, phase transition, and continuing professional development.

We have included a considerable amount of practical advice. Sometimes this is supported by research evidence or formal professional documentation, and we make reference to these sources where appropriate. Most of it, however, is based on the professional experience, observation and reflection of a number of experienced teachers and initial teacher education (ITE) tutors. You may find that the ideas sometimes conflict with advice offered by your tutors, and you need to make judgements which combine our general principles with the knowledge of local contexts which your own tutors bring to their advice. Ultimately we all teach differently, and you need to formulate the solutions which are best for *you* and your particular circumstances. As a new teacher you need be careful how you handle points of disagreement with your tutors or with experienced teachers.

The book is written mainly for people involved in ITE in the United Kingdom drawing particularly on the authors' research and teaching in England and Wales. Many of the ideas concerning ICT pedagogy have not been made available in print previously, however, and the text will be of interest to similar readerships in other parts of the world.

It is not necessary to read the book in the sequence presented. Although the chapters are designed to build progressively, we have cross-referenced extensively so that if you are reading a particular chapter, you can see where to look back to find earlier references to the topic or forward to see how the issues are developed further. We do not attempt to cover every matter which will be of interest or concern to the beginning teacher of ICT. We have focused on the points which are particularly influenced by the nature of the subject, and readers should refer to the core book in this series (Capel *et al.*, 2001) for more detail on general issues.

We have designed the content of the book to remain current for some time, but inevitably, in this rapidly changing field, new developments and initiatives will need to be taken into account. For example, the KS3 strategy for ICT in England is being piloted as we write, and the materials are likely to be published before you read the book. We are confident, however, that our ideas are compatible with the strategy and that the materials will complement the detail provided in this book.

S.K.
J.P.
H.T.

Part I

ICT in Secondary Schools

1 The Place of ICT in Secondary Education

Howard Tanner

The term Information and Communication Technology (ICT) was introduced in the National Curricula of England and Wales (DfEE, 1999) to define a set of tools used to process and communicate information. You may be more familiar with the term Information Technology (IT), which is more often used in the international business world to describe the same tools.

Whatever the terms used to describe the tools, the issues that arise in secondary schools are associated with developing in teachers, pupils and institutions the ability and inclination to use the tools appropriately to control situations in which information is processed and communicated. Processing and communicating information lie at the heart of teaching and learning in secondary schools, and this suggests that ICT capability should be central to effective secondary education.

This feature gives the subject of ICT a special status in the curriculum, and before we consider the subject itself in more detail, it will be helpful for you to consider its wider role.

OBJECTIVES

By the end of this chapter you should be able to:

*   appreciate the scope of ICT in secondary education;
*   distinguish between ICT as: a subject of study, a Key Skill and a resource for teaching and learning;

- appreciate how ICT has developed within the curriculum and the position of Computer Science and ICT as examination subjects;
- identify the roles carried out by ICT specialist teachers, ICT co-ordinators and teachers of other subjects concerning pupils' learning of ICT in school;
- identify the contribution to ICT attainment of learning outside school and explain the digital divide.

WHAT IS THE SCOPE OF ICT IN THE SECONDARY SCHOOL?

In England, ICT is defined for curriculum purposes as:

> the range of tools and techniques relating to computer-based hardware and software, to communications including both directed and broadcast, to information sources such as CD-ROM and the Internet, and to associated technologies such as robots, video-conferencing and digital TV.
>
> (QCA, 1999)

This offers a very broad scope for ICT in terms of the tools which we might use in school. The pedagogical aims of ICT are defined equally broadly and include a wide range of purposes aiming to develop:

> the knowledge skills and understanding needed to employ ICT appropriately, securely and fruitfully in learning, employment and everyday life . . . As with any change in terminology there will be exceptions. Thus qualifications in this area continue to have the title IT, including in particular the IT Key Skill.
>
> (QCA, 1999)

Before we can discuss how to teach ICT in secondary schools it is necessary to be clear about our aims. A range of purposes is implied in the statement by QCA above. We need to be clear about what we want pupils to learn and why we want them to learn it if we are to organise the curriculum effectively. What priorities should you have as a teacher of ICT?

Task 1.1 What place should ICT have in the secondary school curriculum?

Identify the key areas of ICT knowledge, skills or experiences that you think every secondary child should gain during their secondary education. For each of these, explain why you think it should be included.

Table 1.1 What place should ICT have in the secondary school curriculum?

Knowledge, skills, understanding, experience	Justification for inclusion
Knowledge and skills about the detailed working of ICT hardware and software	*Vocational.* Some pupils will gain employment in the computer industry
Knowledge and skills about common tools used in business; for example: Windows, word processors, spreadsheets, databases, the Internet	*Vocational.* These tools will be important to pupils in future employment
Knowledge and skills about common tools which will be used in learning other subjects in the curriculum, for example Windows, word processors, spreadsheets, databases, the Internet	*Key skills.* These tools are necessary for pupils to become independent learners and for other teachers to be able to assume are available for use in other contexts
Experience of using ICT tools to learn about other subjects	*Pedagogical.* ICT can improve the quality of learning in other subjects by removing drudgery, providing good visual aids, increasing motivation, giving access to new worlds and encouraging pupils to work at a higher level
Experience of teachers using ICT to teach their subjects	*Pedagogical.* ICT can improve the quality of teacher–pupil communication through the production of audio-visual aids to support understanding, demonstrations of processes outside the classroom, and providing a focus for group discussion
Knowledge about how computers are used in the world of work, discussing ethical and employment issues	*Social.* Education should prepare pupils to live in a society in which ICT is likely to play an increasingly important role

There is no clear, correct answer to Task 1.1. In fact an examination of how the use of ICT has developed in UK schools over the last thirty years suggests that clear thinking about the aims of ICT has been rare. Rather, we would suggest, the use of ICT has often been regarded as being good for its own sake. We have produced Table 1.1 for Task 1.1 and have grouped the knowledge, skills, understanding and experience which you might have considered under general headings.

The rate of development of information and communications technologies has been stunning over the last thirty years. It has been claimed that the capacity and speed of processing of desktop devices double every eighteen months. If motor vehicle technology had developed at the same rate people would now be driving cars the size of a pinhead which could travel 50,000 miles on a gallon of fuel with a top speed of 100,000 m.p.h.

It would be a good idea to examine our list and critically consider our justifications in the light of the rate at which computer technology is developing. The detailed knowledge and skills gained in Year 7 about computer hardware or software may not still be current when a pupil leaves school at the end of Year 13.

Task 1.2 What is most important in ICT teaching?

Given that so much of the precise and detailed knowledge that might be gained in ICT may be short-lived, re-examine *your* list and decide what knowledge, skills, understanding and experiences are most important in ICT teaching.

The authors of the National Curriculum wrote the ICT orders with the intention of making them as resilient to change as possible for such a rapidly developing area.

Task 1.3 Examine the National Curriculum orders for ICT

Visit the National Curriculum website for England at http://www.nc.uk.net/home.html and follow the links for the National Curriculum for ICT. View the National Curriculum for Key Stages 3 and 4, examining how the knowledge skills and understanding are organised. Identify the four 'themes' used to organise the content.

(If you are not training in England, you will find the curriculum requirements for ICT are different. It will be valuable to consider the curriculum for England, as most of the points that we will make are general ones, but you should also study your specific requirements in detail.)

Perhaps you noticed the absence of references to skills or techniques associated with specific software, such as using frames in desktop publishing (DTP) or creating formulas in spreadsheets. The programmes of study include instead the following themes:

- finding things out;
- developing ideas and making things happen;

- exchanging and sharing information;
- reviewing, modifying and evaluating work as it progresses.

(DfEE, 1999)

Although some knowledge and skills about current technology must be developed in order to gain the experience necessary to understand the potential of digital technology and develop the attitudes necessary for ICT capability, these should be the vehicle for developing ICT capability rather than its focus.

The effective teaching of ICT, whether through special lessons in ICT or through the use of ICT in other subjects, should develop in pupils:

- positive attitudes to the use of ICT;
- confidence in their own ability to use ICT to solve problems;
- a disposition to apply ICT in relevant situations and critically evaluate its effect;
- personal autonomy in their use of ICT for learning and problem solving.

Clearly there is a small number of basic skills and routines which support the development of the key concepts, processes and higher order skills which are necessary for true ICT capability. Rather than focusing on the basic skills or techniques, we prefer to consider ICT capability in terms of broad domains of transferable learning, which must be developed within the context of higher order components (see below) to create longer lasting and more useful knowledge. We suggest that ICT capability requires the development of knowledge in five key components:

- *routines*, such as: using a mouse or double clicking on an application;
- *techniques*, such as: adjusting margins to make text fit a page;
- *key concepts*, such as: menu, file, database, spreadsheet, website or hypertext link;
- *processes*, such as: developing a presentation for English, researching for a Geography project, organising, analysing and presenting the results of a survey in Mathematics;
- *higher order skills and knowledge*, such as recognizing when the use of ICT might be appropriate, planning how to approach a problem, making and testing hypotheses, monitoring progress in a task and evaluating the result, reflecting on the effect of using ICT in a particular situation.

(Kennewell *et al.*, 2000: 20–5)

The different components of ICT capability, listed above, are most typically developed through characteristically different learning experiences.

Basic skills or routines are learned primarily through practice. Techniques may develop slowly through trial and error, but are developed more efficiently by copying the actions of a teacher or other pupil. If skills and techniques are to be transferable they should be encountered and practised in a range of subject areas or problem contexts.

There are relatively few fundamental concepts involved in ICT, and we will discuss these further in Chapter 2. Concepts are developed effectively through pupils' talk and reflection based on experiences that are supported by the teacher.

Processes and higher order knowledge and skills are developed in environments that are characterised by the active involvement of a pupil who demonstrates significant personal autonomy. The pupil should be encouraged to explore the opportunities which are presented, and be allowed to decide which software to use, to plan how to use it, to monitor progress and to evaluate and reflect on solutions. This does not deny an active role for the teacher – the support and gentle guidance of a teacher are vital if learning is to occur.

It should also be noted that the higher levels of knowledge demand that ICT should be used in the context of other school subjects and the real world. The higher levels of attainment in ICT capability are most clearly demonstrated when ICT is used effectively in context. The nature of ICT is complex and we can identify three distinct aspects of ICT within the school curriculum.

THE DIVERSE NATURE OF ICT

ICT may be viewed as a:

- *Key Skill* which like literacy and numeracy underpins learning in a range of subject areas;
- *resource* which should be used by schools to support and extend the nature of teaching and learning across the curriculum;
- *discipline* in its own right like English, Mathematics or History with its own characteristic forms of knowledge, skill and understanding.

(Kennewell *et al.*, 2000, pp. 8–9)

ICT as a Key Skill

Task 1.4 Investigating learning across the curriculum

Visit the National Curriculum website at http://www.nc.uk.net/home.html and follow the links for 'learning across the curriculum'. A number of skills and themes are listed which are supposed to be taught throughout the curriculum. (They are referred to as 'cross-curricular'.) Follow the link to 'search the curriculum' for 'Key Skills'. Make a note of the Key Skills listed. In particular note the Key Skill 'Information Technology' and investigate the links that are made to other curriculum subjects.

Key Skills are fundamental aspects of learning which underpin the learning of a wide range of subjects across the curriculum. The Key Skills within the National Curriculum for England are listed as being:

- application of number;
- communication;
- improving own learning and performance;
- information technology;
- problem solving;
- working with others.

(DfES, 2001a)

Three of the Key Skills are very closely associated with particular subjects within the National Curriculum. For example, 'application of number' will obviously draw on knowledge, skills and understanding developed in Mathematics. However, this does not mean that they will be learned solely in their associated curriculum subject. Although Key Skills are of great significance for effective teaching and learning within schools, they are more often learned on the way to learning something else than by direct instruction.

Research demonstrates how difficult it is to transfer the knowledge and skills learned in one context into a different context (for example, Saloman and Globerson, 1987; Lave, 1988; Lave and Wenger, 1991; Brown *et al.*, 1995). For example, when pupils leave the mathematics classroom and enter the science classroom they often appear to forget all their mathematical knowledge. They do not expect to apply knowledge learned in one subject in the context of another.

Similar difficulties arise with ICT and the IT Key Skill. Any definition of ICT capability must include the demand that pupils are able to use their knowledge, skills and understanding of ICT in other subject areas and in real life.

> **Task 1.5 Reflect on your own use of ICT in other subjects at school**
>
> Think back to your own schooling. Try to think of an occasion when you were able to *choose* to use your knowledge of ICT to solve a problem when learning another subject. If that is not possible, try to think of an occasion when it would have been helpful to use ICT when learning another subject, but you did not do so. What makes it difficult to use ICT in other subjects?

There are, of course, many possible constraints that limit the use of ICT in other subject areas. Many of these are practical, because of limited access to equipment. In time, it is to be hoped, such constraints will gradually ease. However, there are other more significant constraints. You may have rejected a possible use of ICT because you knew that 'they just don't do it that way in that subject' or the teacher may have conveyed the impression that to use ICT would be cheating in some way. The teacher may not have intended to give that impression, but you may have inferred some unwritten rules for the subject from their failure to use ICT when appropriate.

There is a further constraint here. When you are a novice in a particular subject, you usually rely on others who are more experienced to show you how problems may be solved efficiently within that subject. You need to focus all your thoughts on following the processes being demonstrated, leaving little mental capacity for reflection on possible alternative approaches based on your ICT knowledge and skills. The expert teacher must accept the responsibility of showing pupils the potential of ICT within their subject, as it is probably too much to expect pupils to do it for themselves.

The Key Skill of IT demands that pupils should actively seek and recognise opportunities to use ICT in other subjects and everyday life. This requires far more than basic ICT skills and techniques. It requires pupils to understand the potential of ICT and have the confidence and desire to seek opportunities to apply their knowledge on their own initiative. In order to develop such knowledge and attitudes, we believe, the Key Skill demands that pupils should experience the effective use of ICT as a tool or resource in all subjects in the curriculum.

ICT as a tool or resource to support, and extend the nature of, teaching and learning

Enthusiasts for the use of ICT in education have long claimed that the technology has the potential to change dramatically the nature of teaching and learning in schools, and to change it for the better. Some have drawn parallels between the way in which the industrial revolution transformed the physical power of people at work and the ways in which the ICT revolution was to amplify the power of the human mind (Howe, 1983). The expectation that ICT would revolutionise education through the more efficient teaching of traditional school subjects and the development of pupils' thinking has yet to be realised (Stevenson, 1997). However, we may have entered the decade in which the availability of technology and the education and training of teachers reach the point at which such claims may be fairly tested for the first time.

Task 1.6 Using ICT as a tool to support and extend teaching and learning in schools

Consider the potential for ICT in teaching and learning in all subjects.

- What features of ICT support its use as a tool for teaching and learning?
- How would the use of such features within ICT change the nature of teaching and learning in schools?
- Are there any features of ICT that make it especially effective in developing pupils' thinking?

You may have listed some of the features of ICT that the UK government identified in its expected outcomes for teachers following training in ICT in subject teaching:

- speed and automaticity;
- range and capacity;
- provisionality;
- interactivity.

(TTA, 1998)

You may also have included more familiar terms such as programming and logical processing.

The speed and capacity of digital technology have allowed the development of software tools of great utility. Word processors, spreadsheets, databases and graph plotters are examples of generic tools that may be used to good effect in a range of subject areas. The power of such tools lies in their ability to perform repetitive operations swiftly and accurately. When used well, this can free pupils from performing routine tasks, allowing them to focus their attention on higher level problem solving activities. For example, pupils using a spreadsheet in a science lesson to record data and draw graphs and charts are able to focus on the interpretation of the results rather than on the mathematics involved in plotting a line of best fit (Barton, 1997).

The provisionality inherent in such software allows pupils to operate in an exploratory fashion, testing hypotheses (or even half formed ideas), evaluating their impact, abandoning some and modifying others. Unlike many older people, today's pupils are happy to make a mistake on a computer, secure in the knowledge that their errors may be swiftly and painlessly corrected with no loss of face. In many ways they find it easier to do this with a machine than with a person. Computers 'don't boss you around' and 'don't shout at you when you get things wrong like teachers do' as some pupils report (see Kennewell *et al.*, 2000).

Similarly, the swift access to information provided by using the Internet at home frees pupils from the controlled learning environment provided by schools, allowing pupils to access opinions and attitudes other than those sanctioned by National Curricula. The teacher ceases to be the source of all knowledge and becomes just one of many. This poses a number of problems for the pupil in evaluating information coming from 'unofficial' sources. An urgent need for new knowledge and skills associated with the validation of sources is generated alongside increasing pupil autonomy and control.

From the outset, there have been those who have claimed that working with computers would develop pupils' thinking. For example, it was suggested that when using the programming language Logo, pupils would be immersed in a mathematically rich learning environment and thus learn to think mathematically in a more natural way (Papert, 1980). Others have reported the advantages to be gained through paraprogramming such as designing a spreadsheet to solve a problem (Sutherland, 1992).

Many of the positive features of digital technology are associated with its potential to assist pupils in developing into independent, autonomous learners. Unfortunately, pupil autonomy is not the dominant characteristic of secondary education in the United Kingdom. Often the introduction of ICT into subject teaching acts as a catalyst of reform, challenging traditional pedagogy and pushing classroom organisation towards a more individualised model. Such organisation sits more comfortably with some subjects than with others. In some subject areas the introduction of ICT challenges teachers' perceptions of the very nature of their subject, demanding a 'root and branch' change (Goodson and Mangan, 1995). The extent of the change demanded in some areas goes some way to explaining the low level of penetration into subject teaching reported in surveys (for example, Lovegrove and Wilshire, 1997). In many schools, the main impact of ICT is through its position as a subject discipline in its own right.

ICT as a subject discipline

ICT has been established as a subject discipline in its own right since the early 1970s, although a variety of names have been used for it. Typically, subject disciplines have their own characteristic concepts and forms of knowledge. Pupils within a subject discipline are usually required to learn specific skills and processes that are associated with that subject. However, the knowledge associated with the ICT subject discipline is qualitatively different from the formal knowledge found in other, more traditional, subjects. Although there are some low level skills and routines which appear to be at the heart of the subject content, progression demands the development of concepts, strategies and processes which will enable the pupil to identify opportunities, solve problems and evaluate solutions in other subjects and in real life contexts. So although pupils must develop concepts related to computer systems, the higher levels of attainment depend on the ability to apply such knowledge in other situations. However, there do seem to be a number of fundamental concepts and methods of enquiry which characterise ICT as a discipline in its own right.

We can identify a number of fields of knowledge whose content or methods are used by researchers and practitioners in the field of ICT:

- *Engineering:* for methods of selection of materials, tools and techniques with properties required for particular purposes, and for the design, construction and configuration of devices and systems;
- *Mathematics:* for the structures and relationships of logic and algebra which underlie information storage, retrieval and processing;
- *Psychology:* for the ways in which humans interact with machines;
- *Sociology:* for the broader impact of ICT on human activity and relations.

(Kennewell *et al.*, 2000: 104)

Task 1.7 Ideas underpinning ICT as a subject

Are there important concepts and methods of enquiry that characterise ICT as a discipline in its own right? Analyse your advanced study and/or professional practice in ICT and try to identify the ideas which underpin the tools and activities of ICT.

We suggest a number of fundamental concepts and methods which make the discipline distinct academically and which characterise professional practice:

- *data:* binary values which may represent text characters, numbers, colours, vectors, storage locations, etc.;
- *variables:* storage locations which hold data representing particular meanings;
- *instructions:* such as arithmetic operations, comparisons, movement of data;
- *structures:* such as tables, lists, stacks, serial/sequential files;
- *algorithms and procedures:* such as branch, iterate, evaluate, insert, delete, locate, transfer, exchange, search, sort;
- *information systems:* comprising collection, entry, storage, processing and communication of data to provide information for users;
- *hardware subsystems:* input, output, storage;
- *communications subsystems:* buses, networks, protocols;
- *software subsystems:* BIOS, DOS, applications;
- *systems development:* strategies such as analysis, design, implement, test;
- *interaction with social subsystems:* human–computer interaction, security, privacy.

Task 1.8 Aims in teaching ICT

We have identified a number of purposes of teaching ICT: its vocational aspects, its role as a Key Skill and as a tool for learning, and as a means of understanding aspects of the world in which we live. Consider the relative importance which these purposes have for you.

- What purposes have been served by the lessons which you have observed?
- Do you think that all pupils should study ICT or just a few?
- Do you think that all pupils should sit examinations in IT/ICT at GCSE level?

The National Curriculum emphasises the importance of ICT as a Key Skill and in the learning of other subjects. Its study may be in depth as an examination subject or as a Key Skill in Key Stage 4 (KS4) and post-16. Schools vary considerably in the emphasis that they place on it. A number of different teaching roles and responsibilities are associated with differing aims of the subject.

THE ROLES OF SPECIALIST TEACHERS, COORDINATORS AND TEACHERS OF OTHER SUBJECTS

Prior to the introduction of the National Curriculum most secondary schools had a Head of Computing who took responsibility for the Computer Studies subject area and usually also for the ICT resources in the school, which were usually concentrated in a computer room. In many schools it was then seen as natural to give this person the responsibility for coordinating ICT as a resource for teaching and learning in addition to their responsibility for teaching the subject discipline of ICT. However, although the roles of ICT specialist and ICT coordinator are closely linked, and indeed often have a high degree of overlap in some curriculum models, they have distinct purposes and are often separated in large secondary schools.

The role of the ICT coordinator is a school-wide responsibility that may involve the development of ICT as a tool for teaching learning as well as the development of the ICT Key Skill. The nature of this wider whole school responsibility has often led head teachers to reject the head of the ICT department for this role, placing greater emphasis on interpersonal skills than technical expertise. Indeed, the role is sometimes seen to be of such significance that it is taken on by an assistant head teacher who is designated as 'Director of Studies', with responsibility for developing and extending the nature of teaching and learning in the school.

The precise responsibilities of the teachers involved depend on the model of curriculum organisation chosen for the teaching of ICT. In broad terms, models of delivery are either *cross-curricular* or *discrete*. In the former model, ICT knowledge, skills and processes are taught through other subject areas whilst, in the latter, pupils attend separate, discrete lessons in ICT. Cross-curricular models vary in the degree to which ICT is integrated into the schemes of work of the subjects through which it is taught. In some versions, ICT is fully *integrated*, in others it is only *hosted* and taught as a distinct series of lessons which otherwise make few links with the host subject (Smith, 1991).

Task 1.9 What model of curriculum organisation for ICT is employed in your school?

Consider the way in which the teaching and learning of ICT are provided in your placement school. Classify the model of organisation employed in each key stage as cross-curricular or discrete. What advantages and disadvantages do you see in your school's model?

The National Curriculum proposed a cross-curricular, integrated approach from the start, stating strongly that 'it is not intended that IT should be seen as another subject' (CCW, 1990: A3). The logic behind this should be clear from our analysis above. However, the implementation of such an ambitious curriculum development has been beset by difficulties. At that time, only a small proportion had sufficient personal ICT skills to support its teaching within their own subject area (Tanner, 1991). Even as late as 1998, the ITCD project reported that large numbers of pupils experienced the use of ICT in only a small number of subjects and that a significant minority experienced ICT only in discrete lessons (Kennewell *et al.*, 2000). Of course,

if scarce ICT resources are always in use for discrete ICT lessons, there is little incent-
ive or opportunity for other teachers to integrate the use of ICT in their teaching.
However, school inspectors report that cross-curricular delivery works only when
subject teachers are confident, progress is monitored and structures are in place for
motivating and coordinating (Ofsted, 1995: 3).

Task 1.10 ICT roles in your school

Find out which staff have ICT responsibilities in your school (for example,
Heads of Department, Head of ICT, ICT Coordinator, Network Manager,
Director of Studies). What roles or tasks does each one carry out?

The specialist teacher or head of ICT has a key role to play in either the discrete or
the integrated model. The role is different from that of the ICT coordinator, as it
involves the direct teaching of pupils, and preparing them for examinations. Heads
of ICT departments have roles and responsibilities that parallel those of other subject leaders. However, they and other specialist teachers are usually enthusiasts who
should be aware of current developments that they draw to the attention of other
staff, motivating curriculum and pedagogical change as appropriate.

The ICT coordinator, on the other hand, is expected to possess a broad vision of
the potential of ICT across the curriculum and to work productively and sensitively
with a wide range of staff to develop their teaching styles. Furthermore, the ICT coordinator is expected to coordinate policies, schemes of work and assessment relating
to ICT. The role often includes external liaison and resource management. This should
include awareness of the curriculum outside school and the resources that exist in
pupils' homes and in the community that may be used in the service of education.

LEARNING OUTSIDE SCHOOL AND THE DIGITAL DIVIDE

The homes of many pupils now contain a broad range of ICT equipment. The
ImpacT2 project reported that in 2000 the percentage of pupils with access at home
to a computer that was more than a games machine varied from 75 per cent at Key
Stage 2 to 88 per cent at Key Stage 4 (DfES/BECTA, 2001a). Increasingly, children
are becoming networked learners, with 48 per cent of primary pupils and 64 per cent
of secondary pupils having access to the Internet at home (DfES/BECTA, 2001a). The
average amount of time secondary school pupils spent using the computer at home is
eleven and a half hours, but three and a half hours on average were spent playing games.

Research has long shown that pupils who have access to computers at home have
a more positive attitude towards and self-confidence in the use of computers in school
than those who lack such access (for example, Coley et al., 1994; Selwyn, 1997;
Kennewell et al., 2000) and we believe that these attitudes contribute to ICT capability.

Furthermore, pupils who have access outside school have a resource that can support them when revising, performing homework tasks and developing projects for examination schemes.

Computer use at home has a different character from computer use in school. Not only is the technology in use at home often better than that in use at school, at home 'You don't have a teacher looking over your shoulder and bossing you around' (Year 7 girl, quoted in Kennewell *et al.*, 2000: 123). Pupils using computers at home are usually independent learners, working without time pressure, experimenting and exploring in a free, natural learning environment (Papert, 1996). Although many schools state pupil autonomy in learning as among their aims, the extent to which this is attainable in school is limited by their nature as institutions.

Task 1.11 Exploring out-of-school access in your school

Find out what access your pupils have to computers outside school. How many of your pupils use the facilities which are available and how do they use them?

The percentage of pupils with computer access was only 41 per cent among the lowest two socio-economic groups, and 44 per cent among those from single parent families (DfES/BECTA, 2001a). The so-called 'digital divide' between those who have good ICT facilities at home and those who have not is an important factor that you will need to take into account in your teaching.

We have suggested that schools should:

- *collect data* about the extent and nature of ICT resources in pupils' homes and in the community;
- *nurture links between home, school and community*, ensuring that home facilities are used to good effect and supporting pupils without computers by ensuring that good information is available about the resources in the community, or provided by the school out of hours;
- *organise* and *monitor* ICT access outside normal school hours, setting targets for personal ICT use. Supervision of the schools' ICT facilities outside school hours need not be the responsibility of a specialist teacher: alternative means of supervision can be organised using appropriate non-teaching staff;
- *encourage the use of ICT outside school* by setting work which assumes the availability of ICT.

(See Kennewell *et al.*, 2000: 133)

ICT will be a significant feature in the education, training and social life of all our pupils and confidence in its use in a wide variety of contexts will be a necessary condition of their inclusion in that society. Strategies for overcoming the digital divide are discussed further in Chapter 10.

SUMMARY

The scope of ICT in the curriculum is very broad, including aims that are vocational, social and pedagogical in addition to aims associated with the knowledge of the subject discipline and the Key Skill.

ICT appears in the school curriculum as a discipline in its own right like English, Mathematics or History with its own characteristic forms of knowledge, skill and understanding. It also has a place as a Key Skill that, like literacy and numeracy, underpins learning in a range of subject areas. Finally, it is a resource that should be used by teachers and pupils to support and extend the nature of teaching and learning across the curriculum.

Curriculum models for ICT are either *cross-curricular* or *discrete*, depending on whether ICT is taught through other subjects or through separate lessons. Cross-curricular models may be fully *integrated* or *hosted*.

Key personnel within the school have distinct roles and responsibilities for ICT. Specialist teachers are responsible for the direct teaching of ICT, and preparing pupils for ICT examinations. Heads of ICT departments have roles and responsibilities that parallel those of other subject leaders. ICT coordinators have a school-wide responsibility that may involve not only the development of the ICT Key Skill but also the development of ICT as a tool for teaching learning. Teachers of other subjects are responsible for using ICT effectively in their teaching, developing their teaching styles and modelling the appropriate use of ICT in their discipline.

ICT facilities exist in the home and the community as well as in the school. Pupils who have home access to ICT have more positive attitudes, are more confident and see more opportunities for its use. Schools should use the potential for autonomous pupil research and learning which exists outside school. Unfortunately a 'digital divide' exists between the technologically rich and the technologically deprived which if left undisturbed will exclude a significant number of pupils from effective participation in education training and adult life.

FURTHER READING

Kennewell, S., Parkinson, J. and Tanner, H. (2000) *Developing the ICT Capable School*, London: RoutledgeFalmer. Provides a wide view of the development of ICT capability, taking a whole-school approach, and thus particularly helpful to those in management positions.

Leask, M. and Pachler, N. (1999) *Learning to Teach using ICT in the Secondary School*, London: RoutledgeFalmer. Deals extensively with the use of ICT in teaching and learning across the curriculum, covering each subject specialism together with consideration of general issues such as SEN.

Russell, T. (2001) *Teaching and Using ICT in Secondary Schools*, London: David Fulton. A source book of ideas concerning the background to ICT in education, the management of ICT in schools, the place of ICT in the curriculum, and the teaching and assessment of ICT as a subject.

2 The Nature of ICT as a Subject

Steve Kennewell

ICT is a relatively new addition to the school curriculum. The current subject title was only introduced in 2000, and even if we include its predecessors with different titles – Information Technology, Information Systems, Computer Studies, Computer Science and Computer Literacy – the subject has been taught formally for a much shorter time than most subjects. Furthermore, Computing Science has existed as a field of research for a mere half century.

ICT is also one of the Key Skills to be developed through each subject. Some subject areas are well placed to teach certain ICT concepts and skills; for instance, Design and Technology may teach computer control and computer assisted design (CAD), as well as helping pupils with appropriate use of other packages such as word processing. The potential for combining the teaching of ICT with the teaching of other subjects has led to a wide variety of perceptions of the nature of ICT in different schools.

You will find that little research has been carried out concerning the teaching of ICT, however. Unlike Mathematics, Science and other subjects, we cannot turn to a body of literature concerning how its main ideas are represented, what learners find difficult or what makes a difference to the effectiveness of teaching. In this chapter, we are going to analyse what is involved in the subject as it is taught at various levels. Our purpose is to raise your understanding of what is distinctive about ICT as a subject in the curriculum and the implications of these features for teaching the subject.

OBJECTIVES

At the end of this chapter, you should be able to:

• explain the principles of each strand of ICT, explain progression between levels and explain the relative contribution of each component of ICT capability;
• understand the relationship between ICT and other technology subjects as disciplines;
• explain the principles of ICT systems and their development;
• develop awareness of content at advanced levels and identify its foundations in ICT up to intermediate levels and in other disciplines.

ICT CAPABILITY

In Chapter 1 we discussed briefly the content and rationale of the National Curriculum for ICT. We saw that the idea of ICT capability was the basis of the developing knowledge in ICT as a subject and as a Key Skill. The structure was set out by the devisers of the National Curriculum for IT (DES/WO, 1990). They recognised that they could not identify a fixed body of knowledge for the subject, and so the content was represented as five 'strands of progression': developing ideas and communicating information; handling information; modelling; measurement and control; applications and effects (NCC, 1990: C4).

• *Developing ideas and communicating information* includes the use of word processing to draft and redraft written work; the use of DTP for presenting ideas attractively and effectively; the use of graphics in design; e–mail communication to distant locations.
• *Handling information* includes interrogating databases to find numbers and lists of items satisfying particular conditions; creating and editing databases in order to store and retrieve information; analysing and displaying stored data in various ways including graphs and charts.
• *Modelling* includes exploring simulations and solving adventure games; creating stored relationships between variables using spreadsheets and programming languages such as Logo.
• *Measurement and control* involves the connection to the computer of sensors, switches, motors, etc. through suitable interfacing devices, and the use of programming languages or specially designed software to record changes in temperature, light, etc. and to control lights, buggies, alarms, etc. It includes the control of machinery by computers to produced items automatically once the designs are specified using CAD/CAM.

- *Applications and effects* involves the study of how IT is used in the outside world and its implications for the economic, social, environmental and ethical aspects of society.

ICT capability involves knowledge, skills and understanding in all these strands.

IT capability consists in a rounded development in the five . . [strands] . . so that a pupil can:

- recognise in which situations the use of IT is sensible;
- use IT appropriately in such situations;
- evaluate the effects of that use;
- know and understand the range and purpose of applications of IT, and be able to evaluate their effects on individuals and society.

(Birnbaum, 1989: 5)

Task 2.1 Work in different strands

From your experiences of using ICT in academic study, employment and leisure activity, identify activities in each strand that you have carried out.

As we highlighted in Chapter 1, the authors of the IT component of the National Curriculum used very general terms with the intention of making the Attainment Target and the Programmes of Study resilient to change in the technology. They recognised the rapidly changing nature of ICT, and avoided what they felt were ephemeral terms such as 'spreadsheet' and 'word processing'.

The revision of the National Curriculum for ICT in England in 2000 brought about a number of changes to make the Programme of Study easier to understand, and added more explicit references to communicating over a distance. The emphasis on generality is still so great that the Internet is not mentioned in the legal requirements, although it is the basis of current government policy for ICT in school!

Task 2.2 Analysing national curricula

Use the curriculum document for ICT that applies in your national system to identify where the strands of ICT capability are represented in the curriculum elements specified. Is there any aspect of ICT capability that is not covered in your current curriculum specification? Is there anything extra?

The National Curriculum (NC) for England and Wales has a single Attainment Target that specifies eight levels of characteristic ICT activity (together with a further level of 'exceptional performance') which set the expectations for pupils' progression and against which they are judged at the end of each key stage. Through the key stages, you should be able to identify a progression in the demands of the Programmes of Study and Attainment Targets. For example, at level 4, we expect pupils to 'understand the need for care in framing questions when collecting, finding and interrogating information', and, at level 7, to 'select and use information systems suited to their work in a variety of contexts, translating enquiries expressed in ordinary language into the form required by the system'. Also at level 4, 'They compare their use of ICT with other methods and with its use outside school', and at level 7, 'They take part in informed discussion about the use of ICT and its impact on society'.

Progression

Progression in ICT demands that pupils develop greater autonomy and confidence in their selection and use of information sources and tools. They are expected to develop into discerning users of ICT, with increasing awareness of the benefits and limitations of the systems they use. They become able to present their ideas in an increasing variety of ways with a developing sense of audience. They use ICT based models of growing complexity for increasingly complex lines of enquiry involving progressively greater decision making and personal autonomy. Their ability to evaluate their own work grows, and they become progressively more able to discuss and appreciate social, economic, political, legal, ethical and moral issues (QCA, 1998).

For example, during the Whole-school Approaches to Developing IT Capability (ITCD) research project (Kennewell et al., 2000), we saw the programme Microsoft Publisher being used by pupils from Year 3 to Year 11 (and, of course, by student teachers!), but for different purposes. Year 3 pupils were using it to write simple reports on looking after their pets, focusing on the writing process and the important features of animal care; Year 7 pupils were producing a poster for young children concerning healthy foods, focusing on the selection, importing and positioning of clip art; Year 10 pupils were producing advertising material for simulated business projects, focusing on effective design and precise layout for a sophisticated audience; Year 11 pupils were producing material to persuade people to adopt a more environmentally friendly lifestyle, focusing on use of language to construct an effective argument and layout of text and graphics to attract people's attention. Their use of techniques showed a progression that matched the complexity of purpose. Generally this reflected their growing maturity, although the Year 10 group were actually using more sophisticated techniques (this was an IT lesson which aimed to introduce these techniques) than the Year 11 group (this was an English lesson which aimed to develop the quality of their persuasive writing).

It is not necessary for every use of ICT to involve more complex techniques. In addition to progression within the skills, knowledge and understanding described above, the orders also demand breadth of study across each key stage. The breadth of study increases over the key stages demanding that pupils be taught about an increasing variety of contexts, information sources and ICT tools. Pupils use these with increasing efficiency, to explore, develop and pass on information; to design systems and to evaluate their efficacy. Pupils' own use of ICT is also compared with their developing awareness of ICT use in the outside world (QCA, 1998).

Task 2.3 Analysing progression

Consider different groups of pupils that you have observed in school. Can you identify any progression from one year group to the next, either in complexity or breadth of context? Did older pupils use more complex techniques?

Progression in ICT capability comprises the two major groups of factors in Figure 2.1. The first factor involves using an ICT perspective to analyse problem contexts, and progression requires increasing self-regulation, strategic planning, evaluation, deep understanding and transferable knowledge. It suggests confidence with computers and an understanding of the ICT potential of situations. This in its turn is dependent on the second factor, experience of a wide range of problem situations for which an ICT solution has proved appropriate. Progression here involves the pupil solving increasingly sophisticated and abstract problems, constructing an increasingly rich framework of concepts and developing fluency in the use of a widening range of techniques.

Figure 2.1 Dimensions of progression in ICT

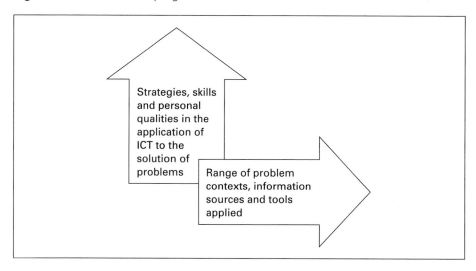

Aspects of ICT capability

ICT capability thus involves more than the secure knowledge and understanding of a wide range of ICT skills, techniques, processes and strategies. It also includes the disposition to construct ICT solutions to problems that are appropriate to the context and are based on knowledge of the opportunities and limitations offered by the systems available.

Task 2.4 Analysing your own learning

Choose a particular software package that you know well, and review the development of your expertise. How did you learn? How was your progression different from that of pupils in school?

The National Curriculum emphasises these higher order skills rather than specific techniques, but in order to work effectively with ICT, pupils will certainly require knowledge of relevant techniques. These are too numerous to list here, although you might try to identify the main techniques needed to use the package you considered in Task 2.4 in order to appreciate the nature of the task. Many of them are specific to the resources used and have a limited life span. However, it is a feature of ICT that you do not have to learn techniques fully before they can be used; usually the software provides prompts through on-screen menus and icons concerning what techniques are available and the options at each stage. ICT capable users should be able to meet new software with a positive attitude and an inclination to explore. Using the concepts which they have developed from their experiences with other software, such as an object which can be selected, or a handle which can be dragged, capable users should be able to explore new systems and work out what to do next as they proceed. Indeed, ICT capable users should *expect* to be able to explore new systems in this way with little assistance from manuals or instructors. It is important, then, when introducing a new software tool to pupils, to start by discussing what it can do and how this may be achieved, rather than merely demonstrating a fixed sequence of techniques to achieve a single outcome.

Frequently used skills and techniques, such as selecting objects and dragging handles, eventually become routine and no longer need conscious attention in order to carry them out. This process of becoming routine enables the ICT user to focus on the content of the problem in hand without having to monitor the progress of a technique. It is therefore important to develop such skills to an automatic level to facilitate learning across the curriculum even if they are not at the heart of the subject and their longer term value is dubious.

Initially, techniques also involve an ICT interference factor (Birnbaum, 1990). Since a part of the conscious mind must be allocated to controlling the technique, it is more difficult for learners to keep track of their goal. This can be overcome through the development of higher order skills of self-regulation and by making the technique routine.

We have seen that techniques are often taught in a single context, which makes it difficult for learners to generalise. If, however, techniques are met in a variety of situations and contexts, the potential for reflection and concept development grows.

It is much easier to use a technique than it is to describe or explain it. However, if you make it possible to describe techniques you are more likely to support pupils' concept development and the transfer of techniques to new situations. For example, when you first show a pupil how to insert an image into a publication, it is helpful to talk about selecting the object by clicking, and refer to handles and dragging when sizing or moving the object. If you use the same words in another context – or better still, prompt the pupil to use the words – you will help them to develop the concepts.

There are relatively few key concepts that underpin knowledge of techniques and processes, and our suggestion of a basic set is given in Table 2.1 together with a brief idea of the meaning of each. In order to work effectively in the classroom or employment setting, however, it is not enough for individuals to understand the concepts and carry out the processes. They need to be able to communicate with other people and engage with texts about ICT, such as guides to software packages. This requires knowledge of standard terminology, conventions and facts. For instance, as well as understanding the function of random access memory, a capable ICT user needs to know the fact that it takes the form of a microchip, the convention that it is measured in bytes, and the relevant terminology such as 'RAM'.

Task 2.5 Analysing desired knowledge

Identify some of the facts, conventions and terminology that you think the capable user of spreadsheets should know.

It is often possible to use different sequences of techniques to achieve the same goal. Some routes will be better than others, however, and users need an understanding of both the goal and the tools available in order to make appropriate choices. Sometimes the choice they make will not produce the desired effect, and they will try a different technique. Reflection on this mistake will lead to learning which improves their ability to make an appropriate choice in the future. An overall understanding of a process, such as developing a publication, which is characteristically made up of a particular set of procedures, will guide their selection of appropriate techniques. Processes are underpinned by concepts; in the example given, the user's concepts of publication and audience will influence the quality of the results.

Knowledge of processes and techniques is not sufficient for pupils to apply ICT to problem situations successfully: the pupil must also choose to use that knowledge, to monitor the progress being made, and to evaluate the solution gained. It is therefore important for pupils to know what knowledge they possess and consequently be more able to decide to use it. A further aspect is how pupils *feel* about using ICT: if they feel positive or confident about using an ICT process they are more likely to choose to use it, and are more likely to persevere in the face of any difficulties they may meet.

Table 2.1 Key concepts of ICT

Concept	Meaning
file	A unit of data which can be saved, loaded and printed
window	An area of the screen which can display part of a file
menu	A list of options which can be displayed and selected
text	A continuous string of characters, including formatting codes
object	Something which can be selected, formatted, moved, resized, copied, deleted and transferred to other locations
presentation	A set of text and objects, animated suitably for communication in screen form
publication	A set of text and objects, positioned suitably for communication in printed form
database structure	A store of data which can be searched and selected information displayed
model	A representation of relationships among variables
spreadsheet	A grid each cell of which can contain a value or a formula
hypertext structure	A set of text and objects containing links which allow quick access to chosen options
procedure	A sequence of instructions which achieve a specified result
monitoring process	A system which records data automatically from sensors at intervals of time
message	A set of text and objects together with a destination and return address
website	A hypertext structure which can be accessed remotely from any location

Source: From Kennewell *et al.*, 2000: 22.

The way in which pupils explore, plan, monitor, regulate and evaluate progress is also important. These are the higher order skills that are common across the curriculum, but their role in ICT capability is particularly vital. For example, in order to create a hypertext web of several linked pages, pupils need to give thought in advance, not just to the design of each page, as in traditional publishing, but to the overall structure and the ease of navigation for the user. As they make progress with the task, they must check links, keep records of links created, and maintain a view of the overall feel that the user will get. They will need to make decisions concerning changes to the design according to the ongoing evaluation. None of this planning and recording need be on paper, of course; they can keep much of it in their minds, and the web composing tool may have all the features needed to supplement their mental capacities.

Table 2.2 Components of ICT capability

	What it is	Examples	Special features
Basic skill or routine	An operation which is carried out without significant conscious thought	*Moving a mouse* or tracker ball to point at a cell on the screen *Dragging* a file from one window to another, or *double clicking* to start a program or load a file	Automatisation makes it natural to transfer skills to other contexts, but the specific nature of many routines makes it difficult to transfer skills to different hardware and software. When resources change, simple procedures are no longer routine and a conscious relearning process is required
Technique	Procedure which still requires a degree of conscious thought. Method known to achieve specified effects	*Copying an element* of a graphic design to make a regular pattern or *adjusting the frame boundary* in order to make a piece of text fit on to a page	Specific to the software tool used, but software designers often ensure that similar techniques can be used for similar procedures in different programs. Techniques, such as copy/paste, may become routine as a result of practice
Facts, conventions and terminology	Knowledge which enables people to communicate about the use of tools	Knowing that *Publisher is a DTP package* (fact), that an object of a page which encloses text or images is called a *frame* (terminology) and that *different tools are used to create text and graphic frames* (convention)	These components of knowledge do not involve understanding, but will be of little use without the corresponding concept
Key concepts	Understanding of features and relationships of main aspects of ICT tools	A concept of *publication* should involve knowing properties of frames and their relationship with text items, graphic objects and page layout	Requires a process of reflection to develop. Not immediately recognisable when observing a user in the way that knowledge of techniques is

Processes	*Multi-stage procedures* for achieving specified goals	The process of *developing a publication* would involve a sequence of techniques such as, in the case of a DTP package: • selecting the page to work on • creating a number of frames • entering text into frames • choosing text features • importing images into frames • adjusting the size/position of frames	The knowledge that links concepts and techniques
Higher order skills	Affective, strategic and metacognitive skills	In relation to the development of a publication, these issues could arise: • seeking opportunities when the use of ICT might be appropriate or effective in producing a publication • planning how ICT resources, techniques and processes are to be used in producing a publication • conjecturing, discussing and testing the strategies and data to be used • monitoring the progress of problem solving activities • making and testing hypotheses • persevering in the face of setbacks • exploring and learning new techniques when required for producing the publication • evaluating the outcomes of using ICT for the publication • explaining and justifying the use of ICT in producing the publication • reflecting on the learning which may have occurred during the process	These are generic skills concerning awareness of own knowledge and organising of activity. They enable pupils to respond effectively to new challenges and new tools

To summarise, we suggest that ICT capability comprises five components, set out in Table 2.2.

Task 2.6 Analysing concepts and techniques

We have started the analysis of the ICT capability components needed for producing a publication using DTP. The process and the higher order skills are shown in Table 2.2. Continue this analysis of the ICT capability needed by identifying the concepts and the essential techniques you would expect to be needed. Which of the techniques would you expect to become routine for pupils?

TEACHING AND LEARNING ICT CAPABILITY

Mere exposure to ICT is insufficient to ensure that learning occurs. There are already signs that, like television, ICT is becoming a familiar feature of pupils' lives and consequently is in danger of being regarded as a medium of entertainment rather than a serious medium for learning. If your lessons focus primarily on low order skills, the lack of intellectual challenge is likely to eliminate both learning and enjoyment.

Pupils' initial ICT capability will depend on their general learning ability, their experience and their access to ICT. In addition there are many social and domestic aspects that will influence the pupil's attitude and motivation to using ICT, the school and learning in general. This attitude can be positive or negative, and will be subject to many influences both in and out of school. When designing a Scheme of Work all the above factors should come into consideration. Work units will need to take into consideration various aspects of the social and domestic experiences. The scheme must also address school policies and features of society such as gender, class, race and even family background. There may be particular aspects that inhibit learning; for example, there may be pupils whose literacy level is well below the level required to read instructions or write reports (see Capel *et al.*, 2001: chapter 4.6). However, such pupils may well be able to use ICT effectively and talk about their work. Indeed, a pupil with reading problems may have an ICT capability level higher than that of the average for the year group.

The development of ICT capability is a progressive process and each aim should be seen as a part of a holistic approach. This should encompass practical, theoretical and experiential learning. Pupils should experience many software application packages and be able to critically select the appropriate package to solve a particular problem. Experience with a number of generic packages such as databases, word processors, spreadsheets will enable the pupils to produce informed solutions to specific problems encountered. But to move between similar packages before the basic concepts have been mastered is likely to lead to confusion and will inhibit the learning process.

You can facilitate progression in ICT capability through increasing the complexity of contexts and using more sophisticated ICT tools in response to the demands of tasks. However, the increased use of sophisticated software *per se* does not constitute progression in ICT capability. It may involve little more than the development of further techniques that the pupil finds hard to use in different contexts. More sophisticated software should be used because the task demands it, and not for its own sake.

A pupil may encounter difficulties in the task or problem situation itself, in the use of the system or software, or in the application of the software to the problem. The pupil must find and overcome difficulties somewhere for learning to occur. If the ICT interference factor is very large, the pupil will have little processing power left to use for the application of the software to the problem or to consider the issues arising in the problem domain (which may be another curriculum subject area). On the other hand, if there are few difficulties involved in either the use of the software or its application to the problem situation, it is unlikely that ICT capability would be developed further by the lesson, although learning in the other subject may be stimulated. The challenge for teachers is to maintain a balance between the factors according to the objectives of the activity.

Initial lessons may focus on techniques; pupils do not usually find these difficult if they lead quickly to a worthwhile outcome. Pupils should then be expected to combine techniques appropriately within an overall process and, in doing this, practise them so that they become routine. These elements can then form the basis for developing problem solving and decision making skills. In, for example, the production of a poster using desktop publishing, the initial paper plan would incorporate some text and suitable graphics. To implement this the pupil would be required to open a document, select frames for the various parts of the poster and then enter and manipulate the text, find and import suitable graphics, save and print. This could then be enhanced by changing the background and fonts, and incorporating features such as word art. These techniques are easily and quite quickly achievable provided the acquisition of the skills is carefully thought out so that the pupil is not overwhelmed by the complexity of the task.

The development of ICT capability occurs in the interaction between social contexts, problem situations and ICT environments as pupils engage actively, and to some extent autonomously, with problems in the pursuit of a designated goal. This suggests that your teaching approach should focus on the development of higher order skills and should emphasise:

- significant pupil autonomy in the selection of tools and resources;
- active participation by pupils in the process of planning and evaluating the use of ICT in problem situations;
- teacher intervention in the form of focusing questions to assist pupils in the formation of generalisations;
- demands that pupils articulate their thoughts about the opportunities and constraints offered by ICT techniques, processes and strategies which they have experienced (articulation may be verbal, written or via e-mail, but should be interactive);

- that teaching should develop pupils' enthusiasm and confidence about ICT;
- that pupils should be given opportunities and encouragement to reflect formally on their ICT learning.

(Kennewell *et al.*, 2000: 24–5)

Task 2.7 Observing variation in purpose of lessons

For each lesson you have observed involving pupils using ICT, whether they are taught by an ICT specialist or by a specialist in another subject, consider the balance between developing ICT capability and learning about the context to which the ICT is applied. How much variation was there from lesson to lesson?

SPECIALIST STUDY IN ICT

So far, we have discussed ICT capability. This is a Key Skill, similar to literacy and numeracy, which is important to learning other curriculum subjects. It may be taught, at least partially, in specialist lessons, but one of its main purposes is to form a foundation for pupils' learning across the whole curriculum. As we have seen, ICT has a status as a discipline of its own as well, like English and Mathematics. This discipline forms the knowledge required to be a developer of systems rather than merely a constructive user. Such knowledge is based on a further set of fundamental concepts from those given in Table 2.1.

These concepts and methods make up the *content* of ICT as a subject. However, the study of ICT up to age 16 often specifies the ways in which ICT is applied to various *contexts*, particularly:

- curriculum;
- business;
- leisure;
- school administration.

The GCSE syllabus of the Welsh Joint Education Committee (WJEC, 2000), for instance, specifies that candidates will be expected to be familiar with ICT applications in:

- shops and money services;
- the electronic office.

We have identified four main strands which have influenced the nature of IT/ICT as a subject of study in UK secondary schools: Computer Studies/Science; commercial subjects such as Business Studies and Office Practice; Design and Technology sub-jects, and Study Skills. Although the authors of the National Curriculum initially placed IT in the Design and Technology orders, their dominant influence seems to have been information/study skills. However, ICT resources were largely under the influence of Computer Science and commercial subjects at the time, and this still influences practice in Key Stage 3 (Kennewell *et al.*, 2000).

Some GCSE syllabuses have a strong vocational aspect (such as those originating from the RSA Examinations Board, now OCR) but the influence of the Computer Science interest group is strong in many examination boards and recently the trend has been towards a more theoretical approach.

The National Curriculum explicitly states that studies in other curriculum subjects should be the main context for the study of ICT up to Key Stage 3, and the change in context for examination courses represents a progression from the familiar context of school to the less familiar context of commerce and work. We shall consider the question of context further in Chapters 5 and 8.

Your role as an ICT teacher is to help pupils analyse the information requirements of these contexts and develop an understanding of the concepts and methods which are needed to satisfy those information requirements. For example, the supermarket system is an appropriate context, but pupils' views of it will be initially limited to features of the checkout such as bar code scanning. Considerable work will need to be done to develop understanding of the purpose and processes involved in point-of-sale transactions, stock control, and purchasing.

It is thus helpful to use a case study approach in which a scenario for ICT applica-tion is studied in terms of:

- the need for information;
- data collection and entry;
- data communication;
- data storage;
- data processing;
- information display.

By considering the purpose of the information system, you can analyse and evaluate each aspect in terms of design issues, techniques used, hardware/software tools needed.

Task 2.8 Analysing an information system for teaching

Choose an information system with which you are familiar and briefly analyse it, using the framework provided in Figure 2.2.

Figure 2.2 Framework for the study of an information system
Source: Based on Kennewell *et al.* (2000, 114)

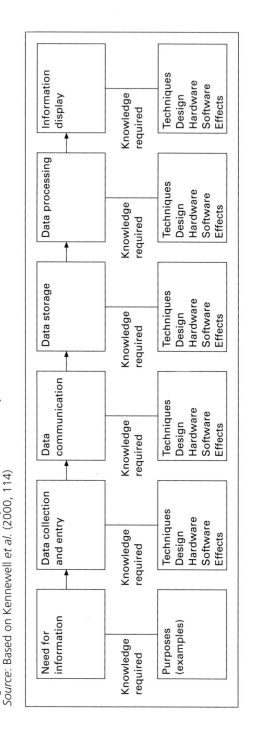

RELATIONSHIP WITH OTHER TECHNOLOGY SUBJECTS

ICT can be used in the learning of all subjects, but there is a close relation between the nature of ICT and Design and Technology (D&T) as subjects. Indeed, until 1995 they were part of the same umbrella subject of Technology in the National Curriculum for England and Wales (DES/WO, 1990).

Design and Technology is also a new subject in the curriculum. It was created in response to the 1988 Education Reform Act. It moved the subject away from the Craft, Design and Technology (CDT) that had been taught in schools throughout the 1970s and 1980s. The subject is one that engages pupils both intellectually and practically. It is based on the solving of real problems set in contexts of which they have some, if only a little, experience, in order that they can develop knowledge, skills and understanding. This is achieved through the sub-sets of the subject:

- resistant materials technology (RMT);
- graphical products;
- systems and control;
- textiles;
- food.

It is an important area of the curriculum as it raises pupils' awareness of what is happening in the ever changing world in which they will take their places. Design and Technology involves the application of knowledge from other areas of the curriculum – Mathematics, Science, ICT, etc. These are all used in practical situations such as measuring, calculating amounts of materials, and using electricity and electronics theory to design and make circuits.

Each area of Design and Technology will divide the subject into two main areas – designing and making. The relative weightings of these two areas altered a little during the 1990s; the present weighting is about 40 per cent designing and 60 per cent making. Most teachers use a design process mechanism to enable pupils to succeed in the subject. The complexity of this process will depend on the ability of the pupil – and that of the teacher.

Designing is an active and reflective aspect of the subject. In order to be effective as designers, pupils need to have active imaginations that are engaged by external stimuli such as the work of professional designers, videos, photographs of existing products. Knowledge of ICT in this area is vitally important. Pupils can have access to images and websites that can provide the stimulus. Further, the use of various packages such as desktop publishing and graphics can provide excellent aids for pupils to produce quality work. Many pupils are unable to sketch or draw well and are therefore reluctant to put their ideas on paper, so ICT can make a significant difference.

The introduction of other ICT software provides pupils with access to industry standard products that they can use easily. Examples of this include software to construct artwork for printed circuit boards (pcb), design packages that are capable of communicating work to a printer, plotter, computer-driven milling machine, sign-writing machine or similar device. All this helps to increase a pupil's design capability by broadening the availability of sources of information and thereby giving pupils more opportunities to use and develop their creativity.

In a similar manner, the making element of design and technology gives pupils the opportunity to explore the properties of different materials – how they can be processed to make high quality products. Again, knowledge of ICT can assist some of these processes. The use of computer aided manufacturing (CAM) can enhance, encourage and build the self-esteem and confidence of pupils. Examples of CAM use in textiles include computer driven sewing and embroidery machines.

One area of design and technology relates directly to ICT. This is systems and control. In this area, computer control is one of the elements taught. The software available for this is now very user friendly. Pupils can quickly learn how to use the packages and design programs to control models they have designed and built. For example, pupils in Key Stage 3 can undertake simple systems such as an egg timer or traffic light sequencing successfully. Pupils in Key Stage 4 can design and make systems to control the movement and storage of stock in a warehouse or a system to control a three-floor lift. The potential is very great, and limited only by imagination and school resources!

Task 2.9 Comparing ICT and Design and Technology subjects

Identify what is similar to ICT capability in either RMT or food technology. What are the key differences?

ADVANCED COURSE CONTENT AND TEACHING

In examination schemes for pupils up to the age of 16, different examination syllabuses and papers reflect the different backgrounds of the examination boards and their senior examiners. Some have a Computer Science feel to them, with the emphasis on how hardware and software works; others have more of a Business Studies feel, with the emphasis on solving business problems. For students beyond age 16, these emphases are reflected more formally in the various schemes available. The two emphases we noted in intermediate courses can be traced through to advanced courses, with an 'academic' branch focusing more on theoretical concepts behind system design (in GCE A level Computing, for instance) and the other 'vocational' branch focusing more on application to increasingly real and complex problems (in the AVCE and GCE A level ICT schemes).

Both branches of advanced study are characterised by more expectation of *analysis* rather than the *description* of systems that is appropriate for GCSE, and the balance of activity may be different from the style which is typical of GCSE. Whilst the development of ICT capability is likely to contain a significant element of *bricolage* (see, for instance, Papert, 1996) progression to more advanced courses in ICT requires a more formal, systematic approach to problem solving. It is therefore important to expose and attempt to resolve any misconceptions which students have developed through their informal learning, and assist them in developing viable 'mental models' (Ben-Ari, 2001) for aspects of ICT such as variable, object, program and the computer itself. This idea will be considered further in subsequent chapters. Many successful schools start the more formal approach to problem solving in Key Stage 4, and Chapter 8 will explore this in more detail.

The more formal branch of advanced ICT emphasises depth of understanding of concepts and more detailed knowledge of techniques in order to gain a high level of control over ICT systems. You may need to plan a higher proportion of structured direct teaching, using explanation, questioning and class discussion to develop pupils' understanding of concepts such as programming, data structures, relational database design and network topology which it would be inefficient to develop through experience and reflection. The more vocational branch, such as the Advanced Vocational Certificate in Education (AVCE) for ICT, emphasises more complex and unfamiliar contexts. You will need to plan extended engagement in realistic settings, through case studies, role play, work placements, independent study and seminars. Structured reflection on experience will be the primary mode of developing concepts. The differences are only in the balance of activity, however, and you should apply the same principles of effective ICT teaching that apply to lower level courses to advanced teaching as well. These principles will be developed in the next few chapters.

Task 2.10 Comparing different ICT schemes

Compare an 'academic' syllabus such as A level Computing with a 'vocational' syllabus such as the AVCE in IT. Choose a topic that appears in both, and analyse the differences in what is expected. You may need to consider the assessment scheme and sample examination questions to appreciate the differences fully. Compare, too, the approach taken by textbooks designed for the different types of course, and analyse the differences.

SUMMARY

The subject of ICT includes the National Curriculum subject of ICT together with more advanced specialist study. National Curriculum ICT involves learning to apply ICT tools of an increasing range and sophistication to a broadening and deepening range of problems. The processes cover a number of strands that provide a foundation for more advanced study. Progression in ICT capability involves development in various components – higher order skills, concepts, processes, techniques and routines – and teaching approaches should pay attention to all these.

Specialist study in ICT involves greater depth of study concerning the nature of the tools and methods of solving problems using ICT. The basis of most aspects of intermediate and advanced courses is the information system, its analysis and design in terms of information required, and the data to be collected, entered, processed, communicated, displayed and stored. Teaching approaches should involve the study of real systems, with practical and theoretical work integrated as far as possible.

FURTHER READING

DfES (2001) *Key Stage 3 Scheme of Work for ICT*. HTTP: http://www.standards.dfee.gov.uk/ schemes/ict2_pdf/. The web version of the government's Scheme of Work for Key Stage 3 which gives a view of progression in ICT through a structured set of teaching and learning activities. Also see http://www.ncaction.org.uk/subjects/ict/index.htm for guidance on assessment and samples of pupils' work at different levels.

Owen-Jackson, G. (ed.) (2000) *Learning to Teach Design and Technology in the Secondary School: a Companion to School Experience*, London, RoutledgeFalmer. A companion volume to this one, designed for Design and Technology teachers, which gives a fuller perspective on the nature of design and technology as a subject.

3 Analysing and Developing your Knowledge of ICT

Neil Stanley and Chris Jones

In this chapter, we guide you in the analysis of what it is that you know about ICT, and we suggest approaches to developing your knowledge in those aspects of ICT with which you are less familiar. Confidence in your own subject knowledge is essential for good teaching. Your awareness of and reflection on what you know and how you know it (your metacognitive knowledge) are paramount. As you learn to teach, you will need to fill gaps in your knowledge and develop a deeper understanding of ideas that may be a little hazy from your previous studies or employment. We recognise that you learn new things in ICT all the time when applying ICT processes to real life information needs, but now you will be learning for *teaching* purposes. It is important that you can represent your ideas to make them suited to the ability of the learners you are dealing with. In doing this, you need to make your points simple but still correct.

OBJECTIVES

By the end of this chapter, you should be able to:

- analyse your own ICT knowledge in terms of capability and concepts;
- identify ways in which you learn ICT and show awareness of differences in learning styles;

- explain the ideas of continuity and progression from early learning of computer games to advanced study of Computer Science;
- understand more advanced concepts and other unfamiliar aspects of ICT knowledge where relevant;
- analyse what you have learned from lectures, books, the internet tasks, projects, discussions, help from others, and helping others.

WHAT IS SUBJECT KNOWLEDGE?

Consider the simple model of different aspects of subject knowledge provided in Figure 3.1.

At the lowest level we have the basic ICT skills that have been classified in Chapters 1 and 2 as processes, techniques and routines. We have seen that these skills are part of a much more complex idea: ICT capability. This involves the marrying of skills with the knowledge and understanding which are used to determine how and when it is appropriate to apply these skills for your own use.

However, ICT subject knowledge is more than this, as you will also need to know when, how and why to apply ICT solutions to other people's problems, and to be aware of a range of applications of ICT which may be found in different fields of human activity.

Figure 3.1 Relations between some aspects of subject knowledge

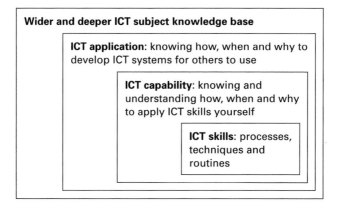

Task 3.1 Your range of knowledge and skills

From your own knowledge base identify: (a) three ICT routines, (b) three other elements of your ICT capability, (c) three elements of ICT application with which you are familiar.

- Where does programming fit into your subject knowledge model?
- What about knowing about how the computer works?
- Do the answers to these questions have an impact on Figure 3.1?
- Is there another level that we can add?

Subject knowledge audit

It is important to realise that your subject knowledge will map into these categories in a way that may be very different from your colleagues. Much of this will be dependent on your past experience. It is important, therefore, to map your experience as fully as you can and to identify those areas of skill, knowledge and understanding of your subject that will enable you to feel fully confident in your subject knowledge as you prepare to teach.

Task 3.2 Identifying gaps in your own knowledge

Use the subject knowledge profile in the appendix or the subject knowledge profile provided in your training institution, to identify the gaps in your knowledge, skills and understanding.

You may consider that there is a layer that underpins this model: knowing how and when, and to what depth, you should teach these ideas.

There is no definitive list of subject knowledge for secondary IT specialists. You could consider the A level subject specifications as being useful starting points for identifying the core of what you need to know in order to establish a strong subject base. You will need to decide whether to concentrate on A level ICT, or whether your previous subject knowledge and experience are suited to A level Computing. You may of course see elements of your own strengths identified in both specifications. You should aim to identify where there are overlaps between the two subject specifications, and to compare these with the subject knowledge requirements of the AVCE subject specification. The appendix gives an example of a subject knowledge audit in use for student teachers on an 11–16 course.

Task 3.3 Range of
subject audit

Look again at the appendix. Are you surprised at the inclusion of any of
these topics? Are there any you feel important that are missing? Are
there any you would leave out?

If you are on a course of initial teacher education (ITE) you may need to give evidence of your subject knowledge, and to identify where you gained it. It could be that elements of your knowledge came from your previous study (including undergraduate modules or employment based training). If so identify these. You could also find that some of your subject knowledge comes from your preparation to teach: in this instance identify the source of your preparation and provide examples of the work you developed for the classroom. You could, on the other hand, be asked to produce model answers to examination questions and projects as evidence, or your course may test you in some other way.

LEARNING ICT

You have probably been using computers and software for so long that you cannot remember exactly how you learnt many of the things you use now. There are also probably many things you have forgotten. It is likely that the things that you remember are those which you use or do frequently whilst the ones that you forgot you learnt for a single specific purpose.

Learning theories

During the last century, various theories were developed to try to explain how we come to develop the knowledge, skills and understanding that we use to make sense of the world we live in and that we apply to the problems that we face. One particular idea is fundamental to our current understanding of learning: constructivism. The central feature of this idea is that learning involves an active process of constructing knowledge, rather than a passive process of receiving knowledge transmitted by others. There are different views on how this construction is influenced, with those influenced most by Piaget emphasising the process of individual discovery and adaptation, and those influenced most by Vygotsky (such as Bruner) emphasising the role of other people and the role of tools (including language). The implications for teachers of these theories will be explored implicitly throughout the rest of the book, but we can summarise them simplistically as follows:

- Except for very simple facts, just telling somebody something doesn't help them to learn it.

- Learners need opportunities to find things out for themselves through active involvement.
- Understanding is generated by thinking about activity, both while it is taking place and afterwards: this is called *reflection*.
- Tasks should be given which require learners to think, that is, not too easy, but should be within their grasp, that is, not too hard.
- Support for learners should depend on what they can do for themselves.
- We should provide 'scaffolding' for activity, that is, help initially and then remove or reduce it when the learners can do things for themselves.

For more detail on these general issues of learning see, for example, Baumann *et al.* (1997).

Increasingly, it has become clear how important the context of learning can be. Knowledge gained in school can be very difficult to apply in 'real world' settings, and learners need help in recognising general principles in what they know so that they can seek opportunities to apply their knowledge in other contexts.

Look at these tasks and discussion points and identify the issues pertaining to your own learning of ICT. Identify also what issues you need to consider as you prepare to teach.

Task 3.4 Analysing your learning of ICT

- *Keyboarding.* Can you recall how you learnt to type using a computer? Did it just happen? Were you forced to learn how to type 'properly'? Did you learn from a typing tutor program? Compare your experience with your colleagues'.
- *Word processing.* Does skill development in word processing just happen? How were you taught to word-process? Are you aware of the rules for presentation, or have you developed an *ad hoc* approach to the presentation of your work? What is the role of house styles? Are there 'correct' ways to present letters?
- *Spreadsheets.* What difficulties can you recall in your initial use of a spreadsheet package? What are cell references? What are the conventions for naming cells? What is the difference between absolute and relative references? How do you calculate percentages in a spreadsheet package?

Learning styles

Newborn babies will make use of all their senses to find out about the world. It is no different when we are adults; our senses are the most important ways we have of making sense of our world. However, by the time we are 11 years old we have developed preferred ways of using our senses to process new information. Some of us prefer to use our eyes, others prefer to listen, and a third group prefer to touch and move things (Smith, 1998).

These three main ways of thinking – visually, aurally and through physical activity – have been used to characterise different preferences for learning:

- *Visual.* Visual learners find it easier to take in new information through pictures, diagrams, charts, films, and so on.
- *Auditory.* Aural learners find it easier to take in new information through the spoken word.
- *Kinaesthetic.* Kinaesthetic learners find it easier to take in new information through copying demonstrations and physically manipulating things.

It is thus important when planning lessons to use a multi-sensory approach, to ensure that we allow the pupils an opportunity to gain knowledge through Visual, Aural and Kinaesthetic means (from now on referred to as VAK. This is not the only classification of learning styles; see Capel *et al.*, 2001: unit 5.1).

Your own learning style will differ from those of your colleagues; for instance, you may find it very easy to transfer your skills from one software application to another whilst a colleague can more easily see different or new applications of a software tool than you can. It is thus important for you first to analyse your own preferences. This will have benefits in two ways:

- You may be able to improve your own learning effectiveness by focusing on the methods you find most fruitful.
- You will gain an awareness that your own learning style may not match those of many of your pupils.

Task 3.5 Learning styles

Determine your preferred learning style using the VAK classification. Do you think that this has influenced the development of your subject knowledge, particularly in the aspects you have found difficult to learn?

When you are teaching, it is crucial that you are aware of learners' differing needs and provide for these in the management of the learning opportunities you provide. Just because you like a particular method, it does not mean that your learners will also find it the best way. Equally, if you are effectively and efficiently to extend your knowledge, you need to do it in your most comfortable learning format.

It is also important to be aware of the development of misconceptions that develop through learning informally by making the wrong link between concepts or ideas and using analogies inappropriately. For instance, many people think that spreadsheet formulas have to use the SuM function, for instance =SuM(9*A5) to multiply the contents of cell A5 by 9. Although this will give the correct answer, it is inefficient and will lead to difficulties when trying to learn about other functions. As you start to plan lessons, you need to be sure that you are not teaching and reinforcing your own misconceptions.

Task 3.6 Misconceptions

- Suggest a reason why the misconception described above is so common.
- Identify a misconception that you have had in your own ICT work or one you have observed in a pupil. How do you think that idea originated?

Progression in your learning

The computer today pervades society and, as you saw in Chapter 1, many children will be brought up in homes where it is part of the basic infrastructure of life. The vast majority will have had access at least to some sort of games machine or console from an early age.

Most children's toys are now computer processor based and the child needs to learn some basic principles of use. Personal computer (PC) and console games require quite sophisticated physical skills for successful use. By comparison, most application packages are slow to respond and give poor feedback. Game play is an end in itself, whereas application packages are used to produce some sort of product; they are true tools. You may be motivated to learn about a new application package for its own sake, but for most people the desire to produce the product is the critical issue, and you may have seen that this is the main goal of pupils in the ICT classroom, too.

As you mature and progress in ICT, your goal shifts away from the immediate physical product towards the idea of an effective system for people to use. For many pupils, this is much less motivating, and you should consider whether you can maintain the motivation produced by the immediate feedback from the computer game when they are embarking on more formal systems development work.

Task 3.7 Motivation for advanced study in ICT

Identify what motivated you to start or continue your studies in ICT up to degree level, or to move into ICT in your employment. Compare your ideas with those of colleagues from different backgrounds, and see whether there any common features.

The idea of progression is complex and requires careful thought. In many schools you will observe different year groups doing very similar tasks. This may not look like progression. However, progression has to be related to the individual learner and the activities may indicate more about the changes in the opportunities now available in the school. We will develop this key idea further in Chapter 4.

Task 3.8 The further ICT curriculum

Many degree subjects are mostly just narrower, deeper, 'harder' versions of their school subject. Is this true of ICT/Computing or does the curriculum change in nature at degree level? If your studies were not in this area, talk to someone who did study ICT at this level.

Do you think a degree in Computer Science a good basis for teaching someone to use desktop publishing at Key Stage 3?

Extending your own knowledge

Information technology as a secondary school subject is perhaps unique in its rate of change – it is only about forty years since the first commercial computers started work. What will you be doing in forty years? Even if you are still teaching, you will certainly be nearing the end of your career. If this rate of change continues, you will require considerable professional development to keep up with the range of applications of ICT and the breadth of uses. New versions of software packages seem to appear at least every two years, and you will need to work to maintain your knowledge in a way that no other subject teacher has to.

Task 3.9 Strategies

List as many ways as possible of extending and updating your knowledge. Form a composite list with a colleague. How many of these do you already do? How many others could you do for little cost in money, effort or time?

Besides traditional textbook sources, you should try to read popular computing magazines, the professional trade publications and journals of teacher organisations such as the Association for ICT in Education (ACITT: see www.acitt.org.uk) and the Computer Education Group (CEG: see www.ceg.org.uk), as well as visiting government, commercial and enthusiast websites. Research is being made increasingly accessible in summary form on the web, for instance by BECTA (www.becta.org.uk/research/

reports). There are various discussion lists, newsgroups and conferences that you can subscribe to. All these may throw up items which may seem irrelevant at the time but that suddenly become useful at a later date, so keeping good records is essential. These sources of support are considered further in Chapter 12.

More advanced theoretical ICT knowledge may be gained from textbooks, continuing professional development (CPD) courses, perhaps at a local institution of higher education (IHE), an institution further afield, or via online courses. Also, many of your colleagues on your course will have knowledge and understanding that you can access, so try to maintain this network when you start teaching. An e-mail distribution list is very helpful for sharing ideas and information.

Task 3.10 Evaluating sources

When you have to teach a topic that is new or less familiar to you, you will need to decide on trustworthy and relevant sources. Think about the sources you have available to you: textbooks, magazines, colleagues, the web, and so on.

Make a list of as many sources as possible. Which do you think are the most likely not to provide faulty information? What criteria do you use?

Developing your pedagogical knowledge

The best way to consolidate your knowledge is by teaching it, and you may find it is useful to note what you have taught as part of your subject knowledge audit. You should reflect on the change in your knowledge which occurs when you plan to teach it. The cycle of pedagogical reasoning (Wilson *et al.*, 1987) involves the following:

- comprehension;
- transformation;
- instruction;
- evaluation;
- reflection;
- new comprehension.

This model includes the process of *transformation* of knowledge: you critically interpret your knowledge, then represent it, adapt it and tailor it. As a result, you no longer have purely subject knowledge; you have developed 'pedagogical content knowledge' (Wilson *et al.*, 1987) which includes how to represent the subject or teaching, how learners learn it (including common misconceptions), how curricular materials are organised, and how particular topics are best included in the curriculum.

Task 3.11 Analysing your pedagogical knowledge

Think back on a topic you have taught (perhaps just to a friend if you have not taught a class yet) and consider how you represented the ideas. Did you just tell them what you knew, or did you think of how to link the ideas with their existing knowledge?

SUMMARY

You have studied ICT as a subject to a high level, and it is valuable to reflect on what you know, how you learned it, what you don't know, and how you might develop new knowledge. Your motivation and interests will be different from those of others, particularly your pupils, and you should also compare your progression in learning with the opportunities afforded to current school pupils. Finally, you should recognise the difference between learning ICT for problem solving and systems development and learning it for teaching. The way you apply the concepts and skills in the classroom will be different from the way you apply them in undergraduate studies and in the 'real world'.

FURTHER READING

Bradley, R. (1999) *Understanding Computer Science for Advanced Level*, London: Nelson Thornes. A substantial guide to advanced content in the field of ICT, considered to be the most authoritative text at this level.

British Computer Society Schools Committee Working Party (eds.) (2002) *A Glossary of Computing Terms*, tenth edition, Harlow: Addison Wesley. An indispensable reference source for the ICT specialist teacher, this book is used by examination boards as the definitive source of definitions and explanations.

Christopher, D. (2000) *Computing Projects in Visual Basic*, Ipswich: Payne-Gallway. Also in the popular Payne-Gallway series.

Heathcote, P. (1999a) *A level ICT*, second edition, Ipswich: Payne-Gallway. An alternative text that provides a good guide to the less formal advanced schemes based on solving problems rather than applying theoretical knowledge.

Heathcote, P. (1999b) *Successful IT Projects in Excel*, Ipswich: Payne-Gallway. One of a series which provides guidance on practical projects in Word, Access, Front Page as well as Excel.

Part II

Developing ICT Teaching Skills

4 Structuring Lessons and Units of Work

Ian Hughes and Steve Kennewell

The next three chapters deal with the essential elements of teaching: planning, preparation and the management of learning in the classroom. They focus on Key Stage 3, as examination courses in Key Stage 4 and above are considered separately in Chapter 8. In planning specialist courses in ICT, you should aim to provide a continuous progression from the pupils' capability at the start of the course towards a target of pupils having a high level of independence as users of ICT and a good understanding of the underlying concepts. Each unit of work must develop particular knowledge, skills and understanding. Each individual lesson should contribute to pupils' progress by incorporating a core element which you expect all pupils to achieve, extension material to challenge the quicker learners, and plans to remedy any lack of skills in less capable pupils.

OBJECTIVES

By the end of this chapter, you should be able to:

- identify teaching aims, learning objectives, key ideas and benchmarks for progress during a unit of work;
- plan for progression in pupils' ICT capability;
- estimate time scales and set out plans for individual lessons;
- evaluate lessons in terms of personal performance, the effectiveness of teaching strategies, the suitability of tasks, and the nature of pupils' learning.

INITIAL STAGES OF PLANNING

Identifying aims and objectives

Aims are the overall goals of pupils' learning that you are trying to achieve during a unit of work. Learning objectives are the specific abilities which you want pupils to develop, and which can be assessed.

Aims should represent the essence of the subject. They should be broad statements giving the overall vision of the ideas you want pupils to learn, such as developing their ability to adapt presentations for different audiences. They should include the higher order skills in ICT such as identifying opportunities and evaluating work, and other Key Skills such as solving problems, working collaboratively and improving their own learning. Some of your aims may be very general and do not always need to be written down explicitly (see Capel *et al.*, 2001: unit 7.1). The subject of ICT provides a good context for helping pupils to acquire the skill of lifelong learning, including the ability to find things out for themselves. It also helps improve pupils' ability to work in groups, as problem solving in ICT generally involves teams. One of the characteristics of ICT is its ability to offer early success in tasks. This helps to raise pupils' self-esteem and, as a consequence, their motivation to learn (see Capel *et al.*, 2001: unit 3.2).

Objectives should provide more detail concerning how the aims are to be achieved and the steps that will be involved along the way. They will need to show progression from the current level of knowledge and skill to a projected baseline that is achievable by all pupils (some perhaps needing extra help) and extension targets for the most able. It is useful to identify strategic stages in the skill development process with easily assessable outcomes. For instance, when teaching to produce publications using DTP, you may have an objective that pupils should be able to select text and picture frames, and position them precisely on the page.

Task 4.1 Observing experienced teachers

Arrange to observe an experienced teacher during a lesson, and find out in advance what the learning objectives of the lesson are.

Be careful how you approach this observation. Make it clear that the purpose of the observation is to learn about different teaching strategies. Be professional; do not make comments on the effectiveness of the teaching unless asked, and then focus on only positive aspects.

During your observation, make notes on the structure of the lesson, the learning objectives and the way the teacher ensured that these were achieved as far as possible. Focus, too, on the following questions:

- How does the teacher share the learning objectives with the pupils?
- How are the resources organised to help pupils meet the learning objectives?

- How does the teacher find out whether pupils have achieved the learning objectives?
- What constraints affect the teacher's work?
- Can you identify particular phases in the lesson – for example, entry and administration, introduction and explanation, task and support, assessment and review? How long does each phase take?

Remember that experienced teachers sometimes make what they do look simple and straightforward. They have the advantage of knowing the pupils well and taking this into account when planning and preparing their lessons.

Discuss your findings with your mentor or tutor. What other issues occurred to you during the lesson?

As a student teacher you should be given clear guidelines as to what to teach and the goals for pupils' learning. These goals will have their roots in the government guidelines, such as the National Curriculum, or in examination syllabuses. The school aims and policies will also have an influence. However, before you start preparing lesson plans you will need an overall picture of what learning is to take place over a unit or topic of work and how this fits into the overall Scheme of Work for the year or key stage (see Capel *et al.*, 2001: unit 2.2; Baumann *et al.*, 1997). Such schemes are important in ensuring that all pupils gain their entitlement to learning in ICT, and in enabling other subject teachers to check what ICT skills pupils can be expected to apply in their own subject. Figure 4.1 shows an extract from an outline Scheme of Work used in one particular school, covering the first term of Year 7.

Task 4.2 Analysing Schemes of Work

Use the extract from the Scheme of Work in Figure 4.1 and identify, if possible:

- the software to be used;
- aims;
- objectives;
- prior knowledge expected;
- how skills are built up progressively;
- key learning points for each stage of the topic;
- differentiation in expected learning: what is expected of more and less able pupils.

Obtain a copy of a Scheme of Work for a topic or year of study from your school, and one from the Scheme of Work on the DfES Standards website: http://www.standards.dfes.gov.uk/schemes2/secondary-ICT/. Take one unit or topic from each source, and carry out the same exercise as above. Identify which features of each scheme that you have looked at will be most helpful to you.

Figure 4.1 Example outline Scheme of Work for the first term of Year 7

1 Introductory unit
Introduction to ICT in the Hall for the whole of Year 7, with forms given out:
- Internet permission form.
- Initial data collection form (Year 7 survey).
- Information relating to network access and Internet letter to parents.

Introduction to include:
- Overview of school computer rooms, network.
- User ID and user area – security.
- Internet access – E-mail – Safety guidelines.
- Do's and don'ts of Internet and e-mail.

Note: concepts should be introduced as part of the practical sessions. Pupils to make their own word processed notes with guidance.

2 DTP unit 1 (using Publisher)
Five or six lessons
Discuss classroom rules and routines.
Collect in Internet permission forms signed by parents and pupils.
Talk through: log on – password change – create sub-directory – load template for 'Rules', type up, save and print.
Set task 'It's me': load template for personal information sheet, enter details, save, proof reading procedures, and print with own photograph.
Introduction to scanner and digital camera for photograph.
(Link with work being carried out in English and Modern Foreign Languages.)
Introduce word processing rules and correct It's me: reprint corrected version.
Extension work. Design and create front page for work folder. Template available for differentiation.
Passport template, fill in with photo. Save and print.

3 Internet unit 1
Four or five lessons
Guidelines for use in school.
Review of the safety presentation.
Carry out survey of Internet access at home.
Question and answer on basic Internet terminology.
Talk through how to access Internet and intranet pages.
Set task: produce information sheet on planets for primary school, using NASA website (link with science).
Demonstrate e-mail and review guidelines.
Set task: send personal information sheet to form tutor.
Demonstrate: headers for name and form, footer for date and filename; borders, etc., to amend and improve DTP done so far.
Discuss: what makes different pupils' information sheets good?

4 DTP unit 2 Christmas cards (audience and URLs)
One or two lessons.
Discussion of how to lay out a card with examples.
Use of wizard to create card layout.
Discussion of what is suitable for young child, friend, elderly relative.
Pupils choose one and use Christmas clip art from intranet or Internet.
Extension: change your card for a different type of person.

Once you have determined the overall goals for the unit, you need to consider:

- *An introduction.* How are you going to capture pupils' interest and motivate them to complete the tasks you will set them? How are you going to explain the key ideas so that pupils understand?
- *Practice or development activities.* How will you support and monitor the pupils' work? How will you cater for pupils' different abilities?
- *Key learning points.* What are the essential elements you expect pupils to have grasped?
- *The assessment of learning.* How will you find out whether they have achieved the outcomes you intended? How will you give feedback on progress?

You should also plan for variety and progression throughout, and we will consider these aspects in detail in subsequent sections.

Selecting teaching strategies

Teaching strategies are the means through which teachers enable pupils to learn. Demonstrating, explaining, questioning, group discussions, role play and pupil presentations are all important features of good ICT teaching in addition to setting pupils practical ICT tasks. They are skills you need to learn and develop as you progress through your training and into your teaching posts. The teaching strategies you use can make a large difference to the success or failure of a lesson. Your choice of strategies needs to provide a means of interesting pupils in the topic, engaging them in learning and enabling them to carry out the tasks associated with the topic.

Every lesson should make use of a range of teaching strategies to ensure that you cater for the different learning styles of the pupils and their different levels of attainment. It is important to ensure that the strategies chosen enable the children to meet the learning objectives of the lesson. As you progress you will develop a repertoire of teaching approaches and be able to apply them critically and flexibly to each teaching situation. This will come with time and experience. It is worth analysing a variety of teaching styles and strategies that you see in your observations and try them out in your teaching. Consider which approaches are appropriate in different situations. Some will work for you and some will not, and it is important to experiment and work on developing the most effective for you!

It does not have to be a purely trial and error process, however. There are certain guiding principles which you can use to help you gain success in most situations. These concern involving pupils from the outset, explaining ideas in ways they can understand, utilising their existing knowledge, asking focused questions, listening and responding to their answers, observing and evaluating how they respond to tasks, intervening when they are working ineffectively, providing just enough help for them to succeed, giving helpful feedback on progress, reflecting on activity and reviewing key learning points (Newton, 2000; Muijs and Reynolds, 2001).

Task 4.3 Variety of teaching strategies

Think back to your observation for Task 4.1. What teaching strategies did the teacher use in each phase of the lesson? Can you identify why particular strategies were selected at each stage?

Identifying assessment opportunities

You should plan to find out how pupils are progressing at particular points during each lesson, rather than waiting until the end of a task to assess their learning. Assessment opportunities occur during the initial question and answer session to introduce the topic or recap key points, whilst pupils are working on the task, and during a plenary session at the end. It is helpful to identify particular points in the task where you will check pupils' work on screen or ask them to bring you a print-out. This enables you to question them and to check whether they are meeting your expectations in terms of outcome and rate of progress.

The facility for developing and improving work is an important feature of ICT, but not all pupils will have the knowledge or motivation to take full advantage of it. Some pupils, however, will overdo the changes and spend all the lesson perfecting their heading if given the chance. Your systematic monitoring process gives you the opportunity to prompt and assist them with their improvements.

Task 4.4 Key learning points and assessment opportunities

For the unit of study that you analysed in Task 4.2, identify further key learning points and identify opportunities to assess pupils' capability.

PLANNING IN DETAIL

Example of the lesson planning process

In order to examine the lesson planning process in detail, we will consider an initial unit on DTP at the start of secondary school. This is probably the most useful aspect to develop first because it is required in many areas of the curriculum. It is also a useful starting point for developing the higher order skills involved in ICT capability.

In addition to studying the Scheme of Work and identifying the lesson objectives, you need to consider the following:

- *Pupils' prior knowledge.* How are you going to determine this?
- *New ideas to be introduced.* If there are several of these, can you introduce them in stages?
- *Context of activity.* What is going to be realistic and motivating?
- *Sequence and variety of activities.* How can you build up understanding progressively using different approaches in order to involve all pupils?
- *Lesson phases.* How are you going to divide up the lesson into different activities?
- *Transitions between phases.* How are you going to manage these?
- *Timing and pace.* How long should you spend on each phase of the lesson, so that pupils can keep up without becoming bored?
- *Review and recap.* How can you stimulate pupils to think back on what they have done and consolidate the learning of key points?
- *Resources.* What will be available, and how can they be used most effectively?
- *Expectations and targets.* What do you expect all pupils to achieve, most pupils to achieve, and just the most able pupils to achieve? How do you communicate this to pupils?

Checking prior knowledge and introducing new procedures

On entering secondary school many pupils may have some of the skills for entering text and graphics on to an electronic page. However, some will not and may need considerable practice initially before the basic skills become routine. They will certainly be unfamiliar with the particular ICT and learning environment that is operated in the secondary school, and issues of primary–secondary transition are discussed in more detail in Chapter 10.

The following points should stimulate your thoughts about the issues to be considered and you will be able to identify many more as your experience grows.

- Do pupils know what is meant by a program? Desktop publishing? Word processing?
- Are they clear about network access, log on procedures and the use of the pupil's own area?
- Are there particular rules for using a computer in the school? Are there rules for entry to the computer room?
- Do they know how to start software, and the first thing to do in a task?
- Should they use a 'wizard' in order to get started, or does this make it more difficult for them to understand the process and develop their work later?
- Where will they save their work? What file names should they use?
- How will the pupils remember what to do a week later when they come back or possibly two weeks later?
- Do all pupils know where each character is on the keyboard?
- Do they understand upper and lower case, and the use of the shift key?
- Can they handle paragraphs, spacing, font and size of text?
- If they all print off similar work, how will you know who owns what?

These are all questions that you will need to consider and incorporate within your planning. It is debatable whether to use word processing or desktop publishing in the first instance. The one that you choose will be the pupils' preferred choice for general unguided work unless they have had previous and confident experience of ICT.

Task 4.5 Introducing ICT

> Use your information about policy in your placement school, together with observations of experienced teachers, to try to answer some of the points raised above. How does your school actually introduce ICT in Year 7?

Deciding on the sequencing and variety of activities

You will need to consider carefully how you will start the teaching of a unit. In our example, you may think of introducing the basic concepts of the computer system such as input and output, but the pupils are keen and want to get on with using the computers. This initial motivation needs to be maintained for all pupils in the class, from the most able to the SEN pupil. Consider how much the pupils need to know about how the computer works at this point, and reconsider the objectives of this initial lesson.

If pupils gain a good initial impression of work in your subject, their motivation for the rest of their time in school is likely to be higher. It will thus be a good idea for them to be able to obtain a print-out of an effective piece of work that they have produced as early as possible. One way of achieving this goal is to use a template. Templates can be set up on the intranet using a DTP or word processing program. The pupil should not easily be able to change the format 'accidentally'. Pupils load a template from the intranet, save a copy of the template into their own area and fill in, for example, name, form and date. Their work can then be saved and printed. This is a useful exercise that covers a number of skills and provides initial evidence of ICT usage. You now need to consider what you use as the content and theme of the template.

Devising the context of activity

As a general rule, practical work carried out by pupils should have a purpose beyond the acquisition of skills, whether it is related to ICT theory, to a cross-curricular theme or to another subject (see Chapter 11); this will foster the idea that using ICT is a tool and not just an end in itself. This will help pupils to utilise ICT in other aspects of the curriculum naturally. In addition, contexts (such as 'healthy food' or Harry Potter characters) that are within the experience of the pupils will enable the ICT process to be more easily assimilated, whilst an unfamiliar context may obscure the ICT process.

ICT skills required across the curriculum can be introduced and developed early on in the Scheme of Work. Progression from this level onwards should be towards a variety of goals, including KS4 requirements, Key Skills qualifications and the production of coursework in other subjects. When using cross-curricular contexts, you should liaise with the relevant subject teachers in order to ensure curriculum consistency.

Task 4.6 Linking with other subjects

Suppose that the History staff in your school are studying the Tudors and Stuarts with Year 8. They have asked you to show the children how they can use the Internet to find source material. You have decided to demonstrate to the children how this can be done, so that when they go to the history lesson they can work independently. Plan your demonstration, using a presentation on a large screen or interactive whiteboard.

Later in Key Stage 3 you will need to move from activities designed to stimulate the learning of techniques towards a more holistic approach where the pupils are asked to solve a problem. The degree of support will initially be great but should diminish through Key Stage 3 as pupils' higher order skills increase. It is important that pupils start keeping a report of each problem solved, noting:

- purpose, audience;
- software selected and why;
- filenames and location, backup file version.

These concepts are useful later in the pupils' schooling and the early development of these administrative tasks will provide helpful tools for the future.

The need for review and recap

ICT lessons are rarely scheduled more than once a week in Key Stage 3. How will the pupil remember what to do next time? There are a number of possible solutions:

- repetitive question and answer to reinforce important facts and techniques;
- handwritten notes by pupils copied from the board;
- printed help sheets;
- online guides that the pupils can access during a lesson or in their own time;
- notes that can be created by the pupils using a simple word processor and built up over time.

The last option has the advantage of not being so easily lost or forgotten, and can even be transferred from one pupil to another should a pupil have missed a lesson for any reason. Furthermore, the reflective activity that this generates will aid pupils' development of concepts and higher order skills. The notes will have to be checked for accuracy and completeness, of course, but this will enable you to identify any misunderstandings or important omissions, and attempt to resolve the problems at an early stage.

It is useful when introducing new concepts to quickly recap previous skills and terminology to reinforce them. Such review sessions are an opportunity for the pupils to show what they know, and will give you an opportunity to establish any gaps or confusion in their knowledge.

Selecting and producing resources

It is important for pupils to have task guides and reference material available so that they do not always have to rely on you or other pupils to help them. Indeed, you may feel that learning to use instructions and reference sources should be one of the aims of an ICT course. However, pupils often have difficulty in managing these in printed form. One solution could be to have a resource sheet available electronically on the intranet. This has difficulties initially in that the pupils would have to open another document and manipulate two windows. However, if this was accepted as the norm, a bank of electronic resources could be made available that was always at hand, thus avoiding the problem of pupils forgetting or losing resources. This opens a wide variety of possibilities, such as worksheets with direct links to a resource page on the Internet. The intranet resources could be made available for pupils to access work from home. In Chapter 5 you will find further guidance on producing such resources.

As for the content of the initial template, it could contain theory work about 'a computer system' or 'the rules of the computer room'. There should be a number of these so that pupils have opportunities to practise techniques and progress through templates, with increasing levels of skill required, combined with a build-up of content. The final template could act as an overall assessment sheet that tests knowledge of the theory of the previous sheets.

Structuring the lesson phases and emphasising key learning points

Before writing a detailed lesson plan you will need to consider a small number of key learning points that form the basis of the lesson and your lessons. These should not all be introduced at the start; instead, try to structure the lesson in such a way as to enable the pupils to comprehend and retain each point. The important goal for the start of the lessons is to make pupils 'ready to learn' (Selinger, 2001: 147). In a Mathematics lesson, merely writing 'Fractions' on the board does not create readiness to learn in pupils, and there is no reason to believe that loading a spreadsheet program on to a large display in the ICT lesson will achieve this effect by itself either. The introduction to a topic, and the recap at the start of subsequent lessons, will need to give pupils a *purpose* and *context* for the learning you intend. This issue will be developed further in Chapter 5.

Before anything else, you should plan to make a clear start by introducing the overall outline of the lesson. This will enable transitions between phases to be anticipated so that there is minimal disruption from one part of the lesson to the next. Each key point necessary for any activity will need to be emphasised before setting the task. If you plan to introduce further key points at a later stage of the lesson, decide how you will judge the right time to do so and how you will make the transition back to task activity. At the end of the lesson, a phase where you regain the attention of the whole class allows you to summarise these key points clearly and review the attainment of the objectives so that the pupils leave the lesson with a method of retaining the essential ideas. This part of the lesson is known as the plenary session (Ofsted, 2001a). The start of the next lesson should also incorporate an element of review.

Timing and pace

The timing of lessons is one of the most difficult aspects of initial teaching. Inevitably in the beginning of your teaching experience there will be times when the bell will catch you by surprise, and you have to rush to review the lesson or give homework whilst the pupils are trying to save work and log off.

Initially it may be an idea to finish a lesson earlier and plan for an extended review. Always allow time for an unhurried briefing of the form 'next lesson we will . . . and by next lesson I would like you to . . .'. It is often useful to give the homework that is written or projected on the board so that pupils can copy down exactly what is to be done, as part of the initial phase of the lesson.

Estimating the time that each phase of the lesson will take is difficult. It is vital to keep an eye on the time and it may be useful to set a watch alarm for five minutes from the end of the lesson. Time spent with individual pupils can be deceptive, and the minutes can easily fly past unexpectedly.

It can be helpful to time various activities during observations; for example, how long does it take:

- to get a class in and settle down?
- for a class to move to computers and log on?
- to move around the class?

Have contingency plans in place in case you run out of activities or the pupils finish more quickly than expected.

The other problem is judging the right pace to use in driving activities forward. You may find yourself rushing through explanations initially, without giving pupils time to think about one point before moving on to the next. This will lead to difficulties at the start of the activity, when the lack of understanding becomes clear. But if you slow down, ask a lot of questions, and continually reinforce key points, you may find that most of the lesson has gone before the practical work starts! Furthermore, pupils take a long time to make progress once they have become accustomed to a slow pace. You should endeavour to pick up the pace of your activities, without seeming to be in a rush.

Transitions

Transitions should be planned and implemented with a high degree of precision, so that you know exactly what you are going to do and say to make your instructions clear and concise. If you wish to stop the class so that you can tell them something, you must make sure that the whole class has stopped and are listening before you continue (see also Capel *et al.*, 2001: unit 2.3). If you are going to demonstrate something to the class, movement from one place to another should be quick and efficient, as delay will lead of lack of control. The detail of class management will be discussed in more detail in Chapter 6.

Expectations and targets

You should aim to identify key learning points and a stage of progress in the task which are achievable by all in the class during the lesson. Make these expectations clear to pupils and, if necessary, remind them later that they are accountable for achieving them. If there are pupils in the class who may be unable to attain your targets because of low motivation or low capability, consider whether the targets should be broken down into shorter term goals. Perhaps you could make it competitive; this may encourage the lazy pupils to pick up their work rate, and could also encourage the boys who like a challenge, but should be balanced with cooperative approaches which may better motivate girls. Also consider pupils who will quickly attain the targets set and identify what they can do next, either as a challenge (extension tasks) or as an aid to others (peer teaching).

Task 4.7 Planning a complete lesson

Now devise a complete plan for the first lesson, indicating what you are going to do and what you expect the pupils to do at each stage. When you have completed it, compare it with our example in the next section.

Figure 4.2 shows a possible solution to Task 4.7, including timings. When you start to teach your first lessons, timing will be difficult to judge. During the lesson, make a note of how long you take helping individual pupils. If you have allocated ten minutes for a practical task you will have a maximum of twenty-five seconds for each pupil in the class! The timings on the plan in Figure 4.2 are the latest times by which each phase needs to be completed if you are to finish on time. If you slip on these timings, you will need to cut something out, so plan in advance which aspects can be shortened or postponed till next lesson. Whatever point you have reached, about five minutes before the end of the lesson you should call the class together to 'round off' the lesson. At the end of the lesson, a positive note on how well they worked will have positive benefits for the confidence of the class next lesson.

Figure 4.2 Specific lesson plan for first lesson of unit of work

Topic from Scheme of Work: **DTP unit 1**				
Date 21/11/01	Duration of lesson: 10.00–10.50		Lesson within topic: 1 of 5	
Class 7 X	Total No.: 24	Boys 12	Girls 12	Age: 11–12

Aims of the unit
Introduce the ideas of DTP, with frames for text and graphics.
Develop skills in proof reading and effective presentation.
Start developing autonomy in managing work and learning.

Objectives of this lesson
Pupils should:
- be familiar with ICT lesson format, computer room rules, supported pair work, and next lesson preparation;
- understand proof reading;
- be able to log on, access their own directory and create a sub-folder;
- be able to load, amend save and print a template.

Resources
Sixteen networked PCs with Windows NT and Publisher 2000.
'It's me' template in Year 7 resources folder on intranet.

Prior knowledge
Pupils will have used Windows PCs before but not network. Some will be familiar with Publisher.

Possible difficulties
Some or all PCs not working – have paper-based 'It's me' templates ready in case this happens.
Some pupils' passwords may not be set up so they will not be able to log on – they will share for now.
Some pupils will have had little experience of loading and saving for themselves.
Identify early, monitor closely and give extra help when needed.

Assessment opportunities: indicated AO below.
Observing them logging on and creating a folder.
Collecting printout to check details entered correctly.

Timing	Teacher activity	Pupil activity	Resource
10.05	**Explain** that this lesson we are going to – • Log on to your area of the network and check that everything works. • Create a folder for your work. • Load in some work, save and print it out. • Collect in your Internet permission forms. • Write down your homework for next lesson.	Pupils should be paying attention, ready to take notes of log on details.	Data projector
10.10	**Demonstration** of logging on to the system using a pupil's ID, emphasise security of password. Then show how to open own area and create directory for own work. **Question** How to create new folder? **Answer** File – New – Folder, change name of folder to e.g. IT.	Take note of own username and password. Answer questions and make note of new folder process.	Data projector Contingency for pupils who cannot log on.

Figure 4.2 continued

10.15	Leave 'filled in' log on screen on data projector. **Instruction** Move to computer allocated with planner and log on to the system, make a new folder for your work. **Place pupils** in alternating gender order at the computer.	Pick up notes and move to designated computer.	One computer per pupil.
0.20 AO	**Rotate round class** quickly checking on pupil progress. **Collect** in Internet permission forms, make clipboard notes against each pupil on whether form collected or reason not, progress and attitude. Note where seated.	Logging on and creating subdirectory.	Class list and clipboard.
0.30	Gather class back round for demonstration. **Demonstrate** load template, save into own area, amend, re-save, partner proof read and print. **Q**: How do we: • Load (from where)? • Save (to where)? • Amend (what)? • Re-save (where)? • Proof read? • Print (how)?	Answering questions. Pay attention to demonstration. Watch back of group and peripheral pupils. Answering questions. Reading handout or writing notes.	Data projector Handout of main points. *or* Instruct-ions on screen for copying.
0.40 ins O	**Instruction**: When I say 'Return to your seats,' load, save and print the rules template. **Circulate round class** quickly checking on pupil progress. Make notes against each pupil on progress and attitude. If any common problems noted, stop class, wait for all to pay attention and give instructions or solution.	Practical work. Pair proof read, support each other. Pupils that finish quickly allocated pupils around the class.	Give out plastic wallets and collect in work produced to place in class folder.
0.45 ins	**Instruction** Make sure you have saved and log off. **Move pupils** back to centre to review main points. **Set homework** Prepare ten sets of facts about yourselves. Also need a photo of yourself. **Explain** that next lesson's theme is 'It's me'. **Praise** good work.	Write homework down.	
0.50	**Instruction** pack away and sit quietly. Dismiss in orderly fashion.		

There are two assessment opportunities highlighted in the lesson plan above. Work collected from the lesson will also give a guide as to the success of the lesson and the pupils' progress. Make a note highlighting any problem areas that arose during the lesson or as a result of the assessment of work afterwards. This will help you to fine tune other lessons. In addition, if you note who sat where (perhaps notionally number the computers around the class) you will be in a position to create a seating plan of the class ready for next lesson. This will aid in getting to know the class; learning individual names has a tremendous advantage for discipline and class management.

Task 4.8 Planning to teach modelling

Now try to produce a lesson plan to introduce modelling with spreadsheets, along the same lines as the example above. Think carefully about the key points which need to be emphasised in order to achieve the objectives.

Progression within the topic

We have considered introductions in some depth, but you will subsequently need to consider how a topic develops. It is not enough for pupils merely to practise the techniques initially introduced, and you need to think about how they should develop their ability to:

- apply the process to other situations;
- understand the underlying concepts;
- plan, monitor and evaluate their work;
- learn new techniques when appropriate.

The next example illustrates how you can build progression into your plans for subsequent lessons. The first step is to decide on the objectives, and for this example, these will be: *Pupils will be able to scan images and text into a publication.*

Next, plan the introduction to the lesson in outline:

- *Explain the learning objective to pupils.*
- *Write it on the board and ask them why we would want to use a scanner. (Saves typing out text from old documents; need to include photographs taken with an ordinary camera or from books – follow up with questions about copyright.)*
- *Recap on the concept of a computer system. What type of a device is a scanner? (Input device.)*
- *Recap on techniques. What do we have to do in Publisher before we can put in any text or graphics? (Create a frame.)*

Then plan the demonstration. It is important to consider what pupils need to do to achieve the learning objective. Break this down into manageable stages to enable you to demonstrate the new skill to the pupils. Think about the resources required for it to be successful. The use of a large computer screen, a data projector or interactive white board is desirable to maximise the effectiveness.

Make sure the resources you require to carry out your demonstration are ready and working properly. Your resource checklist can help you here:

- PC with scanner and associated software;
- projector connected to PC with scanner;
- items to be scanned in;
- pictures and text to be loaded directly into appropriate software.

Plan the pupil tasks. This is the main body of the lesson when pupils will be working on the tasks you have prepared for them. There are a number of questions to consider.

- Will all pupils be able to work on the task? It is unlikely that you will have more than one or two scanners in the classroom. Therefore you will have to consider what tasks the rest of the class will be doing while others gain experience of using the scanner.
- How will you cater for pupils with different abilities? Ensure you know which children have experience of using a scanner and group children in pairs of experts/novices for the work using the scanner. It is important for pupils to know that you want them to support each other and that you value the skills of the more experienced pupils.
- What will pupils do when they are not working on the scanner? If you are introducing a new skill it is sensible for pupils to be working on projects designed to practise and consolidate previously introduced skills. This will allow pairs of children to access the available hardware for set time periods. You will need to be available to support those learning the new skills. If you are able to set up expert/novice pairs the support required will be reduced.

It is important that the tasks set for the rest of the class are teacher-independent to free you to provide support with the scanners. It is likely that pupils will continue with on-going projects previously set while they are waiting for their turn on the scanners. Your task is to:

- support those using the scanners;
- scan the class to ensure pupils are working on the task;
- intervene to support pupils who may be having problems or need support;
- use questioning to check pupil understanding.

Finally, plan the whole-class conclusion, where you will question them on what they have done, what they have learned from it, identify and praise good work, and tell them what they need to do to prepare for the next lesson. Ensure you leave enough time at the end of the lesson for pupils to save their work and leave the room ready for the next class.

Task 4.9 Progression in modelling

For the modelling unit from Task 4.8, plan a second lesson that shows clearly the progression in techniques and concepts.

Identifying the level of content

When first presented with a topic and a class, you will find it difficult to judge the level of content and approach, and well as the pace of progress. You need to consider what progress is expected during Key Stage 3 in each of the strands, both with ICT lessons and in other subject lessons where pupils apply and consolidate their ICT capability. In one school, for instance, the focus is on introducing techniques and concepts in Year 7, on consolidating and broadening techniques and understanding processes in Year 8, and on higher order skills and formalising concepts in Year 9.

In this school, the final term of Year 8 forms a bridge into Year 9. The Scheme of Work concentrates on the set theme of a travel agent and the pupils have to solve the problems of:

- holding information about customers and their holidays so that details related to holidays and customers can be easily found;
- working out the cost of a holiday package and enabling variations of this costing to be calculated;
- advertising the travel agency and presenting a presentation about a resort, including a video clip of a previous client's experience of the resort.

Each problem is to be solved by a small group. They are told that ICT will be used, but they have to decide which generic package should be used to solve the sub-task. They must consider the information needs from the point of view of the user. Pupils' progress with tasks is monitored closely in order to ensure that the tasks are all completed and that the demands on equipment are spread, especially the video equipment that may be limited.

The Year 9 scheme then develops this theme further, but with the focus on information systems which meet the needs of different people (management, staff, clients) within an organisation, as shown in the extract from the Scheme of Work in Figure 4.3.

Figure 4.3 Extract from example of a Year 9 Scheme of Work

Autumn term
1 Review and complete the travel agent work and then move on to the problem of producing standard letters (mail merge of database and word processing, spreadsheet and word processing) for all the people on a particular holiday, giving them:
    (a) the schedule;
    (b) the final payment details.

2 Produce overall report collected in by half-term. Report to include:
    (c) Background information on the travel agency.
    (d) List of objectives to be achieved.
    (e) Separate sections for each of the problems solved to include:
        ● problem to be solved;
        ● software chosen and why;
        ● design stages;
        ● implementation documents;
        ● testing and evaluation comments.
    (f) Outline of each objective as to success of solution.

Use Project Report templates provided in Year 9 resources folder on intranet.

Task 4.10 Identifying progression in expectations through Key Stage 3

Look at the Year 9 Scheme of Work extract in Figure 4.3 and identify the techniques, processes, concepts and higher order skills. Summarise the differences in expectation from that of the Year 7 scheme.
   Compare the expectations in this scheme with those in your placement school and in the DfES scheme (http://www.standards.dfes.gov.uk/schemes2/secondary_ICT/).

EVALUATING AND IMPROVING LESSONS

During the early stages, your main concern will be your personal performance in the classroom, and there are a number of key issues which it will be helpful to focus on.

● How did you feel at the start of the lesson? Pupils can sense when things are not well with a teacher, and this does have an impact on their work and the lesson. If you felt apprehensive, think of a strategy that will help you to relax into the lesson. Remember that, whatever the class, you have had many more years of experience and knowledge than any class you will meet in the secondary school.

- How long did you talk for, was your language easily understandable, did you ask if a word was understood by the class, for example 'society', 'analyse'? Were your instructions clear and simple? Did you talk over any pupils while they were working? These are common areas of difficulty at the start of a teacher's career. Make a point of writing down the words that you will use in the lesson, or even the phrases. Think about words made up of several syllables.

- Was your choice of teaching strategy suitable? If pupils did not react well to your approach, consider whether it was because they were unfamiliar with it, because it was not a good way of approaching the topic, or because you did not manage it well.

- Were the tasks set for pupils effective? If the pupils found it difficult, that may not be a bad thing. You may find that the struggle pays off in the long term, and they are often much more confident next lesson. Alternatively, they may have had difficulty understanding what the task required and what you expected. This can be resolved by clearer instructions and feedback.

- Did you enjoy the lesson or did you feel stressed? If you can enjoy a lesson, and if you show it, the class will relax and tension will be reduced in the pupils and ultimately you. Do not be afraid to smile at a witty remark, but remember that the pupils must never control the class!

- Did you feel in control? You cannot get everything right immediately, and you will learn most if you take some controlled risks. A slight feeling of being out of control can be healthy, as it keeps the adrenalin flowing and makes for a livelier lesson. It is also healthy if you are aware that a class was not quite as you would have liked it. If it was worse than that, then consider why you felt out of control. Did the class get bored, did they not understand, was a task too easy or too difficult? Was the problem with aspects of the class, location or lesson? Did a pupil, pair or small group of pupils cause the problem? If so, what strategies can you adopt to solve the problem? Your mentor or the class teacher may have ideas about why the problem occurred and how to solve it. When you have gained some confidence in your authority in the classroom and you can operate basic procedures routinely, you should focus more on pupils' learning and your management of individuals. It is important that you learn to plan and manage the basic structure of a lesson. However, as time passes, you should enter the second phase of your learning. This is where you are concerned most with the pupils: what they are doing and learning; is it effective; could it be done better or more straightforwardly? Your planning will take these aspects into consideration.

- Did most pupils achieve your learning objectives for the lesson? Did all the pupils achieve a baseline? Did any run out of time? Did any finish early? Did they succeed in the task as expected? If not, then consider why not, and whether the problem was avoidable. You may have had unrealistic expectations, or you may have let the pace slip. If the task was too easy or too difficult consider how it could be adapted or extended.

- Did you interact with every pupil, and were the interactions positive or negative? Did you manage to say something positive to every pupil? Pupils can easily identify false praise, but genuine interest in their work is very satisfying for them.
- Were all pupils motivated and interested? Did they continue to work on the task? If not, try to identify why. Put yourself in their position, and consider how you would have reacted to the situation.

As you gain experience in teaching, the focus of your evaluations will change from emphasis on personal performance to the evaluation of pupils' learning. It is a good idea to continue with the observation of other teachers as your own teaching ability develops, as you will be able to notice more detail and understand better why they are taking certain actions. Chapter 12 offers further advice on evaluating and developing your professional practice.

SUMMARY

The skills of planning and evaluation are fundamental to success in teaching. Curriculum planning can be considered as long term (schemes of work for a year or key stage), medium term (a topic or unit of work) and short term (individual lessons). As a trainee, you may have to implement existing long and medium term plans that are set out in some detail on paper. For short term plans, however, experienced teachers often commit little detail to paper. This may give you some freedom to make choices, and thus greater scope for learning. This book cannot give precise recipes for successful lessons, as there is so much to consider which is special to you and your school. We have explained a number of factors which should be taken into account:

- teaching aims and learning objectives;
- possible teaching strategies;
- assessment opportunities;
- pupils' prior knowledge;
- structuring lessons, sequencing activities and providing variety;
- the relevance of context;
- the importance of recap and review;
- pace and timing;
- expectations for pupils' achievement and specific targets;
- progression in pupils' learning.

In order to illustrate how these decisions may be implemented in practice, we have provided some examples of topic and lesson plans that have been used successfully. We have particularly emphasised the need to plan for progression, and this should be at the forefront of your thinking when planning the next stage for whole class and for individual pupils.

FURTHER READING

Baumann, A., Bloomfield, A. and Baughton, L. (1997) *Becoming a Secondary School Teacher*, London: Hodder and Stoughton. Provides alternative general guidance on schemes of work, lesson planning and evaluation.

Kyriacou, C. (1997) *Effective Teaching in Schools*, second edition, Cheltenham: Stanley Thornes. Develops in greater depth many of the issues concerned with setting up the learning experience in general.

Russell, T. (2001) *Teaching and Using ICT in Secondary Schools*, London: David Fulton. Provides additional ideas for Key Stage 3 plans, including cross-curricular work.

http://www.standards.dfes.gov.uk/keystage3/strands/?strand=ICT. This website is being developed to offer guidance and materials concerning the teaching of ICT in Key Stage 3.

5 Planning Learning Activities and Preparing Resources for Pupils

Dave Hendley and Steve Kennewell

The effective planning of activities that pupils carry out and the preparation of suitable resources are crucial for successful learning. This is the main focus of experienced teachers' short term planning: once the structuring and timing of lessons become routine, teachers' thinking concentrates on the devising, planning and monitoring of tasks to help pupils achieve the learning objectives. Extra care here will pay handsome dividends throughout your teaching career.

We have highlighted in Chapter 4 that you need to take account of a wide range of factors that can contribute to the successful learning of the pupils in your care. In this chapter, we look in more detail at some particular aspects of the teacher's task and consider the factors that lead to success.

OBJECTIVES

By the end of this chapter, you should be able to:

- identify constraints on classroom activity, anticipate difficulties and devise contingency plans;
- characterise what makes a good ICT learning activity;
- plan tasks to facilitate the introduction of new concepts, familiarisation with new skills, the application of familiar skills and the automisation of basic skills;
- identify and select appropriate ways of presenting tasks to different pupil groups;

- design and produce effective activity resources in printed and electronic form;
- evaluate resources for teaching and learning, including ICT and non-ICT resources.

IDENTIFYING CONSTRAINTS AND ANTICIPATING DIFFICULTIES

Taking account of constraints

In developing the unit in Chapter 4 we considered aims and objectives, teaching strategies, prior knowledge, lesson structure, timing, expectations and assessment opportunities. This careful planning will be wasted, however, unless you also consider the constraints on classroom activity and prepare thoroughly for the difficulties which may be encountered.

Time

The overall length of the unit and the time available in each lesson are particularly important constraints in the secondary school classroom. For medium term planning, you should bear in mind that too long on one particular topic is likely to be counterproductive, with the pupils quickly becoming bored and the resulting allied problems affecting learning and discipline. Too short a time spent on a topic, however, will result in many in the class being unable to grasp the basic concepts, resulting in loss of confidence that will also have an effect on learning and discipline. For short term planning, the need to reach a fruitful conclusion to each lesson in time is crucial.

The time devoted to a topic will depend on factors such as pupils' ability, their motivation and the ease with which they grasp new ideas and techniques. It will be determined to a large extent by the agreed Scheme of Work, which will take into account the available resources (for example, the ratio of computers to pupils) and the way the lessons are scheduled. For example, a two week gap between lessons may reduce progress; short lessons require a higher proportion of the time to be devoted to non-learning activity such as entry, exit and registration; a single lesson a week on Mondays will mean that lessons could be lost because of bank holidays; last lesson on a Friday may mean reduced concentration and effort. The teaching strategies and experience of the teacher can also have a significant influence on the time taken to complete a topic.

There will inevitably be a variety of other factors, some predictable, others not, such as network failure, sports matches, holidays, in-service training (INSET) days and pupil or staff illness. Pupils react differently at different points during the day. The morning lessons before break are usually most effective. You will not be able to anticipate all the delays or problems, but the predictable factors must form part of careful planning.

It is advisable to plan lessons with the aim to cover more than anticipated and then not rush to complete the whole in one lesson. Aim to have a minimum target for achievement in the lesson, with extension work available for those pupils who progress faster than others. These factors will also vary not only from class to class across a year group but also from year to year.

The age of pupils

On entry to secondary school, pupils will be familiar with a range of different teaching strategies and may be used to working in a variety of ways, including independently (see Chapter 10). The more formal approaches associated with secondary schools need consideration. By the time pupils reach Year 10 they may have opted for IT as one of their GCSE subjects and be working at a high level of competence. They will also have had more experience of life, and be aware of a greater range of contexts.

The ability of pupils and their grouping

The pupils' abilities have a major influence over choice of the appropriate strategies. Sometimes schools group children according to attainment or ability. High ability groups will need to be engaged in a different way to low ability groups. You will also need to employ different strategies for mixed ability groups in order to cater for the wider range of abilities. Whatever the groupings of pupils, you will be expected to differentiate work to ensure all pupils make progress. You will need to take into account the pupils' literacy, and (in some topics) numeracy. Your language (spoken and written) will need to be appropriate to the pupils, and your voice should be appropriate in tone (see Chapter 6 for more details).

The presence of potentially disruptive pupils will also have a significant influence on the planning of your activities. We will look at strategies for minimising disruption in the next chapter, and it is worth noting at this stage that misbehaviour may be caused by too difficult or too easy a task, by reading difficulties or by expectations of failure. By planning the activities and organising resources carefully, you can avoid most of the disruption often experienced by trainee teachers.

The previous experience of the class

There is nothing more off-putting for a class of pupils than to find themselves repeating something they have already done, either in primary school or in the previous year of secondary school. Detailed knowledge of the curriculum they have followed is essential if you are to ensure progression and development. It is important for teachers to identify what pupils already know, and build on previous experience to take the children's learning forward. Strategies designed to find out what children already know and can do are an important part of teaching. Many pupils will have gaps in their knowledge, and you must be prepared to provide for their needs. This is particularly the case in Year 7, although you will often be confronted by the problem of a pupil new to the school.

The resources available

Despite the high profile given to ICT, the disparity of provision in schools is wide. Some schools will have one ageing network room. Others will have new suites fitted with up-to-date PCs. You may find that you are teaching in a room with insufficient machines for the whole class to use them together. It is essential to think carefully about what you are trying to achieve and how best to get there! It is very important that you know the PCs found in the room, what software is on them, how to access the machines for the class and what steps to take if things go wrong.

The room layout

This is a very important factor to consider. Most computer rooms have the machines around the perimeter of the room so that the pupils face away from you and towards the outside of the room. This is not an easy situation to manage. You will need to devise strategies to overcome it whilst teaching. One solution is to have the chairs arranged around any central tables in the room. The machines are then out of reach of the pupils. They are forced to face you, and this makes your task of introducing the lesson, getting instructions out, having discussions, answering questions and so on much easier to manage.

Learning environment

As a student teacher you will find it harder to influence the appearance of the room but many teachers will be pleased to have some help with tidying papers, organising equipment and renewing displays. The ambience of a room is another important factor in creating an atmosphere conducive to learning. Posters, pupils' work, displays and so on enliven a classroom and make it an interesting place to be. Other aspects of the physical environment, such as noise, heat, light can have a significant effect on pupils' learning.

Task 5.1 Observing the effects of the classroom environment

Arrange to observe a lesson during which you note carefully the way the resources, room layout and general atmosphere influence the pupils' activity and learning. Try to arrange to observe other lessons, so as to see at least one different class in a different room and with different resources. Compare the effectiveness of pupils' learning and draw conclusions about how you might adapt your activities for different conditions.

Devising contingency plans

What if your intended lesson plan proves not to be feasible for some reason? There are many hazards facing the teacher of ICT, and you need to plan for the possibility that the resources you planned to use may not be available. Networks sometimes crash or machines refuse to let children 'log on'. If the ICT facilities have failed, you may still be able to teach the planned topic, but you will need to change strategy so that pupils are discussing and/or working on paper. You should consider in advance how you might do this for every lesson you plan. There will be times, however, when you decide to cut your losses and provide an activity which is not directly related to the planned topic; it is a good idea always to have a set of general revision worksheets or ICT related puzzles available. This may also be the best strategy when a large number of pupils are missing from the class at a vital stage when you want to introduce something new.

Often problems are experienced by individual pupils, and you need to consider what pupils will do if they are banned from the network or unable to log on for some reason. In many cases, a sharing arrangement will overcome the problems temporarily, and you should be ready to implement this quickly and without panic on your part or fuss by the pupils.

REPRESENTING IDEAS TO PUPILS

Before pupils start on the tasks that you have designed, you will normally need to set out the learning objectives, provide some explanation of the key ideas involved, describe the context and expected outcomes of the activity and give instructions on how you expect them to carry out the task. It is important that the pupils are clear about what is expected of them, and what are the attributes of work that you consider to be 'good'. It will be helpful for many tasks, particularly those involving the presentation of ideas to an audience, to show examples of good work, highlighting the key features, and then show some poorer work and ask them to suggest improvements.

These are some specific methods for introducing and consolidating ideas that are used in ICT teaching:

- *Demonstration*. The whole class is shown a new technique or process on a large display away from their own PCs. (Alternatively, the teacher may 'take over' each pupil's screen, using special network software.) For example, how to enter formulas into a spreadsheet.
- *Talk through*. Each pupil follows step-by-step instructions with the whole class being kept together, using suitable support strategies for slower pupils. For example, how to access a file from a particular location on the network.
- *Helpsheet*. Pupils are given a task to carry out, and a printed sheet or computer file provides reference instructions on the new techniques needed. For example, creating a poster using Publisher.

- *Worksheet.* Pupils are given printed instructions to follow and write down what the results are at each stage. For example, formulating database queries to search an existing database.

- *Question and answer.* Working as a whole class, pupils are asked focused questions related to the key points in the current task and then further questions set in a different scenario to test comprehension. For example, downloading images from the Internet into a publication.

- *Investigation.* A situation in which pupils can explore with no fixed outcome; pupils decide on their own task objectives. For example, advising a family on PC equipment to buy.

- *Challenge.* Pupils are given a specific outcome to achieve, but minimal information on how it may be achieved. For example, using an existing spreadsheet model for the effects of different chemicals on plant growth, and attempting to 'grow' the tallest plant.

- *Simulation.* Pupils are given a scenario to represent though role-play, with each pupil having a brief for a particular role. For example, sending an e-mail to someone in Australia.

- *Concept mapping.* Either individual pupils produce a concept map on a topic so that you can assess their understanding, or the teacher collects ideas from the whole class and uses more expert knowledge to assemble them into a more effective map of linked aspects of the topic (see Capel *et al.*, 2001: unit 5.2). For example, a local area network.

- *Discussion.* Groups of three or four pupils are given a problem to solve, or a question or statement to discuss, and each group gives a report to the class (possibly using a presentation package to help structure their thinking and report).

- *Debate.* Two or more pupils are asked to prepare and present arguments for or against a particular proposal, and then other pupils can put further points of view on either side. For example, all secondary school pupils should have their own Internet e-mail addresses which they can use at break and lunchtimes.

- *Hot seating.* The class put questions to an 'expert' pupil, who may have been given time to revise the topic. For example, different forms of storage for data.

- *Expert panel.* An alternative to the above, this approach does not put a single pupil in the hot seat at the risk of ridicule in front of peers.

- *Multiple choice questions.* The options are all quite similar but only one is the required answer, so that fine distinctions need to be considered and misconceptions can be exposed. For example, 'What is a floppy disk – a storage medium, a storage device, RAM or ROM?'

- *Sequencing* involves events or techniques being placed out of order and the pupils have to put them in the correct order. This can be achieved by pupils holding cards of events and being asked to move to the correct place in the sequence, or manipulating boxes on screen. For example, the steps involved in creating a database.

- *Directed activity related to text (DART)* involves pupils reading some material that you provide, but being required to do something specific. For example, identifying the types of software used in a magazine report about a news-agent using ICT to help develop his business (see, for example, Parkinson, 1994).

We will explore some of these strategies in more detail later in this chapter. Chapter 6 provides more details on the organisation and adaptation of particular approaches.

Task 5.2 Evaluating teaching strategies

Consider a particular class and topic you have been involved with. For each one of these strategies, identify advantages and disadvantages for teaching the topic to the class.

The importance of language

Language has an important role to play in the classroom, and you need to consider how you talk to children (Capel *et al.*, 2001: unit 3.1). Language is used to engage the children's interest, to give instructions, to provide explanations, to question pupils, to provide feedback and advice. Good teachers 'talk with' pupils and do not 'talk at' them. They take the time to talk through issues and challenges facing pupils and give them the opportunity to take part in the lesson in an active way. The exchange of views is a good way to develop a relationship with the class and can provide invaluable assessment information. It is good practice to record pupils' views and comments. This shows that you are respectful of their opinions. They may be recorded on a PC screen for further use. However, successful classroom interactions with pupils require careful planning.

You will need to be careful with the level of language you use. Many words you use in formal situations with adults or in university assignments will be unfamiliar to pupils. These can be divided into two types: those which you should help pupils to learn as part of their ICT course, such as 'hypothesis', and those which could be avoided without loss of meaning, such as 'fortuitous'.

Task 5.3 Checking the language you use

When you have an opportunity to carry out some whole-class teaching, ask your mentor to make notes on the words that you use which may be unfamiliar to the pupils. Discuss which ones you should replace and, for those that you do need to use, discuss how you might explain what they mean to the class.

Another essential teaching skill related to classroom talk is that of questioning. Questioning can tell you much about what pupils have learned and will help you challenge children to take their learning further (see, for instance, Kerry, 1998). This is as important in ICT as in other subjects. You will become familiar with pupils' common errors and misconceptions, and you should take the chance to question the pupils in such a way as to expose and challenge ineffective ideas.

Teachers have many different purposes in asking questions (Wragg and Brown, 1993), but the most important is to stimulate and focus talk by pupils. It is vital that pupils have opportunities to talk about their work with you and with each other; this helps them to reflect on their activity, test their ideas out on their peers, appreciate other points of view, and consolidate their understanding. We will deal with whole class questioning about ICT in the next chapter, and more detail and language and questioning generally can be found in Capel *et al.* (2001: unit 3.1).

Task 5.4 Explanations and questions

- Consider how you would explain 'paragraph formatting techniques' to Year 7 pupils. Can you do it purely through questions and the use of pupil volunteers?
- When you observe pupils in primary school, you may notice that pupils carry out simple techniques in inefficient ways. For example, if they want to put a heading in the centre of the page, they keep pressing the space bar until the text seems to be centred. What would you say when you see pupils doing this? Try to devise a sequence of questions that enable pupils to work out for themselves how they should achieve the effect they want.

The importance of context

All new learning is filtered through our experiences of the world. Most important of these are our beliefs about the world. These come from many sources – our upbringing, our culture and the environment we are born into. The classroom is an artificial environment, but as we explained in Chapter 4, it will be helpful to pupils to place them in an imaginary scenario that is as realistic as possible. This principle must be implemented with care, however. If you anticipate that the concepts or skills will be complex for pupils, the context should be a familiar one (see, for example, the 'It's me!' topic in Chapter 4). Alternatively, ICT can be used as a context itself; for example, prepare a database of home computer specifications and set pupils the task of finding the cheapest one which meets a particular household's requirements. When they are more confident with the ideas, you can use contexts with which pupils feel less secure, such as the business world or other curriculum subject topics.

Wherever possible, work within discrete ICT lessons should incorporate a thematic approach where the topic under consideration has a link with another subject(s).

Tasks and outcomes may be linked with the aims of another subject, ICT capability being developed as a means to an end. This will help the pupils to see the ICT in its wider context.

STRUCTURING TASKS TO HELP PUPILS ACHIEVE THE LEARNING OBJECTIVES

Classroom activities should take pupils from knowledge and skills they have and lead them towards something they have not yet learned: you will thus expose a 'learning gap' (Kennewell, 2001). Once you have determined your learning objectives you will need to consider a number of questions.

- *What will pupils need to do to achieve the learning objectives?* For some objectives, such as 'be able to insert clip art images into a presentation', the devising of a suitable task may be quite straightforward. For other objectives, such as 'understand the effects of the Internet on society', you will need to be more creative and think of a variety of ways of enabling pupils to construct their understanding.
- *What resources will you need to enable pupils to achieve the learning objectives?* Once you have decided on the task, the resource implications will usually be clear, but make sure you check every detail in advance, and do not just assume that something which is usually available will actually be there on the day! There may be limited equipment in the classroom for pupils to use. If this is the case you will have to consider what tasks you will set for the class while pupils are using the limited equipment. You need to be sure you know what hardware and software you will need for yourself and the pupils. You will need to be thoroughly familiar with the resources and how they work. It is not enough just to know the features that you are going to teach. Pupils will experiment with different options, they will make mistakes, other unpredictable problems will arise, and you will be expected to help them recover.
- *What procedures will the pupils need to follow?* If you want them to follow particular procedures, you will need to give them clear instructions, ask them questions to check that they have understood the instructions, and monitor their activity to ensure that they are on the right lines.
- *Can you break these procedures down into manageable stages?* Rather than trying to tell them everything at once, it will often be helpful to devise phases of the task, each with a different learning focus. If you do this, however, you will need to involve them in thinking about what they will do next, so that they learn to plan their work rather than relying on you to spoon-feed them permanently.
- *What previous experience have different pupils had?* It is not only the experience that pupils have had in school that needs to be taken into account. It is important to remember that personal computers are now available in many homes and many pupils will have wide experience of using PCs

outside school. Many of them will have knowledge and skills higher than you might expect; however, there will also be gaps in their knowledge and skills.

- *Can you plan adequate differentiation strategies to ensure that all children are taken forward in their learning?* Designing differentiated material can be difficult for beginners to do well and even experienced teachers find it challenging. We will discuss this in some detail in Chapter 9.

- *How will you find out whether pupils have achieved the learning objectives?* You may plan to collect pupils' work in order to evaluate their learning, but this evidence will probably tell only part of the story. Before the lesson ends it is important to build in opportunities for consideration of the learning object-ives set at the beginning of a lesson. When planning your lessons you must ensure you leave time to draw pupils together at the end to assess their know-ledge of the learning objectives, emphasise the key ideas of the topic, prompt the pupils to reflect on what they have been doing, identify what they have learned, and consider how it has contributed to their achievement. This has another purpose, too: you can prompt them to consider how their know-ledge and skills could be used in other fields, perhaps in other subjects, in their leisure activities, or in the world of work.

Task 5.5 Plenary session questions

For the lesson you devised in Chapter 4 on introducing modelling with spreadsheets, plan the questions that you will ask pupils during the plenary session at the end.

Types of task structure

When devising tasks and activities for pupils, you should attempt to give them a challenge. You should not make it so difficult as to be unattainable for them. Your job will be made more difficult or even impossible under these conditions. Your aim should be to create a learning gap that is feasible to bridge with support, or *scaffolding* (see, for example, Muijs and Reynolds, 2001: 18; Capel *et al.*, 2001: 241–2), but not straightforward for them to achieve with their current knowledge.

When beginning teaching you should first devise discrete activities before pro-gressing to coordinated units of work. This section is intended to help in this.

Worksheets and help sheets

Worksheets are a useful resource for teaching and learning, particularly when they are made available for pupils to access from the network rather than duplicated for the class. Care should be taken with worksheets. They are used in every subject taught in schools. They are sometimes overused to the extent that pupils become bored with the method and then learning ceases. You need to ensure that as many pupils as possible can gain access to the requirements of the task and help in carrying it out, so that you can encourage them to use written material rather than always asking you or their friends.

Thus worksheets need to be at the reading level of the pupil, which is often far lower than you would expect. In addition, it is difficult to follow instructions on paper whilst focusing on a screen based activity. Indeed, there is evidence that a printed guide with screenshots is more effective when used away from the computer, provided that the pupils are familiar with the user interface involved. It is not necessary for learners to carry out steps correctly first time; they learn much more from their mistakes than from their successes, as long as they have support available when they cannot see how to solve their problems. Mistakes provide feedback, and learners spend a lot more time thinking about them. The expectations of pupils in ICT should therefore be kept at a high level in order to challenge pupils to try things for themselves, monitor their work and correct their own errors.

Project work

This is a more open-ended strategy, which has benefits and disadvantages. Although you cannot predict what learning problems will arise, you should still plan project based lessons carefully; in fact, the management of project work is harder than briefer and more structured activities. Pupils need to be kept 'on task' and helped more on an individual basis. You need to plan the route through any project for the pupils, allocate time for each section, and keep careful track of each individual's progress.

Group work

Planning parts of lessons so that pupils can sit together in small groups provides a good focus for learning. It has the added benefit of allowing less able pupils or ones who are more reticent in speaking to the whole class the opportunity to contribute without fear of embarrassment. It is important to plan what is discussed carefully, and to brief the pupils clearly on what sort of report you want from them: what points you want them to report on, who is responsible for collecting the group's ideas, and how you want them to present it. You should have very clear learning outcomes so that you can make assessments of what the pupils achieved. You should also move pupils into different groupings so that they do not always work with their friends or rely on the same people. It is important to explain to the pupils why you are doing this.

Providing feedback

This is an important part of the teaching process. Pupils need to know how well they are doing, and what more they need to do to complete work, get a better grade/mark, etc. By engaging individuals in discussion about their work, you can:

- make better assessments of what they have learned;
- provide specific comments on work they have done;
- set targets for further work;
- learn about the effectiveness of your teaching.

ICT activities often provide the opportunity for automatic feedback: if you make the task outcomes sufficiently clear, often the pupils can judge for themselves whether they have achieved what is required and make improvements if not.

Feedback to a whole class is also useful, and you should seek to identify object-ives that all the pupils have achieved so that you can give general praise, as well as highlighting points where improvement is needed. You can stimulate discussion through specific questioning or generally asking pupils to report on what they have done.

PRODUCING AND SELECTING RESOURCES FOR TEACHING AND LEARNING

When looking for good materials to use in lessons, the starting point should be those already available in school. These will usually have the advantage of matching the Scheme of Work and providing tried and tested approaches. If they are in electronic form, you will be able to adapt them to suit your particular style and the class you will use them with. Where good materials are not available, however, or when you want to try a different approach, you will want to look further afield. You may find published materials in your university library, or in your school department's published resource collection. Many of these are in electronic form now, and can also be adapted.

Last, but not least, you can look on the web for materials. These may be websites that the pupils can use directly, or downloadable materials that you can print or put on the school intranet. There are many organisations that have resources available for teachers, with helpful search facilities, though at the time of writing there is no systematic way of accessing them and no quality control procedure.

In any case, you need to consider carefully what are your criteria for adopting resources produced by others. Here are a few suggestions:

- Do they match your learning objectives?
- Is the content accurately represented?
- Do they use the right level of language?
- Will they engage the pupils, by means of relevant context, challenge, and feedback?
- Are they graded or differentiated so as to match the ability of different pupils?

Task 5.6 Selecting appropriate materials

Use the Internet to seek possible materials to help pupils learn Logo programming – suggested activities, worksheets, etc. Identify a particular class and judge which would be most suitable for them in terms of context, language and presentation. Consider what changes you would need to make in order for them to be successful.

Designing and producing effective activity resources – printed and electronic

There are many factors that you should consider when producing printed or electronic resources for pupils. These include:

- the level of language;
- the type of graphic images used;
- the amount of white space;
- the level and grading of difficulty of the concepts;
- the context of the task;
- the progression in challenge which helps to maintain the pupils' interest.

Further guidance may be found in Capel *et al.* (2001: unit 5.2) and in Kyriacou (1997).

Task 5.7 Effective worksheet design

Look at a worksheet or help sheet that is used in your placement school, and consider the factors listed above. What aspects do you feel are effective about this resource? What improvements could be made?

You should plan carefully in order to make the best use of printed or electronic worksheets. If they are not well designed and with clearly thought through activities, they will not be a good use of your efforts. You need to consider what learning outcomes you want pupils to learn in terms of skills and knowledge. You can then design suitable activities to match these.

For example, you may be teaching pupils how to use a CAD package. In order to show the techniques to be learned effectively, you may want to have screen dumps of relevant elements of the package in the resource. Practice in producing these on your word processor is essential. Cropping and adjusting the image is a skill that needs to be second nature.

Many pupils are reluctant to use printed resources. They find reading difficult, particularly when switching between screen and worksheet. You may often be able to provide a resource which can be accessed on screen. Instead of printing a help sheet or worksheet, you can set it up for pupils to access from the network, keep it open in a separate window, and switch to it when necessary. They can use the cursor to keep track of where they have reached in the task. Templates for writing tasks can be set up using DTP or a word processor; spreadsheets can be annotated with instructions and hints concerning the task. The pupil should not easily be able to accidentally change the format, so you should ensure that the template is read-only or that key areas are 'locked'.

Evaluating your own resources

While you are gaining familiarity with pupils' capabilities, you could try out re-sources that you produce on a small group of pupils to get some idea of suitability of the resource and the time it takes to complete. Your tutor will also give you valuable advice, but you will need to develop your own approaches and try them out with full classes in order to develop expertise in effective resource production. In judging the effectiveness of materials you have produced, consider:

- Did pupils use them and find them helpful, or were they discarded while pupils pestered you for help?
- Did they provide the right amount of structure in relation to the objectives – enough support to help pupils with their tasks, and also enough challenge to provide opportunities to learn?
- Did they provide feedback to enable pupils to develop their work, or did you have to keep reassuring pupils that they were doing what you wanted?

USING ICT IN TEACHING AND LEARNING

Teachers of all subjects are now expected to use ICT in their teaching where appropriate to improve pupils' learning. The Teacher Training Authority (TTA) in England has specified a detailed set of standards that student teachers are expected to meet, and teachers of ICT are no exception. The issues are somewhat different for ICT teachers, however, and it is important to focus on the central issue for all teachers: ICT should be used when it is the most effective resource for the learning objectives. This is never easy to judge, but ICT teachers should at least have the deep knowledge of ICT that is necessary to make good decisions.

Why use ICT?

The decision to use ICT should be based on whether it offers features that will enhance pupils' learning. The following features of ICT have been identified:

- *Capacity and range.* The sheer amount of material which can be made available to pupils – information, structured learning material, and data which can be handled – is immense, and can be obtained just as easily from anywhere in the world as it can from the classroom cupboard. Care must be taken to check the validity of the information obtained, however. ICT gives teachers and pupils access to and control over situations which would normally be outside their everyday experience.
- *Speed and automaticity.* ICT enables routine tasks to be completed and repeated quickly, allowing the user to concentrate on thinking and on tasks such as analysing and looking for patterns within data, asking questions and looking for answers, and explaining and presenting results.
- *Provisionality.* ICT allows changes to be made easily and enables alternatives to be explored readily. The fact that pupils can try out ideas and change them if they look bad or before they receive negative comments from the teacher is a tremendous stimulus to creativity and the taking of risks that often lead to effective learning. For many pupils with poor literacy skills, just putting pen to paper is a risky business, and ICT can make a significant difference to the quantity and quality of written work produced.
- *Interactivity.* ICT enables rapid and dynamic feedback and response, which can improve pupils' willingness to evaluate and improve their work as well as avoiding a wait for the teacher to give feedback and encouragement. It is this feature that perhaps contributes most to pupils' feeling of control over their learning and involvement in their work with ICT.

Pupils using ICT

The use of ICT can help pupils to bridge the learning gap by carrying out tedious aspects of the work yet still requiring them to do the important thinking. It can also help them to reflect on their work, and support the higher order skills of planning and evaluating.

There are many advantages for a pupil who can utilise ICT. Many weak pupils can excel when released from the constraints of written work. However, you need to take care that use of the keyboard does not form a new barrier, as the act of searching for the relevant keys can become a serious hindrance to the creative process. In general, if the techniques required are not routine, problem solving and creativity may be hampered.

Pupils are able to access information from around the world, from sources ranging from other pupils' own websites to up-to-date academic papers in the most prestigious universities. But this can generate another difficulty, that of information overload. It is essential that pupils are introduced to the skills of efficient research and critical selection of relevant information. Many pupils will print out a page of information from an encyclopaedia and present it as their work, or as the answer to an assignment, even though it is obvious that they have not read the text and would not understand it if they did. These research skills are particularly useful for pupils if they are weaned on to them from a tightly guided beginning and the constraints gradually relaxed as they develop their skills.

When presented with the delights of a multimedia presentation package, many pupils will enjoy the easy success of their innovative presentations, which initially consist of a cacophony of sounds and animation, often losing the point of the exercise. Pupils will similarly plaster graphics and differing fonts all over a poster or document initially, detracting from the main aim. You should expect them to take a more straightforward approach in the early stages with specific guidelines such as 'A poster with no more than two pictures and two fonts'. They can then suggest extra features, as long as they can justify them.

As a pupil's confidence increases, and the use of 'undo' becomes routine, an element of trial and experiment can be introduced. This is useful when introducing graphics packages, in that the pupils can be given a cursory introduction to the features of the package and set the task of exploring it. Loose guidelines can be given for the task, such as 'Draw a picture of a monster.' This can be extended to 'Copy and paste more monsters', then 'Rotate and reflect.' Versions can easily be saved and previous versions can be loaded after an unsatisfactory experiment.

Simulation software is an effective way of demonstrating processes. For instance, demonstrations of how a web server operates can show pupils the principles behind the process. The program is capable of repetition to help clear up any misconceptions.

If you ask pupils to present their learning to other pupils, you have a powerful way to motivate them and to help them structure and reinforce their learning. It is not merely a matter of repetition; in order to explain to others, the pupils have to think about their own and others' knowledge. This metacognitive process can help them make links between ideas and confront any confusion that they find. It can also help the pupils who form the audience for the presentation, as they may be able to relate to their peers' explanations better than to yours. You need to check that the pupils' ideas are sufficiently correct and complete, of course. More discussion of the use of metacognitive strategies in the context of mathematics teaching can be found in Tanner and Jones (1994).

Presentation software can help with the structuring of ideas, and if hyperlinks are included, enable them to represent linked concepts much better than paper or simple documents. Multimedia features are also valuable in representing pupils' ideas.

Task 5.8 Planning to use ICT

The Internet unit from the Year 7 Scheme of Work in Chapter 4 referred to a task 'Produce information sheet on planets for primary school, using NASA website (link with science)'. Plan the task structure in more detail, and decide how you would present the task to pupils.

Teachers using ICT

As well as using existing ICT learning resources and producing printed/display materials, you should try to experiment with producing your own interactive materials. If you design and produce something yourself using generic ICT tools such as spreadsheets or web page author tools, you will be able to adapt it for other classes and improve it each time you discover more about pupils' learning of the topic.

There are a number of purposes for which you might develop material, including:

- providing information;
- explaining;
- checking understanding;
- problem posing;
- stimulating discussion.

You need to consider whether the features of ICT provide advantages over other ways of achieving these purposes.

Some of the suitable software includes:

- *Managed Learning Environment (MLE) or Virtual Learning Environment (VLE)*. These provide a wide range of features for creating activities for pupils, assessing their work and facilitating indirect communication.
- *Programming language*. This is very flexible, but hard work.
- *Spreadsheet*. This is effective for situations where you need formulas.
- *Animation software*. This is effective for showing sequences of events visually.
- *General web or multimedia author tool*. This can be used at various levels of complexity and features, depending on expertise and needs. Even using Powerpoint with hyperlinks will enable you to achieve quite a range of effects.

Task 5.9 Planning to use an interactive whiteboard

Design a presentation which exploits the features of the interactive whiteboard to help you explain the flow of information between keyboard, CPU, memory and screen.

There are now many sources of pre-prepared material which you can use for your own research for lesson preparation or for pupils to use themselves. You need to evaluate a variety of CD-ROMs and Internet based materials such as 'How stuff works' (http://www.howstuffworks.com), considering the level and accuracy of content, the language used, the relevance to your Scheme of Work, and ease of use by pupils where relevant. You can also develop your own materials for local distribution; web pages, multimedia presentations and research tasks are useful starting points. You should also evaluate resources that claim to support pupils in their exam preparation: BBC Bytesize is good for GCSE revision (http://www.bbc.co.uk/schools/gcsebitesize/ict/).

When should ICT not be used in ICT lessons?

There are some occasions when non-ICT strategies will have advantages, particularly in helping to develop fundamental concepts. The distinctive features of a database, for instance, can be obscured when pupils just see a table on the screen (which appears very similar to a spreadsheet grid or even a basic table structure in a document) or if they see the data in form format, one record on the screen at a time. Manual activity with file cards can give a richer image of the structure and relationships within a database, and searching activity can be understood better if pupils carry out some physical activity (particularly for visual and kinaesthetic learners) with file cards or with themselves, which we describe in Chapter 6.

At higher levels of subject study, too, non-ICT resources are valuable. A level pupils will have used networked computers for many years, but can gain a better understanding of the topologies and their applications by holding pieces of string in different configurations and trying to send messages along them!

Many practical tasks will benefit from being planned first on paper, and this can give you a valuable non-computer activity for homework or when the ICT resources are not available. Multi-page publications and hyperlinked structures gain particularly from pre-planning, so that pupils' ideas can be checked before they embark on complex structures and so that they can more easily keep track themselves of the relationship between different elements of their work.

Task 5.10 Using non-ICT activities in teaching ICT

Observe an ICT lesson which does not involve ICT, or ask your mentor about points in the Scheme of Work where non-ICT activities are recommended. Identify the reason why ICT is not the most effective approach to the learning objective.

SUMMARY

This chapter has further developed the skills of planning and preparation, with a particular focus on the crucial issues of activities for pupils. You should have improved your understanding of the influence of activities and context on learning, and developed your ability to identify constraints, select contexts, design activities, structure tasks, differentiate work, explain ideas and expectations, give instructions, select and produce resources, and use ICT effectively in teaching and learning. The organisation of the classroom and the management of learning are both crucial to success, and you should be aware of the importance of language, particularly in the form of teacher questioning and pupil reflection.

FURTHER READING

See Chapter 4.

6 Organising Learning and Monitoring Progress

Ian Hughes and Steve Kennewell

We have considered issues in the planning and preparation of teaching at some length, and we conclude Part II on the development of essential teaching skills with a chapter concerning the implementation of plans in the classroom. A number of key issues demand detailed treatment, and we use a variety of examples and tasks to help discuss classroom organisation, interaction with pupils, the management of activities, a smooth transition between lesson phases, monitoring pupils' work and behaviour, strategies for improving work and behaviour, and keeping track of pupils' progress.

OBJECTIVES

By the end of this chapter, you should be able to:

- give effective introductions, task briefings, activity instructions, demonstrations, explanations, questions and discussions;
- organise an appropriate working environment;
- devise and set targets for pupils – whole class and individuals;
- group pupils to optimise the effectiveness of the activities;
- manage transitions between different activities;
- monitor pupils' progress in the task and in their learning ;
- intervene at appropriate times in order to improve pupils' learning;
- design and maintain realistic records of task progress.

LESSON BEGINNINGS

Task 6.1 Rules and routines for ICT lessons

The rules and routines applied at the start of the lesson are crucial to the success of the lesson as a whole. Observe a variety of experienced teachers at the start of the lesson and analyse:

- What routines do the pupils and the teacher follow?
- What rules apply concerning pupil behaviour on entry to the class and up to the start of the lesson content?
- How does the teacher ensure these rules are applied?

The start of the lesson should set the scene for the work to be carried out; it also sets the tone of the lesson and it is important that you make clear to pupils the sort of effort and behaviour that is expected. In most cases the lesson should start away from the computers, although this is not always possible because of class layout. You should allocate pupils to appropriate places in the room initially, in order to lay down the ground rules and establish control. Pupils who are allowed to take charge of their seating arrangement from the beginning will feel that they can also control other parts of the lesson. Having fixed positions initially also helps with learning names. This is particularly difficult when you often just see the backs of pupils' heads, but it is vital in establishing your authority and developing a constructive relationship. You can relax the constraints later once a sound relationship has been established and you can rely on pupils to sit down, log on and give you their full attention when you are ready.

Once you have completed the classroom organisation and administration quickly and efficiently, it is important to start the lesson content. Any gaps at this stage will lead to confusion, boredom and a search for alternative amusement by pupils, with the result that it will be more difficult to get their attention when you are ready. Your introductory remarks must be well planned, with the intention of focusing pupils on the lesson objectives and recapping on what you expect them to know from previous work.

Your teaching voice should be appropriate to the purpose of the communication, and it may be helpful to distinguish three ways of addressing pupils:

- *Command voice:* sharp and well projected, for gaining attention and giving instructions to be carried out without negotiation. If your voice is not loud, you may need to adopt an alternative way of making a sharp sound to gain attention.
- *Instructional voice:* slow, measured, clear and to the point, for emphasising and summarising key points and briefing pupils on procedures.

- *Conversational or 'story telling' voice:* soft, well modulated and encouraging, for explaining ideas, describing situations, asking questions and inviting contributions from pupils.

You will need to develop the skill of projecting without shouting or raising your voice. Try to drop your voice to your diaphragm and use this to drive your voice *quietly* to the back wall. Further issues concerning your voice quality and communication with pupils are considered in Capel *et al.* (2001: unit 3.1).

During lesson planning, you should identify key points within every lesson and design a mechanism to enable pupils to record key points for later review and retention. Being told the same point every lesson is wearing on the teacher and demoralising for the pupil. These key points should be progressive, the complexity and number linked to the ability of the pupils. The review of key points should use the instructional voice.

The number and complexity of the teaching points that you introduce at the start of the lesson need careful consideration and will depend on the age and ability of the pupils. Analogies with other skills or techniques already learnt by the pupils will aid learning and also enable transfer of skills to other contexts.

IMPLEMENTING TEACHING STRATEGIES

We have seen in Chapter 4 that there are a variety of teaching strategies that you could consider, and your choice will depend on the nature of the learning objectives. We will consider how to manage some of these in detail.

Question and answer

The skill of managing question and answer sessions is an essential tool for the teacher. It takes time to develop this into a high quality teaching strategy.

Task 6.2 Purposes of questioning

It was noted in Chapter 5 that teachers use questioning for a variety of purposes. From your observations of ICT teachers and your own planning and teaching, identify some purposes of questioning pupils.

A lecture style of teaching is rarely suitable, even for older pupils or more able classes. Question and answer allows a move away from teacher-centred to pupil-centred teaching, and can be a useful tool for motivation and stimulating interest. It is a useful way of checking on pupils' ideas about a concept prior to teaching a particular topic. It is also a useful review or revision tool, allowing you to focus pupils' reflection on the key points. As you gain more experience, question and answer sessions can depart from a fixed, planned path, and you can respond to the class's ideas; for example, in discussing the merits of using a computer for medical diagnosis in a surgery.

There is always the temptation when time is pressing to give the answer. This will lead the class just to sit and wait for you to do so in future. Instead, you need to allow them time to think, then nominate an individual to answer, and be prepared to help them make a response. You also need to consider how you are going to react to a completely incorrect answer which is just a stab in the dark. Do you just say that it's wrong? That may discourage pupils from offering answers in future. Any answer should be dealt with positively, and in most cases you should not make a negative comment related to an answer. You can accept a number of answers without comment except to say, 'Thank you. Who else has a suggestion to make?' It may have taken a pupil a lot of courage to answer a question, risking ridicule from their peers. However, pupils should not be left in a state of confusion, thinking that all the answers are good ones. When you have accepted more than one answer, you can then ask the class which they think is the best – and why!

Control is essential in question and answer; discipline can easily break down if pupils are allowed to shout out all at once and it is also easy for some pupils to 'hide' in a free for all. To aid control, question and answer sessions should be short and snappy most of the time, with extended questioning used for developing particularly important concepts. Until you have a good relationship with a class, you should insist that it is you who nominates the pupil to answer. With younger classes, where many pupils will be keen to answer, you should ask for 'hands up' and then name the pupil you want to answer. If you do not yet know the names (and you should work hard on getting to know them quickly), point to a pupil and ask for their name as well as their answer.

You should normally try to pick on a pupil who has the correct answer. Quite often the pupils will say the answer quietly to another pupil, particularly if the question is not getting the answer looked for, so listen out for pupils saying the answer and this gives you the opportunity to obtain the answer and lift the confidence of the pupil. Another tactic when answers are slow could be to split the class into pairs or groups and ask the group or pair to provide the answer. This reduces the risk for pupils of being seen to give the wrong answer.

If a class cannot answer a question, consider whether it is:

- due to lack of confidence;
- easier for pupils to wait for you to give the answer;
- because they have not understood the question;
- because they do not know the answer.

No answer at all is more difficult to deal with than some incorrect answers. It is usually possible to ask a question that even the least able pupil in the class can answer; such a pupil can then be nominated to give the answer. This helps them to integrate into the class activity and gain in self-esteem. Inexperienced teachers often ask questions which can be answered only by someone with precise knowledge of formal definitions, so try changing the phrasing of the question, either to relate it to pupils' informal knowledge, or to ask for guesses or opinions. If you get any answers at all, they will give clues as to whether the question was misunderstood or whether the pupils lack relevant knowledge. This enables you to ask another question based on the answer(s) that will enable you to focus or refocus on the point you are trying to develop. Further discussion of questioning can be found in Capel *et al.* (2001: units 2.1 and 3.1).

If there is a particular unfamiliar term that you want pupils to associate with an idea or technique, such as 'replicate', games such as 'hangman' can be used to build it letter by letter; even the weakest member of the class can contribute, and it gives you a chance to interact with the class. This also helps with remembering the spelling of the word and makes a contribution to pupils' literacy in general. Word searches can also help, and are valuable resources when the computers are unexpectedly out of action, though they have limited learning value and should not be overused.

Task 6.3 Managing questions

Imagine you have been asked to teach the class about different input and output devices for a computer. You may decide to start with the question 'Give an example of an input device into a computer.'

- Think of different answers you may get, including correct ones, incorrect ones and dubious ones.
- If you were given the answer 'floppy disk' what would your response be and what would be your next set of questions?

Hint: It is the floppy disk *drive* that is the device, and the floppy disk the medium that stores data. This is a common error among pupils.

Discussion

In any form of class discussion, you need to explain clearly what the focus or outcome is to be, and what procedures the class should follow. Otherwise, immature pupils can easily become confused and your well intentioned attempt to encourage whole class talk can degenerate into chaos in which the loudest pupils dominate. The 'snowball' technique is valuable in managing the contribution of ideas from every member of the class. You start by asking pupils to produce an individual list of ideas, then to combine ideas in pairs or groups and consider the question 'Are there any missing from your list?'

The following example of an approach to teaching the basic structure of a computer system illustrates a number of the ideas. It has worked well with pupils who are relatively unfamiliar with group work, and can be extended to more complex topics.

Figure 6.1 Schematic diagram of a simple computer system

A simple computer system can be represented as a set of five boxes as shown in Figure 6.1. As you ask pupils for their ideas about what makes up a computer system, the diagram can be built up visually on the board and explained verbally. You can draw the boxes large enough to hold a list of examples, or set out a separate table for examples of each type of device. In order to generate input and output devices to go on the diagram, a quick snowball exercise can be carried out. You can then ask each group for one item, moving quickly round the class to build up a list. Discussion of whether an item is an input or output device will enable many pupils to focus on the main issues of the lesson. As the list becomes full, the new items become more difficult to identify, so start with the group which has the least number and do not expect every group to have an additional item. Any doubtful items can be used as a focus of class discussion and/or question and answer, which has the advantage of developing pupils' understanding of the concepts. Items not suggested by the class could be offered as a challenge for pupils to decide in which box to place the item, and to justify their choice.

This activity has the advantage that there is a staged build-up of the visual picture of the computer system, supported by a verbal explanation. The pupils have owner-ship of the picture through their interactive participation. The whole diagram can then quickly be reviewed and the pupils copy down the work with their own expla-nation of the key points, which can be collected and marked, ensuring assessment of a grasp of the key points and a basis of review and reteaching if necessary. If an interactive whiteboard is available, or if you build it up using drawing tools in a software package, the diagram can be saved and posted on the intranet for pupils to access electronically.

Class debates are a good way to enthuse pupils about a particular topic, such as the effects of ICT on employment. The pupils are able to focus on the issues and, through listening and contributing to an active and lively debate, formulate concepts. It is relatively easy to get such discussions taking place, but difficulties may arise in con-trolling the direction of the discussion, the process of the discussion and then finishing it, so that normal relations are quickly re-established. Careful and detailed planning is essential so that there is no hiatus, when the control of the class can falter. Firm and swift intervention will prevent any drift towards chaos. You can expect more noise and general activity, and it is important to lay down some ground rules such as:

- no calling out;
- no moving round the class;
- stop and listen on a specific signal from you.

Never be tempted to talk over pupils, and if you have something to say that is important use the command voice to gain attention and then the instructional voice to outline the point clearly.

One format for a debate was described in Chapter 5, but there are a number of alternative scenarios:

- Pairs, with one member of each pair taking one side of the argument.
- Groups could be established where each group has to prepare the arguments or points on one side and then nominate a spokesperson to put one side of the debate.
- If there is a pair that is particularly vocal or confident they could hold a debate at the front of the class.
- You could act on one side of the debate against a pupil, pair or group.

Note that the debate is where one side puts its point of view, then the other side is invited to do the same. The class gives a decision as to who has won the debate. It is not a squabble!

Simulation and role-play activities are particularly useful in that they provide multi-sensory learning situations which enable you to involve many learning styles in one activity. There are many situations that can incorporate this type of activity.

As an example of a simulation, simple database concepts can be introduced by using a set of cards; each card can represent a record and the headings on the cards the fields. Pupils can be allocated to groups, and each group set the task of finding information in the database of cards and timing how long it takes to find the information. This same search can then be demonstrated on the computer and the timings compared. Simple and complex searching can be carried out in the class by asking pupils to stand if they exhibit a particular characteristic such as 'blue eyes'. The Boolean operators 'and' and 'or' can be introduced similarly, for example 'blue eyes and curly hair' and then 'blue eyes or curly hair'. The pupils will see that the latter gives a larger number of matches, thus helping them to understand the difference between the operators. This could be achieved in a PE lesson, so that pupils who exhibit a particular characteristic can be asked to run to a spot in the gym. Similarly activities can be developed for sorting into ascending and descending order, and searching on various criteria. Indeed, the link with PE could be extended so that physiometric measurements are used to compile a fitness database, though be careful to consider questions such as 'Who has shown the most improvement this term?' rather than just who is the best in absolute terms.

Teaching the next stage in database work – devising search criteria to solve real problems – can also be assisted by simulation methods. Pupils take the role of police officers being notified of a crime, questioning witnesses, extracting clues and searching a database of imaginary criminal records to find the culprit. This activity utilises literacy skills and deductive reasoning in pairs or teamwork situations to solve the problem.

Other uses include writing and acting a short play about a social implication such as the dangers of Internet chat rooms and e-mail or the consequence of corrupt data, and a newspaper editor evaluating an article written by applicants trying to get a job in the newsroom. With a younger class, this scenario could be replaced by that of a marketing manager evaluating a poster for an advertising campaign.

Task 6.4 Planning a debate

Write notes on how you might brief pupils for a debate on the issue 'There is no need to learn a DTP package because our word processor does everything we need'.

Introducing new techniques

In Chapter 4 we looked briefly at how you might introduce ideas to pupils, with different strategies being used according to the objectives and the nature of the class. Each of these will require different approaches to classroom organisation.

Demonstration. This seems quite straightforward, assuming that you have a large enough display for the group of pupils you are teaching. Success, however, depends on a number of factors, and you should always consider these questions:

- How will you place the pupils? Can each pupil see the screen?
- What will your position be in relation to the class? Can you see every pupil?
- Can you still face the class while using the keyboard?

Data projectors are becoming more available for use in the class, which can alleviate many logistical problems. If a pupil demonstrates the process under your instruction, difficulties can arise because of differences in interpretation of the instruction or language.

Step by step handouts work very well with limited content or with the most able pupils, but pupils will still tend to seek reassurance that they are 'doing it right' and screen dumps should be included liberally. Pupils following detailed instructions may not learn the key elements of the exercise but just blindly follow the instructions on the sheet, without comprehension. There is also a danger that the exercise could be seen out of context, which could reduce the transferability of any skills learnt. Handouts are useful as an *aide-mémoire* or revision guide but again you should consider the target audience. Most pupils find it difficult to follow detailed instructions and will tend to ask you or their friends rather than reading the handout.

Whole class talk through so that every pupil carries out each instruction on their own PC before the whole class moves on. This is useful to quickly get a class or group to a particular starting point, for example, loading a template, but it is a risky strategy for longer processes. Be prepared for pupils not keeping up or computer problems that will cause the pupil to disrupt your flow by calling out. Consider also the pupils that experiment for themselves or try to move ahead. Instead, ask them to help slower pupils.

Trial and error is feasible for graphics or artwork or with an experienced class, after a brief demonstration of the facilities or potential of a package. Pupils are then instructed to 'play with it' and see what they can do, with loose guidance as to the required outcomes. As long as all pupils succeed this approach has the benefit of increasing confidence, quicker learning, transfer of skill and developing autonomous learning. You will need to plan carefully a plenary session in order to discuss the terminology for the techniques and concepts, and how to combine techniques in order to carry out complete processes.

Cascade involves showing the next phase or a more advanced technique to a small group, then each of the group can show the pupils around them. Alternatively, show the technique to every fifth pupil around the class, and these 'peer teachers' can show the other pupils near to them.

Combinations of the above, for example where you take the class to a suitable point via whole class talk through, then bring the class together for a demonstration and support the pupils on their return to the computer with a handout or notes on the board. This has an advantage in that there is a fall back situation if one strategy fails.

Task 6.5 Choosing the right approach

Discuss with experienced teachers the approaches that they use. Do these vary with different topics? Different classes? Why?

You need to consider how the pupils will retain what they have experienced. One way of doing this is for pupils to open a word processor in a new window and type out their own *aide-mémoire* for each stage as it is carried out. This can be stored as an accumulating bank of procedures that can be called up at any time and even e-mailed to a fellow pupil should the need arise. This can be followed up by giving them a similar task to do, and providing as little support as you can. Instead, you prompt them to refer to their notes and try things out for themselves as far as possible.

ORGANISING AN APPROPRIATE WORKING ENVIRONMENT

Classroom layout

Your ability to control pupils can be largely influenced by the layout of the room. If you are in the centre, there are always going to be pupils who are behind you; you are going to have to move around continually so that there are only a few seconds when any pupil is out of sight. Consider where in the room you can see all the pupils, and they can see you. If, for example, there are two pupils behind an island, consider moving them for the purpose of a demonstration, whole-class questioning or board work. When you turn to the board or to help a pupil with a problem on their computer do you lose contact with the class? If you have to turn your back try to make it on the side with the least number of pupils. Try different stances when dealing with a problem on a computer or writing on the board. Preparing work in advance for an overhead projector (OHP) or data projector will mean that you can face the class continuously. Make sure that you do not have to bend down or turn to operate the OHP, mouse or keyboard.

You cannot keep an eye on every pupil every second of the lesson, but you will need to at least give the impression that you are doing exactly that. Try to make eye contact as soon as a pupil looks up, switching quickly between pupils in order to give this impression, and address comments to pupils in different parts of the room without moving. If you are working with a particular pupil, you will find it easier to keep an eye on the whole class if you stoop down next to the pupil. This stance will also be less threatening to the pupil you are helping. Make a point of commenting to pupils who are in the distance or behind you frequently.

Bags, coats and books all need to go somewhere, particularly on a wet day during the winter. Where are the pupils going to write in their books? If you intend to separate pupils who can be disruptive when together, where can they go so that they cannot try to communicate across the class? Your position within the class is vital in many instances; it is often useful to move around so that pupils are unable to 'hide'. In a classroom situation it is useful to be able to stand behind the back line of pupils, as the pupils are unsure of where you are and are less likely to misbehave.

Task 6.6 Keeping your eyes peeled

Look at various teaching and ICT rooms. In each, place yourself at various points in the room and try to identify:

- Where is the focal point of the room?
- Are there any blind spots or seats where pupils will have their back to you?
- Where will bags and coats go?
- Are you able to move around the room?
- If you give support to a pupil will you lose sight of the rest of the class?

It will be important to give these points attention when you are responsible for organising classes, especially those containing 'difficult' pupils.

Asserting your authority and imposing presence

In order to select appropriate ways of organising the class, you need to consider what your role is to be and how you should carry it out, taking into account the class dynamics. Your role in the class can be as a manager of learning, a presenter of information, an organiser of the pupils or a 'police officer'. It is varied and will depend upon the make-up of the particular class in terms of the age, ability and disposition of the pupils.

As the pupils start to enter the class, your clear and consistent enforcement of familiar rules and routines sets the tone of the lesson and you can be seen as being in control. Placing pupils at a computer or seat within the classroom enhances this. If a pupil starts to comment, that pupil should be stopped – 'It's not a matter of discussion!' Do not get into a debate, move on and ignore the pupil if they continue, say quietly and firmly, 'Be quiet', and move away to emphasise this break in communication. Talking over a pupil who continues may be seen as a conflict situation. If you raise your voice there has to be a big difference between the raised voice and the normal tone. If you are continuously speaking with a raised voice the pupils will get used to it and not respond.

Establish a routine in your class and try to keep rigidly to it, for example pupils should not call out or talk beyond their immediate neighbours. It is important to show quiet efficiency; your lessons should be clearly laid out and in enough detail so that you do not have to stop and think what to do next. It is also important to show confidence: remember you know a lot more than they do. Quiet confidence will give an air of relaxation. If there is tension in the class, it will need controlled release; perhaps the odd smile or sign that you are actually human will enable the class to relax and enable you and the pupils to enjoy the lesson. However, do not try to crack jokes, avoid sarcasm, which is usually lost on younger pupils, and keep a tight rein on pupils who may abuse the relaxed atmosphere.

We have suggested that you set your routine and guidelines for the class, for instance you might decide on a policy of 'no movement around the class', and pupils must adhere to this rigidly: printout can be distributed by you rather than collected by pupils. Any exception to the rule will give cause for debate and conflict. Communication between pupils should be quietly between neighbours. Two people taking normally is quiet, twenty people talking normally are ten times louder, so normal conversation should be kept to relevant matters and should be quieter than normal. As soon as the noise level approaches the point where you can hear individual voices there is too much. 'Working noise' has a different sound from general chatter, and you should learn to detect the difference so that you can intervene early when you perceive pupils stopping work on their task.

There are many ways of issuing sanctions against pupils. A quiet whisper has the advantage of isolation and is not disruptive. There is an old adage that says the more noise the teacher makes the more noise the class makes. A short sharp shout has shock value and tells the whole class that a transgression has been made, but you must immediately drop your volume in order to restore an effective working atmosphere.

Positive discipline enables pupils to work more effectively and enables you to relax and enjoy your lessons. Give praise when pupils reach or exceed your expectations, even with pupils who you would expect to be high achievers, in order to build confidence and respect. An awkward pupil who produces even the smallest good piece of work, with comments like 'Excellent work, now try the next . . . I'm sure you can do it', sets a challenge and is positive. Encouragement, support and individual attention are what some of the more difficult pupils in the class are missing and often they will respond in kind. You can find further guidance on behaviour management in Capel *et al.* (2001: unit 3.3).

Grouping pupils so as to optimise the effectiveness of the activities

Pupils may be grouped for teaching purposes according to a variety of criteria. Care needs to be taken with the 'mix' of the group. There are a number of types of groups and each can have merits, depending on the aims and objectives of the group.

Ability groupings. Cooperation between pupils of similar ability enables the whole group to progress as an entity, given a task that is achievable but stretches the group.

Mixed groupings. The stronger members pull the weaker members along, but difficulties occur when the stronger members are held back or the weaker members 'drop out'. In both situations a team leader often emerges; if he or she leads collaboratively it is beneficial as all can participate and contribute.

However, if the leader is domineering and self-centred it becomes unhelpful. Actively moving members between groups can be useful to fine tune groups, as long as it is seen as normal. Pupils who are lazy will sit back and let the rest get on with the activity, and task allocation within groups is a useful way of making sure that all members of the group participate.

Another reason to influence the make-up of a group is behaviour and this can be enhanced or degraded by friendship groups. Friendship groups or pairs within a group can give some pupils confidence, whereas others could end up chatting about matters unrelated to the task unless the collaboration motivates to achieve the work.

Pairing of pupils can also have positive and negative outcomes; pairs can be mutually supportive, and one pupil can support another who is weaker or has missed a lesson. Care must be taken not to highlight a pupil who is having difficulty because of lack of ability. If one of a pair is lazy the second will carry the entire burden or (worse) just follow the example of the lazy one.

'Peer teachers' can be extremely useful: when capable pupils have completed a task, they can help around the class. The personality of the supporting pupil can again have a positive or negative influence on the effectiveness of this strategy. A sympathetic peer teacher who provides 'scaffolding' and guides his or her classmate to a solution is obviously the ideal, and most pupils can be trained to do it. The antithesis is the pupil who goes around actually doing the work and could even gloat at the ineffectiveness of the pupil being supported and you will need to be alert to this. Although the peer teacher benefits from the reflective nature of the scaffolding process, it may lead to stagnation and boredom if used too much.

Handling the transition between different activities

Transitions occur when a pupil, group or class moves from one activity or task to another. The smoother you can make the change, the less disruption will be generated. After your introduction to the main points of the lesson, the transition to the next phase of the lesson will require careful thinking and planning. There needs to be a clear demarcation point between the two phases, and before any movement occurs, you need to make clear exactly what you want the pupils to do when you give the signal. Your voice should change from the story telling voice to the instructional voice. You may need to specify how they are to move – for instance, who goes first – if space is limited or the pupils are poor at organising themselves.

'When I tell you to move, I would like you to . . . (list a minimal set of points) . . . *now* quietly move to your places.' If you suddenly think of something that you missed, wait until you can regain their attention. While the class are working, bear in mind that casual comments have little or no effect, and it is best to save up points to tell the class in a single intervention rather than saying them when they come to mind.

Do not talk over the class; to make a point, use a 'command voice' which will signal your demand for attention: 'Stop, Listen . . . (wait for all to pay attention, make your points) . . . Carry on.' The point you want to make should be important enough to stop the class; redirecting, focusing, highlighting are all valid purposes. This procedure will also enable you to make an effective transition from individual or group work to a plenary session.

Task 6.7 Managing transitions

For one of the lesson plans where you are giving a demonstration and then setting a practical task, consider the class and the setting (room, equipment, layout) and plan exactly how you will organise a transition from a demonstration to the start of a practical exercise.

MONITORING PUPILS' PROGRESS IN THE TASK AND IN THEIR LEARNING

If you allow pupils to call out or to come up to you with problems, you will have difficulty keeping up with a demanding class. Furthermore, some pupils will not get any attention, either because they are quiet or lack confidence or they deliberately wish to 'hide'. A better strategy is perhaps to circulate round the class 'looking in' on each pupil in turn. If you change your route around the class you will keep the pupils alert.

It is useful to build up a profile of the pupils in your classes. This is most simply done by making regular shorthand notes to yourself about each pupil, perhaps as part of your register or mark book. This is particularly useful if you are asked by a head of year for your views on a particular pupil's work, attitude or behaviour or in preparation for a parents' evening. It will also be valuable when writing reports for parents.

Record keeping needs to be accurate and up to date. It is often useful, particularly for a class that is new to you, to have a clipboard or personal data assistant (PDA) with a grid consisting of a class list and brief notes concerning each pupil's progress. Although it is unrealistic (and unnecessary) to record every step each pupil takes, whilst you are learning to teach ICT it will be helpful to focus on what particular pupils are achieving and make some notes. This can be carried out whilst another teacher is in charge of the class initially. With practice, such focusing will become routine.

During practical work, you should circulate systematically round the class, noting features of progress (for example U for unsatisfactory, C for achieving core target, E for extension), effort (grade A, B, C), and perhaps behaviour (for example, G for good, H for helpful, T for talkative). It gives you a further opportunity to ask and become familiar with the names of the pupils. Keeping this each week enables you to identify at the start of the lesson who will need to be encouraged or set extension work, and may alleviate the need to spend time taking a formal register. It also enables you to give a summary of a pupil's progress should it be required by a form tutor or head of year, and is useful for parents' evenings, particularly if you have some work by the pupils in a folder with a digitised image of the pupil on the front page.

It will be helpful to identify particular points in a task where you ask pupils to see you for a check on the progress and quality of their work. Marking of this key item should help the pupils to assess their own progress and enable you to give feedback as to what they need to do to improve. All comments on work should be supportive and positive. In addition to the individual pupil profiles you will be able to pick up on trends and identify areas of weakness in the class that you will be able to address with the whole class or bring to the attention of the rest of the department for consideration in the Scheme of Work.

Recording pupils' progress related to a completed task can also give valuable information about a pupil. Was it entirely their own work? You should note how much help they received, from you and from peers. Comments on pupils' work should be positive and constructive: 'Very good' may help build confidence but does not give much guidance on how to improve. The pupils should also be in a position to know exactly how marks or grades were allocated.

Scanning the screens in the class will give you snapshots of how the class as a whole is progressing. It is particularly important to give praise and rewards wherever possible to difficult pupils: 'catch them being good' rather than waiting for them to misbehave before you give them attention. These pupils often cause problems because they lack confidence with the work, and if you can identify the source of their difficulties you may be able to help them make progress and gain self-esteem from their achievements. Pupils who finish quickly should also be noted; all too often pupils who are disruptive or cause problems are highlighted and the bright pupil who always does well can receive little or no attention.

Try to involve pupils in reviewing and reflecting on key points. You can use examples of good work to highlight various aspects of the work being done. If this is done with a pupil who usually has few positive experiences, it will have the benefit of increasing the confidence of the pupil and raising his standing in the eyes of his peers. How do you show this work to the class as a whole? It may warrant stopping the whole class; perhaps bringing the class round the computer if the layout of the classroom allows, but if possible a less disruptive method should be used such as a data projector or large screen monitor showing the pupil's work.

You should have some awareness of pupils' general learning abilities, and many schools have records of tests such as Cognitive Ability Testing (CATS). These are primarily used across the whole school to provide an indicator of what Standard Assessment Test (SAT) or GCSE grades should be expected, but can also provide some indication of what rate of progress to expect from individual pupils. This can help you with monitoring progress and setting targets, particularly in the case of underachieving pupils. It is not subject specific, however, and you should not expect it to predict a pupil's potential ICT capability.

There are many other issues concerning assessment, and Chapter 7 will address these in more depth.

Intervening at appropriate times in order to improve pupils' learning

When supporting a practical lesson, if you answer the call of every pupil randomly, or even in order of calling, you will find that you are moving around the class haphazardly. If you move round the class systematically, briefly seeing each pupil in turn, you will see every pupil in the class and you convey an atmosphere of order and organisation. You need to give attention to the ones that are quiet, the ones trying to avoid attention, and others such as those who are used to high achievement in other subjects and will not want to be shown up in front of their peers. Be careful with your position when dealing with pupils – you should be able to check what the rest of the class are doing. If you stoop down at the side of a pupil, you will have a much better view of the class than if you lean over from behind. It is also less intimidating for the pupil.

Take care over the amount of time spent with each pupil. At the start of the task, circulate quite rapidly so that you can ensure all pupils get started and can spend more time on them the next time round. This will help to identify any general misunderstandings early and then you can bring the issue to the attention of the whole class, ensuring, of course, that the whole class is paying attention to the point that you wish to make!

You will become familiar with pupils' common errors and misconceptions and you should take the chance to question the pupils in such a way as to expose and challenge ineffective ideas. For example, if you see a pupil using the backspace key to delete a whole paragraph of text because one word was wrong, ask them whether they can tell you a quicker way of making the change. If they can't, you could show them how, then click 'undo' and ask them to repeat what you have done. Another example is when pupils are learning to enter formulas in a spreadsheet. If a pupil works out the answer and types the number in instead of the formula, ask them to change a value being used to calculate the result. Point out that their answer is now wrong, and ask them to teach the spreadsheet how to work it out. If necessary, show them how to enter the formula and go through the process of changing the value of the independent variable again. Ask them to put in some more formulas in the same way – it's not a good idea to deal with replication until they have repeated the technique of entering formulas several times.

There are various techniques you can use when intervening to support pupils' learning (Kennewell *et al.*, 2000). To help a pupil get an overview of a process, you can show them on the screen, perhaps with the pupil making brief notes. If you need to show how to do something, be careful how you take over a pupil's mouse: for example, say 'Can I use your mouse?' and when they let go, take the mouse from the side rather than reaching across in front of them. To ensure that they comprehend, you can then 'undo' your work and ask the pupil to repeat the process while you check that they can now move forward correctly. It is easy to fall into the trap of doing the work for the pupil, particularly when you are anxious and the pupil is slow. This could result in the pupil being left without the ability to solve the problem should it occur again. When the pupil has done something wrong, it will usually be better to let them correct their mistake, whilst you stay with them and use gentle prompts and questions to help them think. This is often the case when they are 'stuck'. Asking them 'What are you trying to do?' or 'Why did you do that?' may help them think for themselves what to do. You can ask more specific questions ('What menu do you think you might look on?') or make suggestions ('Try selecting the text first'). Actually telling them what to do should be a last resort, as they need to learn how to learn for themselves.

A 'quick fix' (Kennewell *et al.*, 2000: 112) could be valid and appropriate in some cases, to move a weak pupil forward, particularly if the 'stumbling block' experienced by the pupil is not the main point of the lesson. However, the pupil will not be able to repeat the work done by you and this aspect could prevent future progress. If the difficulty is general you may be able to work with one or two pupils and then set them up to disseminate quietly to others in the class.

SUMMARY

In this chapter we have looked at matters of class organisation and learning management. We have focused particularly on the most important phases and methods: the classroom environment, introductions to lessons, choosing strategies to convey key points, and the management of transitions.

We have emphasised the use of oral interaction: by the teacher using different voices to emphasise key points and signal transitions; and by the pupils to encourage involvement in the lesson and stimulate the reflection on experiences which helps concept development and retention of knowledge. We considered methods of grouping pupils and the use of peer teachers.

We also considered methods of monitoring pupils and recording progress within the individual lessons using a clipboard and shorthand notes on the class register together with assessment at key phases within a topic, with the purpose of identifying how well pupils are progressing and providing feedback on how they can improve, individually and as a class. Circulating round the class will enable you to see every pupil. It provides a calm atmosphere that enables pupils as well as yourself to relax and not to get stressed by being pulled from one noisy pupil to the next. The setting of targets was considered to help motivate pupils and clarify expectations of progress that can be monitored and used to assess the need for support.

FURTHER READING

See Chapter 4.

Part III

Aspects of Teaching and Learning ICT

7 Assessing Attainment

Neil Stanley and Howard Tanner

Assessment of pupils' performance is a significant part of the role of all teachers, no matter what their subject. Assessment of attainment is critical to knowing whether or not your pupils are achieving similar standards to those achieved in equivalent institutions. Assessment of progress is necessary if you are to judge whether or not you have succeeded in your teaching efforts. Furthermore, although they may not like to admit it, assessment of their performance is also necessary if your pupils are to become effective learners. They need to know whether their work is meeting your expectations and what they need to do to improve. If your pupils are to become independent learners, taking responsibility for their own progress, they need effective feedback to help them to set targets for themselves.

So far we have emphasised those aspects of assessment which are of interest to learners and teachers in the classroom. However, you will be very aware that there are other stakeholders who are interested in the results of assessment such as parents, governors, employers, local education authorities (LEAs) and governments. Although your interest as a teacher is likely to be focused on the professional aspects of assessment, in these days of accountability you must also pay due regard to the managerial purposes of assessment demanded by other stakeholders.

Assessment should be an integral part of teaching and learning. It should be a key element of your planning and must not be left as an afterthought, as something to be bolted on at the end. In this chapter we will discuss the assessment demands on the teacher of ICT. You will discover that effective assessment is a critical feature of good learning environments and that implementing the best practices in assessment can result in significant gains in pupils' attainment.

Freeman and Lewis (1998: 8) give a list of assessment myths, which include:

- Assessment must always be a competitive process, with learners pitted against one another.
- Collaboration between learners is cheating.
- Assessment happens only at the end of a course.
- Assessment processes must be hidden from the learner.
- If students assess themselves, they are always over-generous.

We need to consider the aspects of learning and using ICT that can help to destroy these myths.

OBJECTIVES

By the end of this chapter, you should:

- understand the purposes of assessment and the various methods appropriate to ICT;
- understand the need to use baseline assessment to inform teaching and learning;
- understand how formative assessment can improve attainment and be aware of a number of effective strategies for formative assessment;
- be aware of the issues involved in assessing ICT capability in the context of other subjects;
- understand how to plan for assessment in teaching and learning;
- understand the issues and processes involved in recording and reporting.

THE PURPOSES OF ASSESSMENT

There are, of course, many purposes of assessment, and different forms of assessment should be used according to your aims. At the beginning of this chapter we listed the main purposes. We think you should distinguish between those purposes of assessment which are essentially managerial in character and those which are professional. Managerial purposes are associated with accountability and the maintenance of the system. Professional purposes are focused on supporting the teaching and learning process.

Summative assessments summarise what pupils know, understand and can do in total over a broad domain at a particular point in time. Typical examples are end of year tests, or end of key stage examinations. Although summative assessment is occasionally useful to you as a teacher, it most often supports managerial purposes. It is formative assessment which supports your professional aims most directly and can make the biggest contribution to improving attainment.

Task 7.1 What professional use is made of summative assessment in your school?

- What summative assessments are made of children's ICT attainment in your school?
- How often are they made and what purposes do they serve?
- Are any of the purposes professional in character, leading directly to improvements in teaching and learning?

Legally, state schools are expected to report pupil progress to parents on at least an annual basis, although in some schools termly, or even half-termly, summative assessments are required. In most subjects, such assessments are based on the results of school tests or examinations summarising the work of the year or the term. However, if you examine your main teaching objectives for ICT, you may come to the conclusion that timed written tests are an inappropriate and inauthentic way to assess most of your key objectives.

School examinations are often quite formal in character and form significant events in pupils' school lives. However, the precise purpose of such summative examinations is not always clear. They are often used as the basis of communication with parents, providing an incontestable item to include on a school report. They may also be used to determine movement between ability sets or bands. You may ask yourself whether the time and emotion invested in such examinations are worth the effort when they add little to what you will already know about your pupils from their efforts in class.

When school examinations have high status, they can motivate some children to reflect on their learning and consolidate their knowledge, although few know how to do so effectively without significant intervention from teachers. There is also evidence that when the focus is on competition and comparisons between pupils, there is a negative impact on the development of many pupils. Whilst competition can be a powerful motivator, the losers in the competition often begin to believe that they lack natural ability, leading them to 'retire hurt', losing the motivation to learn (Black and Wiliam, 1998).

If your school demands periodic summative assessment, it will be useful for teaching and learning only if the results are analysed to identify persistent misconceptions and areas where understanding is weak. A summary mark is not helpful for planning teaching or discussing targets with pupils. It is important for pupils to analyse their performance in detail, setting themselves achievable short term targets in collaboration with their teachers. We believe that continuous formative assessment is far more likely to improve standards in ICT than periodic summative assessment.

Many schools test pupils at the end of units of work. This is not the most effective form of continuous assessment. Formative comments and suggestions, received after the end of a unit of work, are usually too late for pupils to act on – that topic is over and a new one has started! If you assess pupils formatively and give them helpful feedback *prior to the end* of a unit of work, they may be able to act on the advice in order to improve their work. Such formative assessments will become out of date within a matter of days. There is little point in making a major effort to record them – they are intended to be transitory.

In a 'traditional' model of education, the examination at the end of the course determined whether or not pupils had learned the required knowledge. Using *summative* assessment as the sole strategy is particularly unhelpful in ICT, where some pupils may already have the skills or knowledge to pass the examination before undertaking the learning offered. Such a mismatch of learner needs and opportunity often leads to a lack of challenge or progression in learning.

You need a model of teaching, learning and assessment which can take account of the range of ICT experience and ensure that all learners receive an appropriate challenge. Thus before you can begin to plan your learning activities you need to find out what your pupils currently know.

Baseline assessment

Baseline assessment is determined from previous work with that group of learners or from information gathered by testing (formal or informal) or from well thought out questioning when you first meet the class. This form of assessment is necessary in some form at the start of each lesson to enable you to determine what knowledge and concepts have been understood.

Task 7.2 Baseline assessment opportunities

From your observations, think back to when you have watched a teacher start work with a new class or on a new topic.

- What techniques did they use to discover baseline information about the learners?
- Was it necessary to record this information?
- Did every pupil then begin an individually tailored programme of learning?

You may think that the ideal situation for learning would be for each pupil to be assessed prior to a unit of work and then to follow an individually tailored programme. We certainly know of some teachers who try to implement such a regime. However, we think that it pays too little attention to the social nature of learning in schools.

Although having individual learners progress at their own rate appears to be an ideal situation, we have observed that for too many pupils 'their own rate' appears to be very slow or even stationary. Although most pupils are positively disposed towards the use of computers, progression is more rapid if teachers are able to drive learning forwards, setting appropriate short term targets in the light of their knowledge of individual pupils, but dealing with the whole class as a social unit.

Baseline assessment should inform both your planning for the class as a whole and your knowledge of the pupils as individuals, helping you to differentiate when it is appropriate. If you know where the pupils are starting from, and you have clear objectives for learning, you can provide suitable teaching and learning experiences. However, again you are hoping that your baseline assessment will be out of date by the end of the lesson and recording may often be limited to specific notes about particular pupils.

Summative assessment is necessary at intervals during the key stage to support reporting to parents and the monitoring of progress. However, *formative* assessment is of greater significance for day-to-day teaching and learning. Increased emphasis on formative assessment is most likely to result in improved standards of achievement.

Formative assessment

Formative assessment is assessment *for* learning, as opposed to summative assessment, which is assessment *of* learning. Formative assessment must happen continuously for teaching to be effective.

> It is rooted in self-referencing; a pupil needs to know where s/he is and understand not only where s/he wants to be but also how to 'fill the gap'. This involves both the teacher and the pupil in a process of continual reflection and review about *progress*. When teachers and peers provide quality feedback, pupils are empowered to take the appropriate action.
>
> (QCA, 2001a)

In order to maximise learning and ensure that pupils make progress, it is necessary to provide feedback during the learning process. Research suggests that oral feedback is the most effective (QCA, 2001a). However, not all oral feedback is good (Wiliam, 1999). You should not steal the problem from the pupils or take over their keyboards. They must be challenged to think and act for themselves. The best interaction between a teacher and a pupil offers the minimum support necessary for progress to continue. Similarly, praise is often regarded as an obviously good thing. However, although praise is a motivator, it is addictive and seems insincere when overused (Good and Grouws, 1975; Brophy, 1981). Formative assessment intends to modify behaviour and support learning, so oral interactions should be constructive and discuss how work could be improved.

Similarly, when key pieces of work or assignment pieces are marked, you should aim to write a comment in the language of the student, which should be brief, constructively critical and should enable them to move forward. Vague comments such as 'Good', 'VG,' 'Excellent', although supportive, do not enable the student to progress. 'Have you thought about including . . . ?' might be more helpful. Research suggests

Figure 7.1 Linkages between forms of assessment

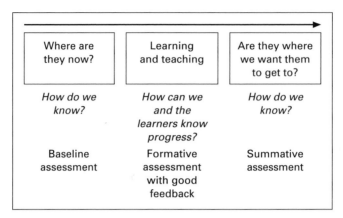

that feedback based on grades or marks also fails to change future performance. A comment suggesting how the work could be improved is far more effective for learning. When both a comment and a mark are used, the mark dominates and the comment loses its impact (see Butler, 1987; 1988; Wiliam, 1999).

Task 7.3 Monitoring and assessing ICT development in your school

Find a copy of the assessment policy for ICT in your school.

- Is the assessment described in the policy mainly formative or summative?
- To what extent does the assessment policy for ICT in your school support the learning process?
- To what extent does it encourage pupil self-assessment and reflection?

Figure 7.1 shows visually how the baseline, formative and summative assessment are linked.

The research evidence in favour of formative assessment is remarkably consistent. Effective formative assessment results in a significant improvement in learning (Black and Wiliam, 1998). Central to formative assessment is that it:

- is embedded in the teaching and learning process, of which it is an essential part;
- shares learning goals with pupils;

- helps pupils to know and to recognise the standards to aim for;
- provides feedback which leads pupils to identify what they should do next to improve;
- has a commitment that every pupil can improve;
- involves both teacher and pupils reviewing and reflecting on pupils' performance and progress;
- involves pupils in self-assessment.

(QCA, 2001a)

The last two conditions would also represent a change in pedagogy for many teachers. The crowded curriculum often leads to little time being set aside for pupils to reflect on their learning and assess their own performance. However, children need to reflect on their learning and assess their own performance if they are to consolidate their actions into general principles and devise strategies to progress further.

We suggested in Chapter 5 that you should explain the learning objectives at the start of a lesson so that pupils will have some idea of what they are expected to achieve. When ICT is being used in the context of subject teaching, the learning objectives should relate to ICT as well as to the other subject being taught. Similarly, it seems only fair to explain assessment criteria to pupils for both the subject and for ICT. This has the effect of helping them to focus on those aspects of their work which you consider to be important.

Tasks which are set for ICT coursework are often open ended and in consequence the assessment criteria are often difficult to interpret. If children are to assess the quality of their ICT work, they must be aware of the nature of a good solution to the task. Currently, many pupils do not understand the criteria against which they are being assessed (QCA, 2001b). Furthermore many pupils have little experience of self-assessment. Children need to be *taught* how to assess themselves. Participation in peer assessment is helpful for this, as it teaches pupils both about the nature of a good solution and about how to assess (Tanner and Jones, 1994). Although time consuming, asking pupils to present their work in a plenary and answer questions about the problems they encountered and the decisions they made helps the class to reflect on the learning process and to formalise the knowledge they developed during the task. Another useful activity, which encourages reflection in plenaries, is to ask a pupil to act as a *rapporteur* to summarise the main points of the lesson and to answer questions from other pupils (Wiliam, 2000).

Some teachers list the main learning objectives of their units of work with tick boxes next to them and ask pupils to assess the extent to which they feel they have properly understood the key concepts *independently* of their success in the tasks. If you think back to your own experiences as a learner, you can probably recall occasions when you successfully completed the task, but felt that you did not really understand what you were doing. When learning is based on an unsound foundation, it is often transitory and quickly forgotten.

QCA (2001b) reports on a technique for self-assessment using 'traffic lights'. Pupils indicate the extent to which they feel they have understood the learning objectives for the term using green, amber and red dots. A green dot means 'I understood this and feel confident.' An amber blob indicates that they have some understanding but are not confident. A red blob means 'I don't understand at all.' This gives teachers feedback on the success of their teaching and helps them to identify areas needing to be revisited. The main benefit, however, is that children are encouraged to reflect on their own learning, helping them to identify suitable targets for improvement (Wiliam, 2000).

You may be concerned about the reliability of pupils' self-assessments. However, our experience leads us to suggest that children are remarkably honest in their self-assessment of their ICT capability, although we would not use self-assessment as our only strategy. Your assessment of ICT capability must not only be reliable, it should also be valid.

Assessment of ICT capability should aim for a judgement based on how pupils perform in a variety of contexts (ACAC, 1996). It is necessary therefore to assess and monitor children's ICT performance in a variety of subject areas if the assessment is to be valid.

ASSESSING THE DEVELOPMENT OF ICT CAPABILITY IN OTHER SUBJECTS

Task 7.4: Assessing ICT capability in the context of other subjects

- ICT is used in the teaching and learning of other subjects. What issues arise in its assessment?
- Does your school have a policy concerning the assessment of ICT capability in the context of other subjects?
- How does your school cope with the assessment of ICT in the context of other subjects?
- Who is responsible for conducting the assessment of ICT capability?

Much of the work undertaken in IT lessons, especially at Key Stage 3, will be either in conjunction with other curriculum areas (co-planned and delivered), or will use what may be termed 'borrowed curriculum', i.e. when IT tools and concepts are taught in the context of some other subject area. With this sort of work it needs to be clear which aspects are being assessed (ICT, subject or both) and who will be responsible for the assessment. A class that joins you from their Mathematics lessons for a series of three sessions on Logo has both mathematics and ICT needs. It is critical that these needs are supported and assessed appropriately.

For summative purposes at the end of Key Stage 3 assessment should be based on the National Curriculum level descriptors, and these give teachers a good indication of the expected standards. However, non-ICT subject teachers are likely to be unfamiliar with the descriptors and will require support in their interpretation.

Assessment of ICT capability is unusual in that task outcomes depend on the technology available and the amount of help provided. This situation is further complicated when some pupils are able to complete tasks at home on their own equipment and with the support of parents and friends whilst others have to rely only on access in school. When ICT is used to perform authentic tasks in the context of other curriculum subjects, it is often difficult to unravel ICT knowledge and understanding from those of the particular subject context.

Many schools have developed portfolios of annotated pupils' work, to indicate the common standards that may be achieved. Portfolios can help teachers to develop understanding of what is being assessed. In order to assess higher order knowledge and skills, it is necessary to use a variety of assessment strategies, including informal assessment through regular observation and questioning of pupils working on IT tasks and by collections of work which show development from draft to final product. This requires careful advanced planning.

PLANNING FOR ASSESSMENT

You should realise by now that assessment is not something that can just happen in a haphazard way, but should be planned for. Indeed, you should see that it is as important to plan assessment as it is to plan teaching, and the two should be planned together, as indicated in Chapter 4.

You will need to ensure that all your teaching episodes have clear learning outcomes – what you want to teach and what you need to assess are inseparable. You should also decide in advance how you are going to judge success against your learning objectives.

As most IT work is based in practical activity it is important to ensure that you don't just end up noting that the class could 'make a PowerPoint presentation'. Remember that ICT capability is about developing concepts and higher order skills and processes – it is not just a collection of low level techniques. If you are assessing against National Curriculum levels in England, the website http://www.ncaction.org.uk/subjects.ict contains valuable guidance.

You may find it helpful to break your learning objectives down into categories. One popular general classification is 'SACK': skills, attitudes, concepts and knowledge. For ICT, this classification can be refined to incorporate our specific structure for the components of ICT capability (see Chapters 1 and 2). For example, in the PowerPoint topic, some of the learning outcomes that might be included are:

- Can open the PowerPoint program (Technique or Routine – Skill).
- Can work in pairs to produce a joint presentation (Process – Attitude).
- Can understand why the amount of text on a PowerPoint slide should be limited (Concept).
- Knows that PowerPoint is a presentation package (Terminology – Knowledge).

- Knows that presentation packages are used in commercial organisations (Fact – Knowledge).

Task 7.5 Assessing outcomes

Each of those outcomes should be assessable. How could you assess that each had been achieved? Do you have a choice of methods?

Your learning outcomes will also need to take account of the range of ability in your teaching group, so you may need to preface your learning outcomes with 'All learners . . .', 'Most learners . . .' and 'Some learners . . .'. Outcomes for a single lesson need to be a sub-set of those describing the whole unit of work. It is unwise to have more than half a dozen learning objectives for a single lesson, and fewer still will be easier to manage.

If you use a system such as SACK you will be able to ensure that your lessons do not focus unduly on any one single category. In particular, many lessons you observe may focus on low level skill development (new techniques and automatisation of familiar ones) and this will constrain the learners from undertaking higher order learning activity. Specifically you won't be stretching the ability of your more able learners.

Task 7.6 Questioning

Arrange to observe a teacher who is known to be skilled at questioning. Make a note of any questions aimed at eliciting higher order responses as opposed to simply maintaining accountability or managing learning.

- How did the teacher deal with pupils who fail to answer?
- How did the teacher support weaker pupils' attempts to respond?
- Did the teacher keep any records of the exchanges?

Your questioning needs also to be thought out in advance: whom you are going to ask as well as what you are asking and how you will probe the answers. Asking mostly closed questions with just simple 'yes' or 'no' type answers will not stretch learners. More open questioning demanding higher order responses such as 'What advantages can you see in that approach?' or 'How do you think data capture ought to be organised?' will generate more higher order thinking. You can ask other group members to add to or clarify an answer: 'Can you add anything to that?' or 'Can you explain that in more detail for us?' Try to ensure that you distribute your questioning fairly throughout the class.

Such questioning can be a valuable form of formative assessment, and it will undoubtedly inform your teaching, but you are unlikely to be able to record individual responses or attainment. However, you may occasionally note an unusually perceptive comment.

RECORDING AND REPORTING YOUR ASSESSMENTS

The problem which we have to face with all assessment and recording procedures in the medium to long term is that people *forget*. People are not like computers. Knowledge which was there yesterday is not necessarily there in the same form today. People learn new knowledge (even when they are not in your lessons). Old knowledge decays away or becomes inaccurate if it is not used regularly.

In the early days of the National Curriculum many advisers developed pupil records based on statements of attainment using tick boxes. These quickly became discredited among teachers, partly because of the high administrative burden they created but, more important, because they were so unreliable. Boxes which had been ticked to indicate that a pupil had a full understanding of a particular concept were useless for planning purposes because pupils persisted in forgetting things (Tanner, 1992)!

The records you keep will depend on the nature and purpose of the assessment. We suggest three levels at which assessment should be carried out, each with a different purpose, focus and methods.

Lesson based assessment

Purpose: to monitor the progress of individual pupils, particularly in terms of techniques and concepts in order to decide how much help to offer.

- Identify the key points and expectations for the lesson, e.g. (1) copying images from the World Wide Web and pasting them into a PowerPoint presentation; (2) understanding how formulas store relationships in a spreadsheet.
- Devise opportunities for pupils to demonstrate attainment, e.g. (1) task which requires selecting an image on a web page, copying, pasting into a slide; (2) task which requires pupils to carry out 'What if?' investigations, and oral questions such as 'When you save a spreadsheet, what things are stored?'
- Set criteria for success and evidence required, e.g. (1) suitable image is pasted at appropriate position in presentation and a printout produced; (2) when carrying out investigations, pupils are observed changing values rather than entering formulas again and when asked what is stored, they mention formulas.
- Ask the class to review what were the main teaching points in the lesson and what they found difficult to grasp.
- Note any implications for next lesson, e.g. (1) demonstrate the technique again, asking pupils what to do at each stage; (2) load the spreadsheet again,

ask them to predict what will happen when values are changed, and then ask them to explain why.

Task-based assessment

A task may take several lessons.

Purpose: to provide feedback to pupils on their skills and identify needs for development. This will mainly involve processes and higher-order skills, but will also help with identifying any techniques and concepts which are not fully grasped.

- Identify the desired outcome of the task and its purpose (e.g. poster to advertise the school play).
- Determine the features required for particular levels, in terms of particular aspects of the process and outcome.
- Share the assessment criteria with the pupils.
- Ask each pupil to review his or her performance against the criteria.
- Collect any products produced for assessment.
- Record attainment against the criteria in your mark book.
- Give the pupil feedback in the form of suggestions for improvement (techniques, process, concepts and higher order skills), *not* marks.

Annual report

- For each pupil, review your records of task based assessments and refer to the complete folder of the pupil's work.
- Decide the overall NC level as a best-fit description of the pupil's attainment represented by the work and records.
- Summarise the comments made about the pupil's ICT capability during the year.

Most schools have a policy of recording/reporting 'effort' as well as 'attainment' in the annual report and this has implications for record keeping at task and lesson level. You will need to judge how much effort each pupil is making. If you set a standard task, the effort may be very little for some of the most experienced, and very great for the least experienced. You should thus ensure that a reasonable challenge is provided for every pupil.

GROUP WORK

It is questionable, even where the resources exist, whether all work should be undertaken by individuals at their own computer. Social constructivist models of learning (see, for instance, Capel *et al.*, 2001: unit 5.1) suggest that working together in a group is beneficial to the learning of each individual. Teamwork is also a Key Skill and ICT allows opportunities for the final product to be far better than anything that could be produced by a solo user.

However, there are issues of assessing an individual's contribution to group work. One strategy would be to have some individual reflective component that can be used to validate group contribution. This is a sophisticated concept but not beyond most young people. Indeed, considerable success has been achieved where learners are asked to comment on the work of their peers as part of the recording process. Figure 7.2 is an example of such a document.

Figure 7.2 Document illustrating self-assessment and peer assessment

PowerPoint Assessment

Name : [redacted] **Form:** [redacted]

TASK	REQUIREMENTS	COMPLETED	COMMENTS
1	Choose an appropriate layout for each slide	18/1/01	I think that I have got a good layout
2	Enter text - colour	18/1/01	I wont all my text black
	- fill	18/1/01	I fill the backsround with black and sreen.
3	Enter graphics – clipart, charts	18/1/01	I have put clipart in
4	Slide transition - effects	18/1/01	I have transation on my slides
5	Custom animation - effects	18/1/01	I'have youscanimation on my slid SOS
6	Input, output, storage devices	1/2/01	I have got on Input output storge it is good
7	Structure	1/2/01	I have change the own of the strucure

Pupil Comment I think that I have made a good Power Point and I think it is very good and also havs good grafiks.

Peer Comment I think that Andy's Slide Show is good. he has chosen alot of diferent input and out put Devises Pictures for it he has chosen meney of Sounds

Teacher Comment
This is a good attempt Andrew. You have used animation and transition to create interesting effects. Perhaps you could think about using the same format for the text and make sure you spell check.

PORTFOLIOS

You will note from Figure 7.2 that an attempt has been made to capture evidence of the process as well as the final product. As software has become more sophisticated we need to get a stronger grasp of how the learner has approached a task in order to provide support and correctly level their ICT capability. You should also note the use of peer assessment and self-assessment to ensure that pupils reflect on their achievements and the teacher's formative comments.

Summative assessment may include judging pupils' work against the school portfolio. However, this should take into account the degree of independence shown by each pupil in the process of development and not just the quantity and quality of their outcomes. A school's assessment policy should be explicit about the role of observation, oral questioning, the product of pupils' work and the effect of peer assistance.

A portfolio of examples of the pupils' tasks provides a suitable tool for this purpose. It is essential to identify in planning how this evidence will be used and against what criteria it will be measured. Figure 7.3 shows how this PowerPoint task was assessed, and Figure 7.4 shows how it fitted into a larger portfolio of activity.

When assessing students' learning by means of a practical task, it is not just the task that must be considered. What also matters is *how* the task has been carried out. How efficient are the techniques used? How much support has the student been given by the teacher or peers? Has the support involved teaching specific techniques, structuring the overall process, or planning and evaluating? It will not be helpful to give students credit for what you or their friends have done for them, but it would be

Figure 7.3 Criteria of assessment at different levels

POWERPOINT – ASSESSMENT LEVELS APPLICABLE TO THIS UNIT OF WORK		
LEVEL 3	**LEVEL 4**	**LEVEL 5**
At this level you are able to find suitable information for your topic from a CD-ROM and you can use the information to create a presentation.	At this level you are able to find suitable information for your topic from a number of different sources and use different forms of information, e.g. text, pictures and sound to create a presentation. To achieve this level you will be expected to produce work of a high standard and you must make sure that your work is at the correct level for the intended audience.	At this level you are able to find suitable information for your topic from a number of different sources and use different forms of information, e.g. text, pictures and sound to create a presentation. To achieve this level you will be expected to produce work of a high standard and you must make sure that your work is at the correct level for the intended audience. Your presentation should have a clear structure so that the slides follow on from each other in a logical sequence. You should also be able to assess your work critically and understand what you need to do in order to improve on it.

This unit of work will be assessed by:

- Your own evaluation and comments from your peers
- Teacher assessment (by watching your slide show)
- Teachers' observation of your practical work

Figure 7.4 Assessment summary for Key Stage 3

KS3 ASSESSMENT

ICT PoS	Description of assessed work	Task	Level	Comments
3a, 3b 4a, 4c 1a,	PowerPoint presentation	Create a multimedia presentation on topic of own choice, using information from a variety of sources.		
1a, 1b, 1c	Data handling – • CD-ROM searching using 'The Way Things Work' • Ability to interrogate database using simple and complex queries • Data collection, creating and amending a database demonstrating accuracy and consistency in the work	Answering set questions and devising own questions. 'Survey' and 'Greenlea' database files – interrogating, interpreting information Creation of graphs/charts Devising own questions for others to answer		
2b, 2c, 2d	Logo – • Basic shapes • Use of REPEAT command • Use of procedures • Use of variables • Extension activities	Draw square, triangle, rectangle, circle Draw shapes and patterns using REPEAT Draw own shapes using procedures Draw shapes using variables Mickey mouse, traffic lights, etc. Own programs		

unfair not to acknowledge their learning if they subsequently show the ability to do it for themselves. Your assessment records will thus be vital in helping to make a judgement, but support offered in the early stages should not detract from later achievement.

EXAMINATIONS

We have considered assessment through open–ended practical tasks and projects, considering that these represent reasonably authentic performance settings. The aim of this type of task is to maximise the *validity* of the assessment, that is, we are assessing what we want the students to learn. However, it is difficult to ensure that all students have the same opportunity to demonstrate their capability, owing to differences in resources, support and judgement of performance. This reduces the *reliability* of the assessment, that is, the independence of the result from the particular setting or marker.

In order to overcome this problem, most public examination schemes require a more controlled assessment process. Some schemes, such as Computer Literacy and Information Technology (CLAIT), European Computer Driving Licence (ECDL) or the Teacher Training Agency ICT tests for qualified teacher status in England, include a practical test; others, such as GCSE schemes, include a written examination. However, whilst these can increase reliability, their validity is often very suspect compared with authentic tasks: they assess the ability to answer examination questions, rather than the ability to solve real problems. They often have little to do with ICT capability as we defined it in Chapter 1.

Figure 7.5 Overview of curriculum, teaching learning and assessment

Thinking about assessment

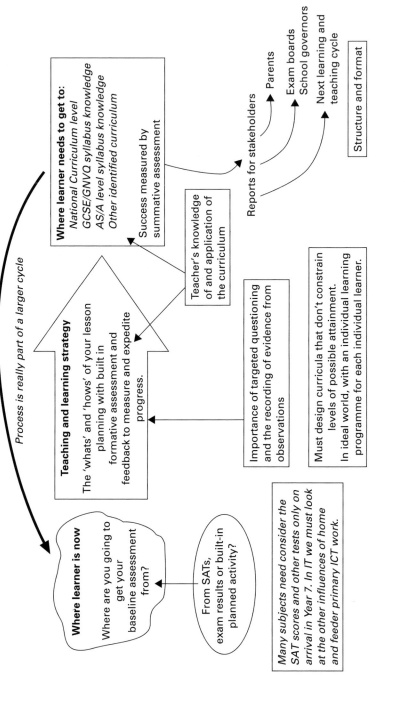

SUMMARY

The purposes of assessment may be divided into those which are managerial and those that are professional. Summative assessment is usually focused on managerial aims whereas formative assessment, assessment for learning, is focused on professional purposes.

It is through the use of effective formative assessment that standards of attainment are most likely to be improved. Effective formative assessment demands that pupils learn the skills of self-assessment. Effective assessment requires careful planning. You may find it helpful to analyse your learning objectives and plan your assessment of pupils using the SACK system.

The recording of assessment data should pay due regard to the fact that all assessment is transitory. It represents a snapshot of a moving image. The most useful forms of assessment are out of date by the end of the lesson and there is little point in making detailed records.

School policies for monitoring and assessing ICT development across a range of contexts should include a wide range of strategies and focus on higher order skills and processes. However, greater emphasis on formative assessment is likely to result in higher achievement. Pupils should be encouraged to reflect on their work to formalise the ICT knowledge gained in the lesson. Pupils should be taught skills of self-assessment, as they help them to understand the criteria of success and to set appropriate targets for improvement. Figure 7.5 illustrates the relationships involved in the overall assessment process.

FURTHER READING

Torrance, H. and Prior, J. (1998) *Investigating Formative Assessment: Teaching Learning and Assessment in the Classroom*, Buckingham: Open University Press. Provides general principles and guidance on methods of formative assessment in general.

8 Teaching Examination Courses

Chris Jones and Ian Hughes

The teaching of examination courses is often seen as the most challenging and perhaps the most rewarding aspect of teaching. Seeing your pupils succeed in public examinations is one of the joys of the profession: a reward for all the effort you put into the learning process. The role of the teacher is very important in enabling pupils to succeed. In this chapter we will be exploring many of the key issues that you need to consider when beginning to plan effective examination preparation for your pupils.

OBJECTIVES

By the end of this chapter you should be able to:

- recognise that pupils enter examination courses with prior knowledge, skills and experience;
- balance and combine theory and practical work;
- select, produce and use case studies of ICT systems;
- use ICT in the teaching of theory;
- teach pupils research and presentation skills;
- develop pupils' abilities as critical ICT users and effective ICT system designers;
- guide pupils on the principles of coursework projects;
- prepare pupils for examinations.

PROGRAMMES AND PROGRESSION AT KEY STAGE 4

ICT is a curriculum requirement for all pupils at Key Stage 3 and there is also an entitlement for all at Key Stage 4 in England. What this means in practice is that some pupils will study for an examination in ICT at Key Stage 4, others will continue to be taught ICT through a non-examination course, whilst others may have little or no specific ICT teaching.

Task 8.1 Analysing KS4 provision

In your placement school identify:

- The number of groups and number of pupils studying ICT at Key Stage 3.
- The number of groups and pupils taking ICT as an examinable subject at Key Stage 4.
- The schemes and syllabuses offered at Key Stage 4.
- The progression policy established by the department: how do pupils choose ICT, and how are they accepted on to the course?

You should find in your analysis of the results that in KS4 examinations for England and Wales there are a number of levels of entry and modes of delivery:

- higher;
- foundation;
- intermediate;
- short course;
- full course;
- three and six unit programmes;
- Certificates of Educational Achievement.

For each of these you may find that, dependent on the type of examinable programme offered in your placement institution, some pupils begin a full course and drop down the various layers as lack of progress causes them to fail to achieve, or manage to keep up with, internal deadlines.

These internal deadlines are important since they enable the teacher to see the progress of the pupils in relation to our requirements and expectations, and help identify those pupils at risk of failing to achieve their potential. Most schools carry out some baseline assessment, either subject specific (see Chapter 7) or of general 'cognitive ability' (see Chapter 6), which are used to help identify what targets should be set for pupils at GCSE.

Task 8.2 Familiarisation with progress monitoring and examination processes

- How does your placement school implement target setting for pupils?
- How is the progress of pupils monitored during their examination course?
- When are mock examinations used? Are they developed in house, or are past papers used?

Try to obtain a copy of the examiner's report – this will be useful for a later task. Ask whether you can see the coursework moderation report. What are the department's policies on internal moderation within the department?

Schools which gain excellent GCSE results generally have high expectations of pupils, and require most pupils to engage with content and skills beyond the minimum required by the syllabus. This requires careful management of the GCSE course.

BALANCING AND COMBINING THEORY AND PRACTICAL WORK

The teaching of ICT combines the teaching of knowledge about ICT and skills in using ICT. Much of the teaching that you will observe, and that you will be asked to do yourself, will concentrate on the development and acquisition of skills. ICT lessons have been found to exhibit a range of strengths of focuses on purpose (Hammond and Mumtaz, 2001). A 'strong' focus on purpose involves tasks with high authenticity for pupils and an emphasis in teaching on the suitability of the tools used in relation to the outcome of the task. A 'weak' focus on purpose involves tasks that do not lead to outcomes perceived as useful by the learners, but instead allows the teaching to emphasise the procedures involved in operating the tool. Student teachers typically try to plan lessons with a strong focus on purpose, but are often constrained by time and schemes of work that prioritise the focus on procedures (Hammond and Mumtaz, 2001). You should recognise and help to overcome these constraints so as to keep as strong a focus on purpose as is feasible.

Some examination courses are very prescriptive concerning the nature of the tasks set and in the approach to producing the documents that are to be assessed. Pupils may well be very successful in meeting the requirements set out, but all they have achieved is to prove that they can follow instructions. They can produce a letter booking a holiday to Tunisia and can set up and manipulate a database for an estate agent. But very often, what they cannot do is to identify independently the need or opportunity for writing a letter or creating a database.

Task 8.3 Identifying the relation between knowledge and skills

As you progress through your observation of teaching to your own teaching of examination classes, develop a checklist of processes and techniques being developed and the facts, concepts and contexts that will help to make these skills relevant.

A very useful starting point for any planning for teaching examination courses is the syllabus/specification or course document. You need from the outset to identify from the syllabus which elements of the course are theoretical in nature, which are practical and which offer opportunities to ground the theory in practice.

Table 8.1 shows some examples from a typical GCSE subject specification document. Each example represents a separate assessment objective – but highlights, in the left hand column, the general area of knowledge, concept or skill. The right hand column indicates what the pupils should know, and what they should be taught.

Table 8.1 Extracts from a syllabus (based on AQA 3521)

1 Candidates will be expected to understand the purpose of, and to have experienced the use of, software packages with the facilities detailed right	A database package that involves the concepts of records and fields, allows the insertion and deletion of fields, allows the insertion and deletion of records, allows editing of information with records, allows a simple search on one criterion only, allows a complex search on two or more criteria, allows control of content of reports by selection of fields, allows control of the format of reports
2 (a) know when, where and why different methods of data capture are used	Candidates must understand the use of questionnaires, data capture forms, data logging, feedback, OMR, OCR, MICR, bar codes, magnetic strip
3 (a) searching, sorting, matching and merging files	
4 The Data Protection Act	Candidates should know the provisions of the Act: requirement to register, responsibilities of data users, rights of data subjects, exemptions (full and partial) and their effects. Understand why electronically stored personal information is potentially easier to misuse than that kept in conventional form

> **Task 8.4 Analysing syllabus requirements**
>
> Read through Table 8.1 and identify the difference between each of the expectations about what pupils should be able to do, know and understand.

For the next set of tasks you need to work with an examination course document. You may choose to work with an examination course that you may be teaching. In that case you should ask for a copy of the relevant documentation. If you are not teaching an examination syllabus at the time you are working through this chapter the choice of examination course is up to you. You can choose from:

- GCSE ICT;
- Vocational GCSE in ICT;
- AS and A2 ICT;
- AVCE ICT.

You can choose to get the documentation by writing to the appropriate examination board, ask for copies from your head of department or subject mentor, or download a copy from the examination board website.

> **Task 8.5 Creating a coursework analysis document**
>
> Identify the area of the examination documentation that deals with course work. Set up a grid that identifies the processes and techniques that pupils need to develop in order to complete the coursework elements for each of the modules or units of the course. This is to be a working document, and you will be adding to the grid as you progress through this set of tasks and activities. It will develop and could, or should, change as your knowledge of and skill in teaching and learning increase. Your choice of software and the design of your layout are therefore going to be important. Now identify the knowledge that underpins the practical elements of the course and add these to the grid. Do these knowledge elements need to be covered before or after the practical elements?

Your document now needs to look at other elements of the examination documentation. You have looked at skills and the knowledge that underpins those skills. Based on our second activity in this chapter, and from the close working relationship you are beginning to develop with the exam specification, you should be aware that you need to look at the knowledge about ICT that is not related to skills.

Task 8.6 Developing your coursework analysis document

Consider those elements of the course that are just about the *facts and concepts* and identify where these will fit in. Add them to your grid. Now you need to look at the table you have produced and ask yourself the following questions.

- Can we group knowledge about ICT and skills elements together?
- Can you build in opportunities for progression in your teaching and learning?
- Have you covered all the knowledge and skill elements required for each of the assessable components of the course?
- Have you identified everything that needs to be covered prior to submitting or embarking upon project work?

Make any amendments to your grid that you think are necessary in response to your thoughts about the questions you have just explored.

This should form the basis of an extensive Scheme of Work for the examination course. This, naturally, goes beyond what you need to develop for your own teaching practice. But it does lay down solid foundations for your own planning and preparation. You should now be very aware of what needs to be taught in order for pupils to be fully aware of their own developmental needs as you work together in exam preparation. These examination courses run over an extended period of time – one or two years will be the norm. In completing these tasks you should have identified all the key components of the course and be able to think about how you will be able to structure the teaching and learning experiences over the time scale of the course. The question that you then should ask yourself as you master the first stage of decoding the exam documentation is whether the course can be structured to ensure that all the components are covered before the examinations are scheduled.

SELECTING, PRODUCING AND USING CASE STUDIES OF ICT SYSTEMS

Case studies are very useful vehicles for developing knowledge about the application of ICT in different situations. In simple terms a case study presents a story or a scenario which encourages pupils to interact with the knowledge, skills and concepts built into the case study. Often they are encouraged to explore an issue from another person's point of view, or to act out a role in order to interpret what they are reading or what they are being asked to find out (see Chapters 5 and 6). A case study of the role of ICT in supermarkets can, for example, give an indication of what shopping was like in the past. We could use the corner shop in *Coronation Street* as an example of what all shopping was like, then provide information about shopping today and ask pupils to research further evidence. We would want to include issues and topics such as electronic point-of-sale (EPoS) and its effect on stocktaking, sales and distribution networks, warehousing, just-in-time. We could look at the role of the bar code in all this and its effect on the consumer: we now get detailed receipts. The impact of debit and smart card technologies is also important.

Case studies provide pupils and teachers with excellent opportunities for relating the theory to practice. They are also useful in providing pupils with evidence and ideas for their project work. As a teacher of ICT you need to develop a whole series of case materials that can help you in your support of pupils in their choice of, and their progress through, their projects.

Task 8.7 Case study topics

What areas are case materials likely to be useful for? Create a list of ideas for case studies in the following categories:

- ICT and control;
- ICT in business organisations;
- ICT in banking;
- the development of the Internet;
- ICT in the home;
- Administrative uses of ICT.

Check with the exam documentation for more examples.

Having developed a list of ideas for case studies you need to take one of the topics you have identified and to develop your own case study. There are a number of case materials in ICT textbooks. Look at those in your placement department and/or university library. The development of your own case study could be based on your comparison of these examples. The guidelines for some GCSE courses in ICT incorporate a set list of case studies that you can also draw upon. You should research relevant and topical materials for your cases. Remember, in ICT systems and approaches can change rapidly: what was relevant last year may not necessarily be relevant this year.

Once you have decided upon and developed your scenario you need to look at past examination papers as well in order to devise questions and tasks which will enable the pupils to interact with the case materials and to demonstrate their knowledge and their understanding of the topic in question. Consider how you can combine the case study work with related practical tasks; for example, a stock control database for the supermarket or a control program for an automatic door.

Task 8.8 Producing a case study

- Create your own case study, using the principles identified above.
- Identify which assessment objectives are covered by your case study: how does it support the subject specification?
- Review past papers and project ideas and derive a series of questions, tasks, activities, research opportunities, essay titles and discussion ideas which will enable a pupil to fully engage with the topic in question.

Having completed all this, you need to plan to use a case study with a small group of pupils during your observation and preparation period in your placement institution. Naturally you will need to negotiate this with your placement supervisor and your head of department or subject mentor. Make sure that it is related to the topic area being taught and that the objectives of the case study relate closely to the examination course assessment objectives. Look also at the chapter about teaching methodology for more information about this area.

USING ICT IN THE TEACHING OF FACTS AND CONCEPTS

As a teacher of ICT you should be using your own knowledge and skills to develop a range of teaching and learning materials which present information to the pupils in an interactive way, rather than relying solely on textbooks and teaching notes to try to transmit information to the pupils. The points we have discussed above about the currency of curriculum materials certainly apply here. ICT is changing all the time; very few textbooks will make reference to digital versatile disks (DVD) as storage media. We can turn to books on our shelves that go into great detail about paper tape and punched cards. These are interesting in terms of their historical value, and demonstrate how quickly things change. The oldest of these books dates from 1973: very old in terms of books about ICT, but relatively recent compared with one of the classic novels we have which were printed in the 1870s. If we were teachers of English literature we could certainly use our own classic texts to help us prepare for our teaching: we can't necessarily do that as teachers of ICT.

You need, therefore, to identify opportunities for presenting work to pupils in ways that can engage them in the knowledge and the concepts that you are covering. So, what approaches can you take to using ICT to teach the theory?

You need first to identify CD-ROMs and Internet-based materials. (How stuff works, http://www.howstuffworks.com, is a good example at the time of writing.) You can also develop your own materials for local distribution – web pages, multimedia presentations and research tasks are useful starting points. You should also consider resources that claim to support pupils in their exam preparation, such as BBC Bytesize (http://www.bbc.co.uk/schools/gcsebitesize/ict/).

Task 8.9 Identifying ICT resources

Talk to your school based tutor or head of department and find out what ICT based resources they use on a regular basis. Carry out some research of your own and develop a list of appropriate and useful resources that you can use.

● What CD-ROMs are available to help you in your planning and preparation?
● Which websites are useful?
● What resource materials can you develop to help you in this area?

Compare lists with some of your colleagues so that you can consolidate and extend your own.

Once you have done this you need to build in opportunities for using some of these resources during your teaching practice. Remember that you do not have to be on line to give your pupils an interactive experience in their use of the computer: you can download whole or part websites for use on the school intranet (subject to permission from the copyright holders). It is easy to forget about your own knowledge and expertise when planning for teaching. The more you plan to incorporate your own teaching of ICT within the knowledge and skills that you possess the more confident and able you should begin to feel. And remember the more you use ICT as part of your planning, preparation and delivery the easier it will be to generate evidence that you have met the ICT Standards (for student teachers in England).

The other way in which ICT can be used effectively to help pupils learn facts and develop concepts is for them to be expected to make their own summarising notes using word processing, concept mapping or presentation software. Indeed, we have seen that this can be fruitfully initiated in Year 7, but if pupils have not adopted the habit during Key Stage 3, you should teach them to do this at the start of Key Stage 4. It may be best to start with work in small mixed ability groups initially, so that less capable pupils can be supported by those with good higher order skills. For each topic, you can ask one group to present their summary to the class, then you and the other pupils can suggest improvements to the content and process. In addition, all pupils benefit from the evaluation of this presentation.

TEACHING PUPILS RESEARCH AND PRESENTATION SKILLS

For pupils developing and preparing work in examination courses, the research they undertake and the way they present their work are both very important elements, and they greatly affect their performance in all the examinable components. The preparation and presentation of course work are critically important.

As a teacher of ICT, you need to be very confident yourself with the attributes and opportunities available to you in word processing and DTP packages. You should not assume that because you are ICT capable you know how to produce effective publications! Many ICT and Computing pupils produce really ugly and technically incompetent publications using word processing and desktop publishing. There are rules for preparing and presenting effective written work, and you need to make sure that you find out what they are and to apply them.

Task 8.10 Principles of producing effective documents

Obtain some books concerning document and publication design and identify the rules and conventions for effective text based presentations. It will also be very useful for you to look at the document processing modules and units in some of the examination courses available at Key Stage 4. Developing your own understanding of the requirements will be very helpful to you in effectively developing opportunities for pupils to do well in their work.

Once you have identified the rules for written presentation, you need to establish criteria for all pupils to apply to their own written presentations. Your teaching can help them to be effective in various ways:

- establishing and using templates that the pupils can access;
- using headers and footers as appropriate (they give us information about the document being developed);
- decide on fonts and font sizes;
- teach pupils about the importance of impact and appropriateness;
- noting and acknowledging Internet sources of text and graphics;
- considering the role of proof reading and the preparation of different versions of a document (showing how a document has progressed is useful, and in some cases required, evidence);
- evaluating each other's work and reporting how you have reacted to the evaluations made;
- recognising that the audience is as important as the purpose of the document.

You need also to think about colour and its impact on the audience. Colour contrast is important. The size and the shape of fonts are important also. Consider in some detail with your pupils the design, structure and layout of the multimedia and web based presentations you may ask them to develop. Again you need to establish a house style and then stick to it. Include the application of the conventions as part of your assessment criteria.

> **Task 8.11 Guidelines for presentations**
>
> Draw up a set of guidelines for the development of a slide presentation using suitable software. Assume that the presentation is to be shown using a data projector.
>
> - Are you going to apply a template?
> - Are you going to specify a font?
> - What combinations of colours are you going to exclude?
> - Provide examples of what works and what doesn't work – and identify why.

There are a number of approaches that pupils can use to demonstrate effectiveness in their research. The use of Internet search engines has become very important as a research tool in schools. They have inherent dangers, and disasters can occur in the classroom if we do not manage the process properly. The policies for acceptable use of the Internet should be established at the start of their secondary schooling, and it will be wise to review them during Key Stage 4.

> **Task 8.12 Internet search engines**
>
> - What are the principles and practice of Internet searching that are applied in your placement school or college?
> - Do they have firewalls in place?
> - Which search engine is most favoured by your placement institution?

Once you have determined your answers to Task 8.12, you need to plan to teach your pupils how to frame effective enquiries, to help them to progress from simple to complex searches, and to understand and apply the concepts of filtering down and filtering out.

> **Task 8.13 Refining searches**
>
> - What other Internet searching techniques are useful?
> - What is the role of Boolean logic in searching? Do your pupils need to know about it?
> - Does our approach to an Internet search change if we use different search engines? Compare Google (http://www.google.com) with Yahoo (http://www.yahoo.co.uk).

You should not underestimate the importance of paper based research. Summarising and note taking are important skills that are easy to neglect. Far too often we can fall into the trap of assuming that the pupils have been taught them elsewhere. Maybe they have, but pupils are very good at pigeonholing! Skills they have been taught in other subject areas may well be assumed to be relevant only to that subject. As teachers we need to remind our pupils of what they know and that their knowledge can be useful in other subject areas. So if you are going to ask pupils to take notes from a video presentation or to summarise a magazine or Internet article you need to make sure that you have prepared them adequately.

- The use of templates is helpful here.
- Watch the video yourself, and compile a series of questions that the pupils should answer so that they compile a set of notes.
- Use cloze procedures so that pupils fill in the gaps and so complete a summary that you have begun.

You can also develop an exam course file where newspaper cuttings, web addresses, pictures, videos and reviews can be stored. Then when pupils need to carry out some research you have a set of resources that can be used to kick start things. But having done this you should make the pupils as responsible for the upkeep of the file as you are. This will teach them that research is an interactive process and involves contributions from them as well as what they 'borrow' from the sources.

Research and presentations often mean that pupils are making use of the work that others have done. When pupils are presenting work for their examinable component we need as teachers and as examiners to be as certain as we can be that the work they are presenting is their own. Referencing is important here. Plagiarism is an issue in examinable courses and pupils can be failed or have their work downgraded if there are suspicions about its source. Your pupils need to be clear where they sourced information from and that they acknowledge the derivation of their materials.

Successful preparation in terms of note taking and summarising is an important tool in helping your pupils to avoid these pitfalls. We have seen instances where pupils have been asked to carry out some research using a CD-ROM based encyclopaedia. One pupil duly carried out some research and applied some skill in cutting and pasting both text and images into a word processing package. The finished document was duly handed in as *bona fide* work, and marked by the teacher as 'good work'.

The skill that the pupil applied was useful in terms of the application of cutting and pasting from one medium/application to another. But in terms of the actual processing of information the skill equated to the photocopying, or even the copying by hand, of huge chunks of text and passing them off as their own. No teacher would accept a photocopy of a page from an encyclopaedia as a pupil's own work. We shouldn't therefore accept work from a pupil that has not been processed in some way.

Developing pupils' abilities as critical ICT users and effective ICT system designers

Pupils should develop a critical attitude to the work they are producing. ICT offers opportunities always to do something better and your pupils should avail themselves of these opportunities. There are tools which should be used and which you as a teacher should encourage: templates, spell checkers, word counts are examples. However, one of the misconceptions that you will need to confront is that spell checkers will correct your work. What they do is to highlight errors, and to suggest alternative spellings. If you do not know that you have a misspelling, and do not recognise any of the alternatives offered, the spell checker is of no use. It also falls down when pupils add their misspellings to the dictionary! This just recycles mistakes and should encourage you to check the contents of the user dictionaries regularly.

You need also to encourage pupils to look at their work and the work of others with the eye of a designer. You, and they, need to always ask the question 'What message are you, are they, intending to convey?' And then to follow it with the question 'How does the presentation impact on this message – does it support or conflict?'

The best way to support pupils in their criticality is to offer a range of models for evaluation. These are important tools for reflecting on what has been produced and what can be done to improve or to amend the work. You have already begun to establish some of these with respect to word processing and desktop publishing. You have also set criteria for the effective use of presentation software.

Task 8.14 Developing guidelines for other software

Establish the similar guidelines for evaluating the effectiveness of:

- spreadsheet presentations;
- database models;
- websites.

Pupils also need to be critical in their approach to the use of the software. They need to be certain that the software meets the requirements of the tasks/projects they are undertaking. As a teacher you can establish from the outset a resource analysis document that requires pupils to identify for their work:

- the software they used and why they chose it;
- the audience;
- the purpose;
- the file name;
- the backup location;

- the references they made;
- the sources they need to acknowledge.

The ability to deal with this question effectively is central to success at GCSE. Pupils need to be clear about what it was exactly about the software that made it the right tool for the job. If they concluded that it was not exactly right (because of the limitations of the software made available to them by the school) they need to be able to say so as well.

A common problem area here is the confusion that many pupils have in differentiating between spreadsheets and databases. Some of the confusion arises in that they often use flat file databases, which look like spreadsheets, or use the database functions in a spreadsheet package. You need to help the pupils to distinguish between the concept of a table structure (which can be implemented in word processor, spreadsheet or database) and the functional concepts (such as formula, graph, sort or search) that are associated with particular types of software. Your pupils need to be clear about what it is they are doing and be able to explain why.

Task 8.15 Misconceptions in software classification

Identify some of the misconceptions pupils may have in differentiating between word processing and desktop publishing packages.

Much of the work that pupils will carry out will revolve around the principles of effective system design. This is a problem that professional system designers have to deal with, so we need to establish realistic criteria for pupil work at a level appropriate to the examinable course they are following.

Task 8.16 Guidelines for system development

Look again at the guidelines offered to you in the exam documentation.

- What does the document say with regard to effective system design?
- What do the pupils have to produce as part of their system development?
- If it is simply a set of documents, what are the assessment guidelines for the documents they have to produce?
- If the requirement is to develop a system to solve a 'real world' problem, what do pupils need to produce in order to solve the problem itself, document and support the solution and meet the requirements for assessment?

We also have to be clear about the level of the work the pupils are producing. Look at the exemplar materials offered by the examination board and identify the statements about pupil performance at each of the levels.

Guiding pupils on the principles of coursework projects

You need to identify the proportion of time you can allow for coursework projects. They are important but you need to consider how the development of the course work relates to the knowledge that needs to be taught.

It is all too easy to spend a disproportionate amount of time on the coursework elements. The danger of missing out on elements of the knowledge that may be assessed in the terminal examination is considerable. There are many occasions when this happens: the pressure on both teachers and pupils to complete the course work can get in the way, as it counts for so much.

You have already begun to deal with this in your analysis of exam course documentation, and there are other practical approaches which can be adopted.

Task 8.17 Displaying coursework requirements

Create a set of classroom display materials that identifies the key components of course work as exemplified in the exam course documentation.

You should set up a project management table for each pupil for whom you are responsible. You need to be sure that every pupil is aware of key deadlines and completion dates. Many of the ideas and concepts inherent in the project will be alien to the pupils you are teaching. Sometimes you may find that even the most basic ideas will impose barriers to learning and to progression because the pupils do not have the experience that we often take for granted to support their attempts. What often gets in the way is inability to realise what is needed to complete the initial tasks of a systems analysis, and this is enough to thwart pupils and lead to a falling off of their confidence in the subject, to discipline problems and a low level of work and progress. Your setting up of individual project management tables for pupils and your breaking down of larger projects into smaller, more manageable, components will prove to be helpful in alleviating these problems.

Remember that the examiner and moderator will not see the project in action even though both you as teacher and your pupils may want to spend most of the time getting the implementation phase to work! Success is determined by the quality of the documentation and what the pupil says about their project. So you need to make sure that the pupils get the documentation right and that you encourage them to make it a regular feature of the work. Most pupils have greater difficulty in producing the documentation than in the practical implementation. It may not be sufficient just to inform them that it is the write-up that gets most of the marks, and you will need to provide some structure to support the development of their higher order skills. Writing frames, for instance, have been found valuable in stimulating pupils' reflective writing (Deadman, 1997). Your task subsequently will be to withdraw your structure and encourage pupils to write up independently.

Task 8.18 Structuring project documentation

Produce a writing frame, template or outline for project documentation that provides an appropriate structure and prompts for a particular exam scheme. You may find it useful to look at the examples for A level projects in, for example, Heathcote (1999b).

You need also to be realistic about the types of project that work. Look at the advice from the examination board, particularly examiners' reports; very often it is the simplest projects that give pupils the clearest opportunities of success.

Task 8.19 Identifying suitable projects

Draw up a list of example projects for your pupils. Think about the range of software that can be used and about the range of 'real world' applications that can be developed.

You need also to be realistic about what you can support. Add further resources to your course file: it will be useful also at this point to look at the locality in which your teaching placement is situated. What resources and ideas can you glean from the local community?

PREPARING PUPILS FOR EXAMINATIONS

Successful preparation for examinations starts way back at the planning stage. You need to check your schemes of work thoroughly against the course specification. Look at past exam papers and the published mark schemes. You may be able to obtain copies of these from your placement school. You can also order them from the examination board or download them from examination board websites.

Task 8.20 Analysing examination questions

From the examination papers identify:

● what it is, exactly, that the pupils have to answer questions on;
● the format that the questions take.

In exam preparation you need to give your pupils plenty of opportunities to recognise the types of questions they might face. If the examination is in a multi-choice format you need to make sure that the pupils recognise such a format and that they have the knowledge and skill to interpret what differentiates the correct answer from the rest of the range presented.

If short answer questions are offered, you need to identify with your pupils how much they need to write. For example, if the question is simply asking for four examples of storage devices for four marks the requirement is for a simple list of four storage devices and no more – one mark for each different item which actually is a storage device (and not a medium!). Even the most basic of responses by pupils may generate a positive response from the examiner. If a question is left blank, an examiner cannot help, but if a cursory or slightly confused answer is given, an examiner can make a judgement about a pupil's level of understanding and possibly award marks. If, on the other hand, the question asks for two advantages and two disadvantages of CD-ROM as a storage medium, more elaboration will be required. Single words such as 'faster' or phrases such as 'more efficient' are not usually accepted, and more detail is expected: faster at doing what? Compared with what other devices?

Areas in which you as a teacher can make a positive impact in your preparation include advising pupils (and following up on the advice) that:

● simple answers should be accompanied by an example;
● brand names should not be used: 'Word 97' is not an answer, 'word processor' will be expected;
● illegible writing may result in no marks;
● opposite answers to questions that ask for advantages and disadvantages will merit only one mark rather than two;
● they must make sure that the exam rubric is followed.

Some exam courses will require longer answers in the form of a report or an essay.

In longer answers ensure that your pupils are used to justifying what they say. If they say, for example, that control systems in the supermarket ensure that food safety regulations are adhered to, require them to give examples of how and why this is the case. It is often a good idea to underline the main points in a long answer so that they are clear to the examiner, or to use bullet points to highlight key issues quickly and efficiently.

Task 8.21 Learning from examiners' reports

Look at the last examiner's report for your examination course. What errors and misconceptions did pupils display in their responses to long answer questions?

This is not about teaching to the test, but about giving pupils confidence. If they recognise the format of the examination they are less likely to be worried about the actual content. You need to plan some time in your Scheme of Work for revision – summarise the knowledge that has been gained at regular intervals, surprise the pupils with verbal questions that require them to recall work they have undertaken. Look at the difference between the criteria for the different levels of achievement in the syllabus: the higher levels of achievement don't necessarily require the pupils to write more. But the writing needs to be focused on the key words and key concepts for the level: make these a regular focus of your teaching and a conspicuous feature of your classroom environment!

Task 8.22 Displaying helpful posters

Develop classroom display materials which focus on key words and concepts in ICT.

SUMMARY

In teaching exam courses you need to balance the principles of effective teaching and assessment with the demands of the exam schemes that you are following. The setting of targets, both long and short term, together with deadlines for submission, is important in helping pupils to achieve their potential. Providing structures within which pupils can write reports of their work is helpful, but teaching pupils to develop their own research, note taking and project management skills will bring long term benefits.

FURTHER READING

Doyle, S. (2001) *Information Systems for You*, third edition, London: Nelson Thornes. A popular textbook for reference by teachers and pupils, as is:

Evans, P. (2001) *GCSE Information and Communication Technology*, second edition, Ipswich: Payne-Gallway.

www.ocr.org.uk, www.aqa.org.uk, www.edexcel.org.uk, www.wjec.co.uk. The websites of the main examination boards in England and Wales. They provide guidance and exemplification specific to their schemes, with many downloadable documents.

www.qca.org.uk. The website of the Qualifications and Curriculum Authority (QCA), which provides general guidance on assessment issues and government regulations.

9 Differentiated Teaching and Providing for Special Educational Needs

Chris Jones

The students in your classroom do not comprise a homogeneous mass. Each student in your care is an individual and regardless of classroom arrangements each of them will have different needs that you should bear in mind when planning for teaching and learning.

OBJECTIVES

By the end of this chapter, you should be able to:

- plan to motivate and ensure progress for the most and least capable, and give attention to different pupil groups systematically during lessons;
- plan to balance differentiation by task, by outcome and by support;
- manage mixed and homogeneous ability classes and grouping within the class;
- seek and use information concerning pupils with specific difficulties in learning or access to the curriculum and provide targeted support.

PLANNING FOR MOTIVATION AND PROGRESSION

It is the teacher's responsibility to develop a Scheme of Work and a series of lesson plans, which aim to motivate learners, and which have within them opportunities for progression for the most and least capable learners.

One way of achieving this is the use of *high impact teaching* (Babbage, 1998) to capture interest from the outset. High impact teaching is about making targets clear and attainable, about focusing on the people not the content, and about putting the learning into context.

Part of the planning that you need to do should focus on your use of language. You need to think about the impact of how you phrase things, how you ask questions, and the subject-related jargon that you use as you develop knowledge, skills and understanding in the classroom. Language is obviously our major medium of communication, but for some it can present itself as a barrier to learning. It would be useful for you to talk to a school literacy coordinator about the work that is being done to promote literacy across the curriculum. You should follow up that discussion with the head of an ICT department to see what is being done within the department. These discussions should lead you to think about the various aspects of language use that cause problems for learners. If we focus on vocabulary for a moment you should identify two aspects that need particular attention: general vocabulary and subject specific terminology.

You will find that students do not understand words and phrases that you take for granted, for example: establishment, identify, innovation, development, analysis, independent . . . The list is endless and you need to think carefully about meaning and context. There will be many other words and phrases that they cannot spell, such as 'business', 'a lot' and 'analysis' (again!).

Subject specific terminology has problems, but if pupils are to be successful in the subject, the terminology needs to be used correctly. You need to identify the specific terminology that you want to cover and find out about departmental conventions, and expectations. For example, is it 'disc' or 'disk', 'programme' or 'program'? We prefer the American spellings which represent the subject rather than the national norms, but you need to check that against the conventions the students are used to within their learning environment: changing things can disrupt their learning.

In each of your Schemes of Work and lesson plans you will need to identify opportunities for tackling issues of specific terminology. What terminology are you going to use? How are the words spelt? What do they mean? Can you explain them in lay terms and give examples of how they are applied?

Task 9.1 Using appropriate language

In your classroom observations identify how the teachers are dealing with terminology and jargon. How are they making their language accessible? What strategies are they using to ensure that the students they are teaching understand and can access the content of the lesson?

Motivation and progression also comes from identifying students in lessons who need support from you, or from others. This support is essential for students who cannot progress. The interaction they have with you can help them in instances where they come across a new concept or when they have forgotten a particular skill. Your interaction may well be important for two other groups of students: those who need support to complete, and those who require extension activities to remain motivated.

Elsewhere you will have covered issues relating to coursework and completion issues. In each lesson you teach there will be students who, for one reason or another, fail to complete the tasks allocated for that session. In your planning and preparation you need to identify which students they are and to tackle the issue of their completion rate.

You will also meet students who consistently meet all the targets you set for them and exceed your expectations. You need, for these students, to identify opportunities for extension work which guarantees to extend their knowledge, skills and capabilities and is not just seen as 'more of the same'. If a student is meeting the requirements you set for them, why should they have to do more of the same type of work when they have demonstrated clearly that they have met the requirements of that level of work? You need to be looking at the requirements of the next level of attainment and to be developing tasks and activities which enable these students to meet a new set of requirements within the context you have established for the work of the rest of the class.

For example, if you ask students in general to use simple queries to explore a large database, a follow-on task could be to provide specific students with the opportunity to explore complex queries. This may well be what you are planning to go on to with the rest of the class later in your Scheme of Work, and when you do, you can assess the understanding of the students who had explored this area in the previous lesson. By enabling students to progress from simple to complex lines of enquiry you are moving them from one level of attainment to another, and providing real opportunities for continuity and progression.

Task 9.2 Support at different stages of the task

In your classroom observations make detailed notes on how the classroom teacher provides support for students to:

- progress;
- complete;
- extend.

A skilled teacher will ensure that a lesson progresses smoothly and it should be clear to you that there are different stages in the lesson as it moves from its beginning to its end (see Chapter 4). Weaknesses identified during the inspection of ICT lessons have included a too rapid move from introduction, discussion and discourse to practical activity (Goldstein, 1997). Teachers who do this too regularly are limiting the scope for knowledge and capability development in the students they teach. You need to plan lessons that provide a balance between the introduction, the development activities and the closure.

Observe a lesson and identify the key phases of the lesson. How does the teacher's view of support come across during each of the phases?

After completing this, develop your own lesson plan for the one you have observed. Identify clearly the type of support you are planning to give the class as the lesson progresses. How does the support you give during an introduction differ from that which you give during the development phase of the lesson? Is there a difference between this and the support you give during the closure?

Part of the process of high impact teaching and for the development of student autonomy during Key Stage 3 and beyond into public examinations is the development of project work skills. Students need to be able to work independently and to break down the components of a major project into manageable units. You will need to decide how far you want to go in targeting the help that students will need. Some of the decisions you make will affect the group as a whole and some will affect only individuals. You need to decide when it is appropriate to give help and when it is not. The requirements established in the subject specifications will be important here. Very often it is not information that students need but a question that helps them to focus and then to make their own decisions. For example:

Student   I don't know what to do next.
Teacher   What does the question ask you to do?
Student   I don't know what you mean.
Teacher   Let's look at the task. What does it say? Read it out to me.
Student   It says, 'Based on the figures presented above, calculate the total cost of the skiing trip per student and for the whole group.'
Teacher   So, what package are you going to use to begin to complete this part of the project?
Student   I don't know.
Teacher   You're asked to calculate. What package have we used before to work with figures?
Student   A spreadsheet?
Teacher   Yes. Do you know what to do now?
Student   I have to use a spreadsheet and input those details to get the answers I need?
Teacher   Yes. Make a start and I'll be back in five minutes to check how you're doing.

DIFFERENTIATION IN THE ICT CLASSROOM

Since it is clear that our classrooms are made up of students from a variety of backgrounds it is important to recognise and make the most of opportunities for balancing differentiation by task, outcome and support. You will also need to act upon other opportunities for differentiation as they arise.

Differentiation by task is best exemplified by the use of language moderated worksheets and tasks where all students are following the same type of activity but are working at different levels. If you annotate all your planned student work against the National Curriculum levels of attainment then planning for both differentiation and progression should become more straightforward. Using different types of worksheet in a class can give rise to a problem in that some students may feel they are being singled out because of their low achievement and you will, therefore, need to consider how to deal with the issue sensitively. You should also consider the role of hyperlinked documents as a means of enabling students to target their own level of work and to progress within a restricted or extended range of tasks, activities and knowledge based instruction.

Task 9.4 Differentiated resources

Identify some advantages and disadvantages of differentiated worksheets and activities. How can the use of hyperlinks help pupils of different abilities?

This raises the question why all pupils are often expected to be doing exactly the same thing in each of the lessons you take. Certainly it makes it easier for you to manage and to organise, but it also makes it easier for you to ignore the needs of the individual and to teach to the centre and ignore the margins. The use of problem solving strategies in the ICT classroom should enable, or indeed allow, you to develop a series of mini-projects that develop knowledge, skills and capability within a defined range. This should also ensure that, although the 'product of the learning tasks' is different for different groups of students, the learning outcomes are the same.

Task 9.5 Differentiation by task

Choose a topic, perhaps one that you are being asked to teach during your teaching practice, and develop a series of differentiated tasks that cover the development in ICT capability required. These should target different levels of attainment.

Rather than have pupils working on different tasks according to their ability, you could consider an approach where all pupils work on the same tasks but the levels of achievement will be different. This is called *differentiation by outcome*. Here the students are all working on the same activity – but there is a sense of progression in terms of knowledge, skills and capability as the students work though. You need to identify the minimum level of completion that will satisfy the learning outcomes of the lesson. You will need to ask yourself, 'Can I guarantee that every student will be able to reach this minimum level in the time allocated?' As before, being clear about the levels of attainment will be very helpful to you.

This approach is integral to assessment in GCSE and in Vocational GCSEs. The grade descriptors and examples in the specification documents provide useful examples of differentiation by outcome. Look specifically at the difference between a foundation paper and a higher paper at GCSE. You should notice a progression in the questions and a distinct overlap between one paper and the other. The notion of a minimum level is clearly exemplified here. The further a student progresses through the questions and tasks the greater the opportunity for displaying the characteristics exemplified by the higher level statements of attainment. The next task gives you an opportunity to take the model exemplified in the examination papers and to apply it to your own planning and preparation.

Task 9.6 Determining criteria for outcomes at different levels

Examine a task that has been given to students in one of the classes you have been observing. Establish criteria for the task that describe what a student has to do to pass, to pass with merit and to pass with distinction. Use National Curriculum levels of attainment where relevant. If the task is part of a teaching programme which leads to an examinable qualification, apply the marking criteria set out in the subject specification.

We have already looked in this chapter at how you as a teacher can provide support for your students in their learning. Differentiation by support is an important aspect to be considered in your planning and preparation. Can you plan your movement around the classroom? One way of doing so is to have a clear picture, based upon assessment, of where each student is at any point in your Scheme of Work. Getting students to identify targets and plan their activity for each lesson will also be helpful.

You may be working in a school that makes use of learning mentors or classroom assistants. The classroom assistants will be working, by and large, with specific groups of students. Some may be targeting students with specific learning difficulties, some may be targeting literacy and numeracy issues, and others may be working with students identified as 'gifted' and 'talented'. You need to ensure that you are aware of the targeting that is going on in your placement school and identify how you can best plan for their inclusion.

As a subject specialist you are also going to need to check what the classroom assistant will need to know in order to be able to work with the students who have been targeted.

Task 9.7 Working with other adults in the classroom

What effect can learning mentors or classroom assistants have in the ICT classroom? Does their knowledge of what you are doing have any bearing on your planning and preparation? Should you include them in your lesson planning?

Draw up a set of operational questions that you need to explore with an 'adult other than teacher' who might work with you in your classroom. Discuss the results with your peers and with your school based tutors and amend your list as necessary.

If you have particularly able students in your classroom, you need to identify opportunities for differentiated work at higher levels and to help such students develop their learning through appropriate action planning.

There will be many occasions when, by being observant and sensitive to what is happening in the room, you will be able to support individuals and groups. Students' progress can be enhanced considerably through the occasional helpful and encouraging remark and the well directed challenge to consider how they might improve.

Task 9.8 Seeking opportunities for differentiation

Observe an ICT lesson and make a note of the opportunities for differentiation that were acted upon.

- What category of differentiation was applied?
- How could others have been built into that lesson?

There are other elements of differentiation that you can build into your lesson planning once you are aware of the composition of the classes you are teaching (see Table 9.1). You will need to undertake some form of assessment in order to be able to do this.

Table 9.1 Ways of differentiating by task or support

Resources/Information   The provision of different resources or information to extend or support the same task. *This group should use these books/this equipment/this source material. That group has a first task of locating your resources from the library/this resource box/the Internet/ this CD.*

Input   You start the lesson from the same viewpoint for all students. You can then set some students the task directly and for others break the task down into smaller steps. *OK, you can start now, whilst I have a further word with . . .*

Grouping   Here you set common tasks but ensure that the make-up of groups is designed to support particular pupils either by mixing ability to encourage peer learning, or by ability to allow you to plan for specific teacher intervention. You need to make specific use of your assessment information. Which students will benefit most from this grouping? Why is it important for them?

Extension   A common task with individual or group having an extra challenge built in – higher performance (*I want you to think about using absolute references here*), quality (*Once you have created your poster I want you to think carefully about the audience and how you can improve the impact the poster will have . . .*) and length (*In your description of why you chose this software to solve the problem I want you to aim for about 150 words*) . . .

Pace   Students are given different times in which to complete the task. *I'm expecting you to finish in twenty minutes. Don't rush, I'm expecting high quality stuff. You'll probably take a little longer – that's OK. It's the quality that counts.*

Role   Within group work, you plan to give students specific roles to carry out, based on their ability, behaviour or prior attainment (*Mary, can you coordinate the activities of the group? Sanjay, I'd like you to help James with setting up headers and footers on his report*).

Recording   A common task but the recording demands are different according to prior attainment. *When you've come to a conclusion I'll want you to record your findings in rough and then let me look at them – in a neat version – neatly, including a diagram and some recommendations for altering the program.*

As a teacher of ICT you will be expected during teaching practice and beyond to be able to manage classes regardless of their ability and make-up. This will mean that you will have to be able to demonstrate that you can plan for teaching all the classes you have been allocated, and that you will be able to apply the school rules on classroom behaviour fairly and consistently.

Task 9.9 Identifying students with different types of need

Identify for each of the classes you have been allocated for your teaching practice:

- the range of ability within the classroom (minimum level of attainment, modal level of attainment, highest level of attainment);
- those students with specific learning difficulties;
- those students identified as being gifted and talented;
- those students whose work is falling behind others within the group.

As you begin to prepare your lessons, you should show evidence that you have considered this information in detail: how are you going to address the needs of these students in your planning and preparation?

TEACHING STUDENTS WITH SPECIFIC LEARNING DIFFICULTIES

You should also seek and use information about the students in your classes who have been identified as having specific difficulties in learning or access to the curriculum. Increasingly, schools are implementing policies of inclusion in the mainstream curriculum for such pupils. You should find out as much as possible about the systems available within the school concerned for students with specific difficulties in learning.

Part of the school's response to students with specific learning difficulties will be the development and application of Individual Education Plans (IEPs). As a subject teacher you should know which of the students you are teaching have IEPs and which learning needs the plans are targeting. Some of the plans will be targeting behaviour; others will be related to learning or ability issues. Knowing about these should, again, help you to reflect upon and apply the issues we have discussed earlier in this chapter. You may be able to obtain information from the usual class teacher, or direct from the school's Special Educational Needs Coordinator (SENCO). You will find further details of the issues involved in identifying special educational needs and planning for the inclusion of pupils with special educational needs (SEN) in mainstream education in Capel *et al.* (2001: unit 4.6) and Baumann *et al.* (1997).

Naturally some of these issues are general in their focus and impact upon you as a subject teacher. Your response should always begin with the students as the central focus. At the beginning of this chapter we introduced the notion of high impact teaching. One of the principles of this is putting the students first and the subject second. We can, in ICT, support the students in their learning through the subject itself. Sometimes we can use peripherals that enable students with specific learning difficulties to gain access to learning. At other times we can simply change the desktop environment.

Task 9.10 Resources for specialised learning support

Identify what specific resources there are within your placement school's ICT department for dealing with specific learning difficulties or improving access to the curriculum for those with physical disabilities:

- hardware;
- software;
- curriculum resources such as worksheets;
- cross-curricular resources.

When considering support for students with specific difficulties in learning or access you should plan for including an adult-other-than-teacher (AOT) in the classroom. Coordination is needed to ensure that the pupils gain as much as possible from the combination of your general support for learning ICT and the specific support for their learning difficulties.

SUMMARY

We have considered a variety of issues concerning the optimising of learning in relation to pupils' specific characteristics. Two main aspects of planning are central to success:

- catering for a variety of levels of capability among pupils in any class, not just in relation to ICT, but in relation to literacy and other basic skills.
- being aware of pupils with specific learning difficulties, and working with special needs staff to ensure they gain the maximum amount from your lessons.

FURTHER READING

Bourne, R., Davitt, J. and Wright, J. (1995) *Differentiation: taking IT forward*, Coventry: NCET. Identifies ways in which ICT can support teachers introducing differentiation into their lessons.

Lambert, D. (1994) *Differentiated Learning*, London: Institute of Education. A booklet specifically written for the student teacher concerning the issues faced in implementing differentiation.

Part IV

Improving the Teaching of ICT

10 Building on Pupils' Knowledge from Primary School and Outside School

John Parkinson

This chapter is about helping pupils to make progress in their learning by taking into account what they have learnt in the primary school and the ICT work they have done at home. Teachers, both primary and secondary, sometimes underestimate the extent of pupils' expertise. In addition to their school based learning, pupils learn from their friends and relatives and by finding things out for themselves by 'playing' with a computer. This all has a bearing on the work that we ask pupils to do. If they are presented with a curriculum that involves a considerable amount of repetition of old skills they are likely to become bored and their learning will be adversely affected.

Most people consider that being able to use a computer is an important skill for obtaining a job after school or for going on into higher education, perhaps on a par with learning English and mathematics. Most parents do not want to see their children left behind and those who can afford to do so are often prepared to spend relatively large sums of money to buy the equipment. Head teachers are supplied with earmarked funds to help them update and increase the number of machines available to pupils. Frequently these funds are supplemented from other sources such as the parent–teacher association (PTA) to make sure that the best resources are available. The PTA is often prepared to support primary schools in this way. In fact many primary schools are doing quite sophisticated work with computers and are examining innovative ways of using them in teaching.

However, the 'digital divide' (see Chapter 1) may often be seen clearly in differences between primary schools, with schools in disadvantaged areas often showing a technological deficit by comparison with those in leafy suburbs. Your school may well draw pupils from both advantaged and disadvantaged primary schools and home backgrounds, resulting in a broad spread of background experience.

As with all subjects, there is a wide range of pupil competence at the start of Year 7 and the teacher has to consider how best to deal with the situation so that all pupils have the opportunity to make progress. A number of things need to be done to make sure pupils have a good start to their career in secondary school. It will involve working closely with colleagues in the primary school to develop an understanding of the nature of the teaching and level of learning that takes place there. It will also involve finding out about the types of activities pupils do at home and using the information to plan your teaching. While this may sound like a tall order, you will find that it is possible to prepare a curriculum that will set pupils tasks that will challenge them and help them to develop their expertise.

During your period of school experience and in your first few years as a new teacher you should be looking at how teachers build on pupils' experience from their primary schools and from the work they do at home. You should be involved in primary–secondary continuity activities and consider how to improve the effectiveness of the liaison between your school and its feeder primaries.

OBJECTIVES

At the end of this chapter, you should be able to:

- show awareness of the KS2 ICT curriculum and primary teachers' approaches to teaching ICT;
- understand methods of developing primary–secondary links;
- plan for continuity and constructive discontinuity in the ICT curriculum across the transition;
- identify the characteristics of ICT use at home;
- organise computer club activities and support ICT use in home-work clubs.

ICT IN THE PRIMARY SCHOOL

Class teachers in primary schools generally have the responsibility of teaching all curriculum subjects to a particular group of pupils. They are expected to develop their pupils' ICT capability, and to incorporate ICT into the teaching of all other subjects. The number and type of computers available vary considerably. In a reasonably well equipped school you should expect to find one or two computers per classroom, sometimes augmented with desktop PCs on trolleys and by portable computers that can be booked for specific purposes. An increasing number of schools have electronic whiteboards and data projectors. The National Curriculum for Key Stage 1 and Key Stage 2 gives you a general overview of the ICT work carried out in primary schools, but it will not give you enough information for planning. Schools interpret the National Curriculum in different ways, depending on the resources available and the expertise of their staff. Table 10.1 gives an idea about the types of

Table 10.1 Examples of the type of work pupils may have done in the primary school

Word processing and desktop publishing   Word processing is used extensively for activities such as writing poems, stories and letters. DTP packages are used to produce posters, flyers and front pages for project work. Pupils are able to move text around and modify it. They know simple routines such as checking the spelling and altering the layout of the text.

Multimedia   Pupils are able to use a multimedia authoring program to organise, refine and present a set of linked multimedia pages which incorporate images, sounds and text.

Database   Databases on CD-ROMs are interrogated to look for patterns of data. Pupils are able to construct a simple database, for example one containing the names and key features of dinosaurs.

Spreadsheet   Pupils learn the use of spreadsheets and how to input data and simple formulas. They do calculations involving addition, subtraction, multiplication and division and use simple functions. They are able to produce graphs (mainly bar charts or pie diagrams) from the data.

Internet   Pupils are introduced to the principles of searching for information on the Internet. They examine a number of sites in detail, extracting information to compile a report. They know how to copy text and pictures.

Control   Pupils learn how to switch devices such as buzzers, lights or small motors on and off. They go on to write a sequence of commands to control a set of model traffic lights (available from educational suppliers).

Data logging   Pupils have some understanding of how computers can be connected to sensors to monitor changes in temperature, sound, light, etc. They monitor changes in the environment over a few days and are able to comment on the data obtained.

activities that are carried out in many primary classrooms. You can obtain a clearer picture of what may be expected of pupils by looking at primary ICT resources and books that have been written specifically for teaching this age group (for example, Smith, 1999; Leask and Meadows, 2000). To gain an understanding of the general strengths and weaknesses of ICT teaching in both the primary and the secondary sectors you should look at the annual reports of Ofsted and Estyn. In recent years their findings for primary schools have shown that:

- Pupils' ability to use ICT across the curriculum varies widely.
- The basic skills that pupils learn early on in their schooling are not developed as well as they could be at Key Stage 2. Pupils tend to repeat or practise unchallenging activities.
- The quality of teaching with ICT continues to improve rapidly.
- Pupils are good at preparing presentations using graphics, text and sound.
- Pupils are learning some ICT skills through the teaching of other subjects.
- Pupils' keyboard skills are generally poor.

- Pupils are using the Internet and electronic mail effectively in a small, but rapidly increasing, number of schools.

(Ofsted, 2001b)

The best way of finding out what happens in the primary schools that feed your secondary school is to visit them, talk to the teachers and pupils and observe pupils working on computers. You can arrange this through your mentor and/or the person in charge of primary–secondary liaison in the school.

Task 10.1 Observing primary school ICT work

Arrange to spend a day in one or more of your school's feeder primary schools. Find out about the type of work that pupils do and the levels they achieve. For example, you could complete the following grid:

Application	What the best pupils can do	What average pupils can do	What the least able can do
Word processing and DTP			
Multimedia			
Databases			
Spreadsheets			
Internet			
Control			
Data logging			
Other			

Make a note of the range of hardware and software available. How do the staff in the primary school perceive ICT? (Just another subject to teach, a way of helping pupils to learn, useful up to a point, etc.?)

CONTINUITY OF CURRICULUM AND PROGRESSION IN LEARNING

The transition from primary to secondary school is a big step for most 11 year olds as they come to terms with a new teaching environment, new teachers and new friends. Teachers put a lot of energy into making the process run as smoothly as possible and helping pupils to settle in and feel happy and secure. The organising generally starts in the summer term prior to arrival in the secondary school, with Year 6 pupils spending a day visiting the new school, meeting teachers, having sample lessons and getting to know their way around. When the pupils arrive at the start of Year 7 they are put into classes based on information about friendship groups and there is usually a period of induction where pupils get to know one another and learn about the rules and routines. During their first year the PSE lessons concentrate on issues that concern Year 7 pupils such as bullying, making new friends and doing homework. All these activities are concerned with the social integration of pupils into the new environment but this is just one of a number of bridges that need to be crossed to ensure that pupils continue to make progress in their academic and personal development. Galton *et al.* (1999) have identified five bridges that schools need to consider in supporting cross-phase continuity:

- the social bridge;
- the bureaucratic bridge;
- the pedagogic bridge;
- the management-of-learning bridge;
- the curriculum bridge.

As an ICT teacher you can do a great deal to help in each of these facets of the transition process.

Social aspect

The social integration of children is generally achieved very well by schools. Teachers are very concerned that the pupils are happy in their new environment and do as much as possible not to put pupils into situations where they would feel uncomfortable. One of the things that pupils look forward to on their induction day is their visit to the computer room and to work on 'superior' machines. It is worth while spending time beforehand making sure that everything is in working order and preparing an interesting task for them to do. During the session you can talk to them about the system and make them feel relaxed and 'at home' with the equipment.

Year 7 pupils can, in many ways, be the best ambassadors for the secondary school. If a message comes from a Year 7 pupil it is believable, whereas the same message from a teacher may be thought of as overemphasising the good points and missing out the bad ones. A way of making use of this is to ask the existing Year 7 pupils to prepare material for the school website specifically aimed at new pupils. These could be on topics such as 'What I really liked about my new school', 'Things you need to remember', 'How to avoid getting lost'. Another idea is to invite the Year 6 teachers to ask their pupils to write questions to the Year 7 group and then e-mail the top ten questions which will be answered by the Year 7 pupils. Obviously there will need to be teacher guidance but you may be surprised at how sensible the pupils can be.

Dealing with the bureaucracy

Over the six or so years that a pupil spends in a primary school a tremendous amount of data is accumulated. The question is how much of it should be transferred to the secondary school and to whom it should be sent. A school is likely to want to transfer information related to:

- academic records (for example, national curriculum levels, reading scores);
- personal information (for example, age, siblings, home background);
- any special needs that a pupil may have.

It will be the job of the primary–secondary coordinator or a deputy head teacher to decide how this is to be done and where the information should end up. But an ICT expert can provide considerable help and advice on organising an electronic transfer system that runs efficiently and keeps the sensitive data safe.

On a subject level, ICT teachers need to have information on pupils' capability. If primary schools were to send samples of each pupil's work in each of the main areas of study, secondary staff would quickly find themselves overwhelmed with the amount of material. One way of overcoming this problem would be for the primary school to send a record of the level achieved by each pupil together with some sample materials, showing the work of a good, an average and a low achieving pupil. In this way you can quickly get a picture of pupils' capabilities.

The pedagogic bridge

In the primary school, pupils are mainly taught by one teacher for all curriculum subjects, whereas in the secondary school they have to get used to the idiosyncrasies of ten or more teachers. You will have to help pupils to feel comfortable with your teaching style by being consistent in what you do and making your intentions clear. Pupils need to know what is expected of them in your classroom and how to relate to your teaching approach.

Helping pupils to manage their own learning

ICT is unique in the way it offers pupils the opportunity to extend their learning. Pupils are encouraged to try things out and experiment with techniques in a way that no other curriculum subject can offer. ICT can play an important role in helping pupils to develop important learning skills that can be used in all aspects of school life and beyond.

The need for curriculum continuity

> Increasingly pupils enter secondary education with very different experiences of ICT and this presents significant difficulties to teachers in planning to meet all of their needs.
>
> (Ofsted, 2000)

Repetition of work can result in pupils becoming bored and demotivated. It also takes up valuable curriculum time and reduces the opportunity for pupils to carry out more advanced work. There will, of course, be the need to revisit concepts that have been taught earlier and to consolidate and build on them but this should be more than simply doing the same sort of activity all over again.

Task 10.2 Information transfer

What information would you like to receive about each pupil from the primary school? For example, would you find it useful to know about:

- the list of activities carried out by pupils;
- the extent to which pupils were allowed to develop their learning on their own;
- the National Curriculum levels achieved by pupils;
- the ability of the pupils to carry out higher order skills (for example, planning, choosing, hypothesising, evaluating) and their understanding of processes (for example, communicating information, handling information, modelling);
- the pupils' attitude to ICT;
- pupils' competence at using the keyboard?

Would you also want pupils to carry out a self-assessment of their ICT skills?
How would you use the information obtained?

YOUR ROLE IN HELPING TO ACHIEVE CURRICULUM CONTINUITY

Curriculum continuity is difficult to achieve in any subject area and it has been a cause of concern for many years. A number of initiatives are being tried out to improve the situation (for examples of KS3 strategies, see http://www.standards.dfes.gov.uk/keystage3, local meetings of primary and secondary schools), frequently involving large sums of government money. It is seen as important because:

- repetition of work can lead to a reduction in motivation and the development of negative attitudes to the subject;
- pupils do not make the progress expected of them during Key Stage 3;
- curriculum time can be lost, leading to problems in completing the KS3 Programme of Study.

For curriculum continuity to be effective, teachers need to exchange information about what is taught, how it is taught and the level of understanding achieved by the pupils. This requires a great deal of collaboration and communication between the ICT coordinators in primary and secondary schools. The following reasons are usually given by the coordinators when the liaison between the two sectors is not as good as it should be:

- Secondary teachers may say that obtaining useful information from the primary school is difficult. It either sends too little, making it of little value for planning purposes, or too much, making it impossible to select useful information. Difficulties can also arise when information is not received from all the feeder primary schools.
- Teachers are busy people and have to be selective in how they spend their time. If an ICT coordinator does not see this as a priority s/he will spend little time organising it.
- In some urban areas secondary schools receive pupils from a large number of feeder primary schools. The primary schools may vary widely in the resources they have and in the ICT capability of the teachers. This makes the job of organising curriculum continuity particularly daunting.

You can understand why some teachers simply give up when faced with the complexity of the situation. These teachers would make some assumptions about the type of work carried out in primary schools, perhaps by looking at the KS2 Scheme of Work (http://www.standards.dfes.gov.uk/schemes/it) and then treat all the pupils the same.

Task 10.3 Curriculum continuity or discontinuity?

Discuss with your mentor why some schools believe it to be advantageous to use a 'fresh start' approach. What do you see as the drawbacks to adopting this approach? Do you think it affects some groups of pupils more than others (for example, less able–more able, boys–girls, compliant–disruptive, positive attitude–negative attitude)?

Ofsted and Estyn (the school inspection bodies in England and Wales) show an interest in continuity of curriculum in all subjects across Key Stages 2 and 3 during inspections. What comments did they make when the school was last inspected?

Before we consider ways of achieving curriculum continuity, it is worth while first reviewing what it is. A curriculum that provides pupils with continuity of experience would:

- acknowledge and revisit learning experiences from the primary school and build on them (the spiral curriculum);
- provide new opportunities for the pupils to learn;
- help the pupils to improve their confidence and ICT capability;
- provide challenges for pupils to help them to make progress in their learning.

A linked KS2–KS3 curriculum is not something that needs preparing only once and can then be used in perpetuity. As you are well aware the world of ICT is rapidly changing and what the current Year 6 group can do may be significantly different from the achievements of the previous one. The initial preparation of the curriculum will be the most difficult task but annual review is essential.

It is the job of the ICT coordinator to organise the liaison with the primary schools and develop the curriculum but s/he will require your support and help, even as a newly qualified teacher (NQT). In addition, there is plenty that you can do to ensure that pupils are not exposed to repetitive work. What follows is a list of activities in which you could get involved and make useful contributions.

Setting up meetings with partner primary schools

It is important to get off on the right foot when you arrange a meeting of a group of teachers. You may be surprised how quickly people can become uncooperative when their ideas or practice are challenged. Some secondary school teachers can be rather arrogant and, as the curriculum experts, try to dictate what should be taught in the primary school. This approach is unlikely to lead to a satisfactory outcome. A more open approach, looking at what is currently being done and what changes need to be made on both sides, is likely to lead to better results. It is also worth considering:

- where to hold the meeting (using a different location each time gives teachers the opportunity to view each others' ICT resources);
- who will act as chair (this should not necessarily be the secondary person);
- who will act as secretary (a difficult but essential job to make sure that each member of the group carries out the agreed work).

While the main focus of the meeting could be to look at ways of providing pupils with continuity of experience it could also look at how the schools could work together in partnership for the benefit of all concerned.

Schemes of Work

Chapter 4 discussed the Scheme of Work (SoW) as a long term planning document containing a sequenced list of teaching activities with key features and learning outcomes. The Qualifications and Curriculum Authority (QCA) has produced a Scheme of Work for teaching ICT at both Key Stage 2 and Key Stage 3 in England. Each unit in the KS3 scheme builds on specified units in the KS2 scheme. Both schemes can be downloaded from the web (http://www.standards.dfes.gov.uk/ schemes) or purchased in printed form from QCA. One way of developing continuity would be for all the teachers in a partnership group to agree to adopt both schemes. Assuming that the QCA authors have done their homework correctly, the teachers would then have workable documents that would ensure continuity throughout the two key stages. This may be acceptable for some groups of teachers but others may not find the Scheme of Work in keeping with their own philosophy of teaching or may simply object to the principle of a government body producing a prescriptive teaching document. The solution then would be either to modify the QCA scheme or to produce a Scheme of Work from scratch using the National Curriculum as a guide.

   It may not always be best to plan for continuity. In some instances it is better to recognise that there will be discontinuity, and to plan to take advantage of the strengths of the different teaching approaches in each phase. Using this approach, primary school teachers know how far they are expected to take pupils in a strand and secondary teachers are confident in the knowledge that they can build on pupils' understanding from that point.

Joint project for Year 6 and Year 7

One way of helping pupils to appreciate that their secondary school work is building on what they have achieved in the primary school is to devise a project that they start in Year 6 and complete in Year 7. It could be as simple as collecting data about themselves and looking at different ways the information can be presented.

Sharing secondary school resources with the primary school

From time to time, pupils from the partner primary schools can be invited to carry out specific activities at the secondary school. As well as helping to develop good relations with the feeder primary school it can prepare the pupils for the time when they change school (Wardle, 1998).

Discussion meetings about standards of work

It can be of significant value to all concerned when the focus of a cluster group meeting is the assessment of pupils' work. It helps everyone to come to a common agreement as to what is meant by level 3 or a level 4 piece of work and what a pupil would need to do to attain a higher level. The discussion could go on to examine methods of keeping records of pupils' performance and the transfer of records from one sector to the other.

Support from the local education authority

Much of the organisation can be done through staff working for the LEA. This is particularly important when primary schools feed a number of different secondary schools. The LEA should be able to smooth over the problems of competition between the secondary schools for pupil numbers and stress the importance of working together to help all pupils to learn.

Task 10.4 Continuity in Schemes of Work

Look at the KS3 Scheme of Work for ICT in your school. Identify how continuity is built into the scheme, paying attention to continuity across the primary–secondary divide and then across the KS3 work. You may see continuity in terms of:

- more examples of a particular type of work (increasing the range of experiences);
- increased complexity of tasks;
- learning entirely new procedures.

THE IMPACT OF HOME COMPUTERS

Pupils who have a computer at home are likely to be more confident in handling the equipment and software in school than those who have not. Ready access to a computer has a big impact on pupils' attitudes. They can see the potential of the machine to carry out different procedures and they are, generally, not afraid to try things out. Regular users are also likely to develop good keyboard skills and be able to use the mouse efficiently.

Playing games is the largest area of use for both boys and girls but it is slightly more popular with boys. Girls tend to spend more time on e-mailing friends. But all children spend a significant amount of time on the sort of activities that we want them to use in school. We found the breakdown of use to be: word processing, 82 per cent; retrieving data from a CD-ROM, 64 per cent; revision programs, 44 per cent; the Internet, 26 per cent. (Kennewell *et al.*, 2000).

The availability of computers at home

The number of pupils with access to a computer at home is increasing all the time (see Chapter 1). Buying a computer is a significant financial outlay for any family and the burden does not necessarily stop when the basic hardware has been purchased, particularly if the adults agree to pay a monthly fee to an Internet service provider (ISP). There are probably many reasons why families devote a significant amount of money to this one area of home life, such as those identified by Sutherland *et al.* (2000):

- to assist children's learning in school;
- to make up for a perceived shortage of up-to-date technology in schools;
- to support children in preparation for a technologically rich future in the world of work and leisure;
- to keep up with 'other families';
- to enable exploration of the technology;
- to support parent/s' work or study;
- to provide interest to 'keep' the children in the home;
- to provide entertainment through games.

Children like to have the very latest gadgets and, while opening up Internet access may be one reason for upgrading a computer, improving the capacity of the computer to play more sophisticated games may well be another.

Having a computer is one thing but being given the space and the time to use it is another issue entirely. In some homes there will be competition for the computer and members of the family will devise strong arguments as to who has the right to use it. Problems could also arise if the computer is kept in the same room as the television and the family do not want their evening viewing disturbed, or when it is kept in a bedroom, particularly if the room is occupied by an elder brother who may be of the opinion that it is his property. Research indicates that computers are more likely to be used in support of school work when they are positioned in a 'public' location in the house rather than in a bedroom (Downes, 1997).

You need to take these factors into account when setting a computer based homework task and give pupils a reasonable amount of time to complete it.

Task 10.5 Parents' questions about home computers

If you were asked for advice by a parent on home computer use by children what answers might you give to the following questions?

- Where do you think is the best place to keep a computer?
- How long should my son/daughter spend on the computer in the evening?
- What do you know about chat rooms? I don't want my son/daughter getting into trouble or meeting unsuitable people.
- I don't know what s/he gets up to when s/he's up there on the computer. Do you think it's safe on the Internet?

The differences between home and school use of computers

The attitude that pupils have to computers at home may be quite different from that used in school. At home pupils see working with computers as fun; it can be one of their play or recreational activities. Computer games are exciting and can be quite challenging in terms of the attributes they require of the player, such as persistence, remembering information, observational skills, hand–eye coordination and keyboard dexterity. Chatting through e-mail is also seen as a fun thing to do. There is no teacher standing over children telling them that they have misspelt a word or that there are grammatical errors. But, while e-mailing, youngsters will experiment with different techniques such as changing the layout, adding pictures and sound. They are learning in a relaxed, unintimidating environment on tasks that they see as valuable. In school the situation may be different. The tasks that you ask pupils to do will not have any of the excitement of games software and you will not be able to reproduce the intimacy of writing to a close friend. In school, teachers are governed by the National Curriculum, assessment requirements, timetables and deadlines. None of these exists at home. Wellington (2001) points out that learning using ICT at home has the following characteristics. It is:

- voluntary;
- usually carried out alone;
- undirected and unlimited;
- haphazard, unstructured and unsequenced and has many unintended outcomes (sometime difficult to measure);
- available on demand (more or less);
- learner centred, with the learner clearly in control.

If pupils are asked to carry out tedious IT tasks in school or are provided with computers that do not meet the demands of the job, they are likely to become disaffected with their ICT lessons.

> **Task 10.6 Exploiting home computers**
>
> What sort of learning tasks would you set for pupils to complete at home? How would you assess these tasks, bearing in mind that (1) pupils may be simply copying information from the Internet or a CD-ROM, (2) they may be working with a friend and sharing ideas? Thinking in terms of the future, what do you think will be the long term effect of increasing numbers of home computers on the school curriculum and on the whole process of teaching and learning?

Implications for teaching ICT

The school population is divided into two groups, those who have computers at home and those who have not. The former group, an increasing majority, tend to have positive attitudes to using computers, are confident in carrying out procedures and generally see the benefit of computer use in everyday life. The latter group tend to be anxious about using computers in school and are willing to let a more competent peer take control when working in group situations. You are faced with the tricky job of providing situations where both groups can make progress in their learning and where positive attitudes to the use of ICT can be maintained and negative ones eliminated. Here are a number of suggestions:

- Pupils with computers at home can have their enthusiasm for ICT lessons dampened if the activities they are asked to do are not challenging. In designing tasks for these pupils you need to plan around how you can use their existing expertise and consider how you could get them to solve problems, develop their imagination, memory and thinking skills. A lot of what these pupils have learnt at home has been through play, and you will find it useful if you can devise activities that continue to promote a sense of learning through play. Such pupils may also become frustrated if the school equipment is significantly slower than their computer at home. School financial constraints may limit the frequency of replacement of computers. You may need to turn to other means for ensuring that the system is not overloaded and is kept in good working condition.
- You need to think about the messages you convey to the pupils through your questioning and general interaction. You want to develop a classroom culture in which all pupils feel valued and are able to participate. Make sure that the 'home computer group' does not dominate the answering of your questions. You can do this by asking questions of named individuals and using a variety of question types, some that require previous knowledge but others that ask things such as pupils' opinions, the reasons why certain things are done and questions that require them to use information from other subjects.

- In some situations it is necessary, owing to the lack of equipment, to ask pupils to work in groups at one computer and you may regard this as an imperfect situation. However, on other occasions you may recognise benefits to be gained by asking pupils to work in pairs or small groups at a computer in order to generate discussion and debate. In these situations the 'classroom experts' can assist the others, but it is important to ensure that the 'experts' do not dominate the situation and do all the work. Your instructions to the class and your vigilance during the work should ensure that there is a good division of labour and that there is some job rotation. In order to avoid over-reliance on any one expert it is a good idea to change the membership of the groups regularly. You need to be aware that some expert boys tend to dominate computer groups and should take action to stop this happening.

- At the end of an activity you will find it beneficial to get pupils together to share ideas and reflect on the activities they have participated in and the support that the ICT has provided.

- It may be necessary to teach some ICT processes and terminology explicitly, especially to those pupils who are from a technologically deprived background.

- ICT specialists should recognise that a part of their role is to help develop the culture of ICT across the curriculum by offering advice and support to teachers of other subjects. Hopefully this will help to promote ICT as a medium of learning and convey the message that it is of significant use in all aspects of education.

- Nurture links between the home and the school, helping parents in homes with computers to develop the ICT knowledge of their children and supporting those who do not have a computer by ensuring that useful information is available about the resources in the community or provided by the school out of normal hours. Consider: (1) workshop evenings for parents; (2) after-school or lunchtime computer clubs; (3) producing a regular ICT newsletter giving news of what sorts of things the pupils are doing, achievements, news of updates of the school website, links with other schools, useful websites, etc.

Task 10.7 Surveying pupils' access to home computers

With your mentor's permission, devise a short questionnaire to give to pupils asking about computers in the home. In designing your questionnaire you will need to be sensitive to pupils' feelings and recognise that they come from a wide variety of family backgrounds. You could find out about: the type of computers; the type of software; the sorts of things pupils use their computer for; how long they spend on the computer, etc.

SUMMARY

This chapter has highlighted some of the problems faced by secondary school teachers in having to teach pupils from different ICT backgrounds. In order to deal with this situation you will need to have some knowledge of the type of work pupils have covered and the level of their attainment. In order to help pupils improve their ICT capability you will have to provide them with activities that build upon their prior learning and provide sufficient academic challenge to maintain motivation.

FURTHER READING

DfES/BECTA (2001) *Using ICT to enhance Home–School links*, London: DfES. A booklet reporting an evaluation of how ICT influences home–school links.

Facer, K., Furlong, J., Sutherland, R., and Furlong, R. (2000) 'Home is where the hardware is: young people, the domestic environment and "access" to new technologies', in I. Hutchby and J. Moran-Ellis (eds) *Children, Technology and Culture*, London: Falmer. This chapter gives some insight into the culture of home computer use.

Pachler, N. (1999) 'Linking school with home use', in M. Leask and N. Pachler, *Learning to Teach using ICT in the Secondary School*, London: Routledge Falmer. This chapter provides some useful guidance on linking school and home use of the computer.

Schagen, S. and Kerr, D. (1999) *Bridging the Gap? The National Curriculum and Progression from Primary to Secondary School*, Slough: NFER. This research report deals with the issues of progression in general across the KS2–KS3 transition.

11 Supporting the Teaching and Application of ICT across the Curriculum

Howard Tanner

In Chapter 1 we discussed the diverse nature of ICT, which may be viewed as a Key Skill that underpins learning in a range of subject areas, a resource to support teaching and learning across the curriculum, and a discipline in its own right. The Key Skill of ICT demands that pupils actively seek and recognise opportunities to use ICT in other subjects and everyday life. This requires far more than basic ICT skills and techniques. It requires that pupils understand the potential of ICT and have the confidence and desire to seek opportunities to apply their knowledge, using their own initiative. In order to develop such knowledge and attitudes, we believe, the Key Skill demands that pupils experience the effective use of ICT as a tool or resource in all subjects in the curriculum.

Most ICT schemes of work contain links with ICT activities in other subjects. Many schemes plan both the introduction of ICT skills and their subsequent application in other subjects. Others take the position that skills are best learned in the context in which they are to be used, and plan to teach specific ICT skills at appropriate points in the curriculum of other subjects. However, because secondary schools have a curriculum structure that is based on discrete subject teaching, either model poses major challenges to curriculum coherence, monitoring and assessment.

In this chapter we explore different curriculum models and discuss ways of working with colleagues from other subject disciplines to ensure that the ICT Key Skill is developed in a wide range of contexts and that ICT is used effectively to improve teaching and learning in all areas of the curriculum.

OBJECTIVES

By the end of this chapter, you should be able to:

- analyse the merits of different curriculum models;
- understand ways of teaching for the transfer of principles and skills across different contexts;
- identify possible links with other subjects, and devise and use activities in ICT lessons that are set in other subject contexts;
- understand how to collaborate effectively with colleagues who teach other subjects;
- understand how to support teachers of other subjects in their lessons.

THE ICT CURRICULUM

Different curriculum models for the teaching of ICT

There are many effective models for delivering the ICT curriculum, spread along a continuum with different proportions of discrete and cross-curricular teaching. Each has its particular advantages and disadvantages.

Cross-curricular models are able to offer authentic tasks for teaching and assessment (Birnbaum, 1990), allowing pupils to learn Key Skills in contexts that represent appropriate uses of technology. This naturalistic approach has the potential to remove some of the traditional difficulties of knowledge transfer from one subject domain to another. Given our desire for children to learn to use ICT as a tool or resource, and to evaluate its impact, this is at first sight the most appropriate model of learning. However, in reality, organising and managing such a curriculum is a complex task. The coordination of teaching and the monitoring of pupils' progress may be difficult, potentially leading to a negative impact on pupil attainment if not well managed (Goldstein, 1997).

Discrete courses are often planned in terms of both competences and subject demands. They are sometimes scheduled as a brief, intensive input at the start of Key Stage 3. This is the 'kick start' approach and provides a common core of knowledge and skills for pupils who arrive in secondary school with a wide range of prior experiences. Other models for discrete courses plan in regular modules throughout the key stage, or a regular lesson throughout each year. Two different approaches may be characterised here. In a centralised approach the discrete course aims to provide the whole ICT curriculum. In a core skills approach the discrete course aims to prepare pupils for coordinated provision in other curriculum subjects (NCET, 1996).

The danger with models based on centralised discrete courses is that skills and knowledge may be taught divorced from application and the contexts chosen may be inauthentic or inappropriate owing to ICT teachers having insufficient depth of knowledge of the subject matter concerned. For example, copying out text from a book is an unsatisfactory way to develop word processing skills, whereas analytical writing in the context of History may be a more appropriate use.

Cross-curricular or permeated models may be 'integrated', with ICT adopted by other subjects as appropriate to their schemes of work, or 'hosted', where ICT is added as a scheduled sequence of lessons within their timetable (Smith, 1991). Where subject teachers are confident and enthusiastic about the use of ICT in their subject teaching, integrated models provide opportunities to develop realistic applications in authentic contexts. There is a danger, however, that where subject teachers lack confidence in their own use of ICT, or where the dominant pedagogy in their subject is highly teacher-centred, ICT objectives may be seen as incidental or unimportant. Similarly, although 'hosted' models may be very effective when the outlook of subject teachers is positive, there is a danger that the ICT activity may seem inauthentic and more of a bolt-on extra.

> Cross-curricular delivery of ICT works only when subject teachers are also confident with ICT, pupils' progress is monitored and structures are in place for motivating and effectively coordinating delivery. Where ICT is taught as a separate course, coverage of the programme of study is more rigorous; but often there are insufficient opportunities to apply the ICT skills so acquired to work in other subjects.
>
> (Ofsted, 1995)

When ICT was introduced in the National Curriculum an integrated, cross-curricular model was seen as ideal, and it was specifically stated that ICT should not be seen as another subject to teach, with its own demands on scarce curriculum time (CCW, 1990). However, few schools now have fully cross-curricular models for Year 7, although some 30 per cent use that approach in Years 8 to 11 (DfEE, 1998).

In the ITCD project (Kennewell et al., 2000) we found that in the schools which were most successful in developing a whole school approach to ICT, the schemes of work for most other subjects included clear specifications regarding the role and use of ICT. Specialist teaching was then planned to support the application of skills elsewhere in the curriculum.

Effective schemes of work included clear expectations for learning key concepts, techniques and higher order skills within ICT. Guidance and examples were provided concerning contexts, activities and assessment. There were clear links between ICT documents and references to the use of ICT in other subject schemes of work.

Task 11.1 The curriculum model

Consider the model chosen by your placement school.

- To what extent is it cross-curricular or discrete?
- To what extent is ICT used in the context of subject teaching?

Choosing a model

We consider it most important that the model chosen suits the size of the school and the outlook of the staff. A cross-curricular approach may be very effective in a small school where the staff communicate well. Where subject teaching staff lack confidence, more discrete teaching may be necessary to ensure curriculum progression within ICT. The most appropriate curriculum model will usually combine the carefully planned application and development of skills across the curriculum with some regular discrete teaching by specialists.

Cross-curricular models are often supported by some initial specialist teaching in Year 7 in order to overcome any possible variation in experience in the primary school. However, primary schools are rapidly becoming more ICT capable and this problem is becoming less significant. Even so, there remains a need to ensure that there is an appropriate focus on the ICT Key Skill at the start of secondary school and short basic skills courses can often ensure that pupils develop the important concepts and techniques that teachers of other subjects would expect them to have when using ICT in their lessons.

Where provision is based on centralised specialist ICT lessons, ICT teachers often find themselves expected to teach aspects of all the other subjects in the curriculum as they strive to find a wide range of contexts in which ICT can be used. Clearly this is not an ideal situation and ICT teachers may sometimes inadvertently misinterpret subjects in which they lack specialist knowledge and experience. To alleviate such problems partially, it may be helpful to ask each subject area to make a contribution to the ICT scheme of work in the form of activities based on its discipline which it would like pupils to experience.

For example, in one school in the ITCD project (Kennewell *et al.*, 2000) an investigation of tiling patterns in mathematics was used to provide an authentic application for a spreadsheet. The activity was started in a Mathematics lesson, and the preparatory work was then brought to the specialist ICT lesson. The ICT teacher had discussed the task with the Mathematics teacher and was able to focus on its mathematical objectives as well as specific ICT objectives.

We observed several other examples of successful collaborative planning between subject departments and ICT, such as using ICT for data logging in a scientific experiment. In other subject areas ICT was often used for the application of taught concepts and the consolidation of ideas, bringing together information from conventional teaching with information from databases and web sources. Other teachers used ICT lessons to search for information which was to be used later in conventional lessons.

Even when a high level of collaboration has occurred as reported above some problems remain. Learners are notoriously poor at transferring knowledge and skills learned in one context to a new context. Pupils may not see the knowledge and skills gained in the ICT lesson as applicable in the context of another subject. This attitude is encouraged if the lesson is being taught by an ICT teacher in an ICT room rather than by a Mathematics teacher in the mathematics suite. If the ICT Key Skill is to be of any use, the teaching that occurs must encourage the transfer of principles and skills.

TEACHING FOR THE TRANSFER OF PRINCIPLES AND SKILLS

The National Curriculum for ICT is not expressed in terms of specific ICT techniques. The authors based the curriculum on general concepts such as communicating and handling information, modelling, measurement and control to express their aims. Much of the focus is on higher order skills such as:

- planning to use ICT;
- making decisions concerning appropriate resources and techniques;
- monitoring progress;
- evaluating outcomes.

Learners are expected to recognise when the use of ICT would be helpful, use ICT appropriately in such situations and evaluate the effect of using ICT (Birnbaum, 1989).

The focus on higher order skills represents a challenge to traditional teaching approaches which often aim to 'spoonfeed' facts rather than require active problem solving under the control of the pupils themselves. Our aims demand that teachers prompt pupils to think for themselves how to apply ICT to a task, rather than telling them how to perform specific tasks. For some teachers this would represent a major shift in teaching style.

Nevertheless, to use ICT effectively, pupils must master specific skills and techniques. These may be quite numerous in the context of a particular piece of software. However, techniques and skills that are taught out of the context of authentic tasks often appear mundane or pointless. Fortunately such techniques may often be learned in the natural course of performing a task. Most modern software provides sufficient prompts and guidance through on-screen menus and icons for a self-confident user to make rapid progress through authentic tasks. In fact, one of the defining characteristics of the ICT capable pupil is the self-confidence to explore and evaluate a new piece of software, learning new techniques and skills for themselves. Opportunities for pupil led exploration and evaluation of new software environments must be included in the ICT curriculum if ICT capability is to develop.

Frequently used techniques eventually become automatic and the user is then more able to focus on the content of the task without having to monitor the progress of a technique. However, although such skills and techniques appear to be at the heart of the subject content of ICT, progression demands a deeper understanding based on concepts and processes. When techniques are taught in a single context it is difficult for pupils to generalise appropriate mental models about computer systems. If techniques are to be transferable to new situations, pupils should experience them in several situations. There should be breadth and balance in the range of ICT applications, as well as in the curriculum as a whole.

A wide range of applications and contexts is a necessary but not sufficient condition to ensure the progressive understanding of key concepts. While a task is being performed or a problem solved, the focus of the pupils' attention is often on immediate concerns and task specific objectives. Pupils need to have opportunities to reflect on the techniques they have experienced across a range of contexts in order to develop general principles if transferable knowledge is to be developed.

It is much easier to perform a task than to talk about the processes involved in its performance. Encouraging pupils to talk about how they used ICT to solve a problem and to evaluate its impact assists in the development of ICT concepts. You can help pupils to express their ideas about the general principles involved in ICT application. You should model the skills of planning, decision making and evaluating in your interactions with pupils. You should also structure the questioning of pupils during the performance of tasks to focus their attention on key concepts and transferable processes.

One of the most significant points in a lesson should be the plenary session, for it is here that you can support a period of collective reflection on what has been learned. Set time aside to allow pupils to make presentations of their work, focusing the attention of the class on key issues in the problem solving process and evaluating products against general criteria. Use this evaluation stage systematically to communicate expectations concerning what constitutes a high quality outcome. The plenary session also provides an opportunity for formative assessment and target setting.

As you question pupils about their work during the plenary session, the pupils will gradually learn to ask similar questions of themselves and learn the skills of self-assessment and evaluation which are necessary for progression in ICT.

Task 11.2 How do you ensure that pupils are able to apply their knowledge of ICT?

Examine your ICT scheme of work and any policy documents provided by your school. What advice is offered about teaching approaches when using ICT? Talk to your mentor or the Head of ICT and ask what teaching approaches they recommend to ensure that pupils learn how to apply their ICT knowledge.

In the ITCD project (Kennewell *et al.*, 2000) we identified a number of key strategies designed to help pupils to generalise and develop the conceptual understanding necessary for transfer of ICT learning across the curriculum:

- Alert pupils to the key ICT teaching points in whichever subject they were met.
- Challenge inefficient or naive methods of achieving goals.
- Use questioning to focus attention on general principles and concepts.
- Discuss possible applications of the concepts and processes in other contexts.
- Model the higher order skills of planning, monitoring and evaluation.
- Provide opportunities for teacher supported collective reflection in plenary sessions.
- Use formative assessment, self-assessment and target setting.

The most effective teachers of ICT were clear that they were teaching principles and processes, not merely how to use specific programmes or techniques. They were keen to identify a range of opportunities across the curriculum for applications of key concepts and general principles in authentic contexts.

FORGING LINKS WITH OTHER SUBJECTS

Although our aims demand that children experience the authentic use of ICT in a wide range of contexts, the adoption of ICT is very variable across subject departments within schools, with some subjects only rarely making use of ICT (Kennewell *et al.*, 2000). This may be seen partly as a result of the dominant culture to be found in some subjects, particularly with respect to teachers' views about what would constitute appropriate subject content and learning processes. In some subjects the use of a computer is seen as almost inevitable, whereas in others the use of ICT may be regarded as inconsistent with the character of the discipline. For example, although D&T teachers might regard the use of ICT as part of their subject (see Chapter 2), some English teachers might regard computers as too impersonal for their subject. Still other teachers might regard the use of technology in their subject as a 'dumbing down' process, removing the need to practise basic skills such as graph plotting or dictionary work. Such attitudes are often due to a lack of ICT capability on the part of some subject teachers, whose inexperience with appropriate software prevents them from seeing the potential to teach effective lessons, which address suitably challenging subject objectives.

Task 11.3 Which subjects make the most use of ICT and what for?

- Ask the ICT coordinator which subject areas and teachers use ICT most often in their teaching.
- Ask two of the teachers who use ICT regularly to explain what tasks they ask the pupils to perform. How do they organise their teaching?
- Discuss their aims for the sessions. What are their motives in using ICT for the lessons rather than more traditional approaches?

Pedagogy is very resistant to change. Very few teachers change their teaching styles on introducing ICT; rather they tend to modify their existing practice to incorporate the use of a new tool. The introduction of computers is greeted most enthusiastically when teachers are able to maintain their preferred lesson structure and subject teaching objectives (Goodson and Mangan, 1995).

It is often claimed that the introduction of ICT into subject teaching is easier to achieve in subjects where an individualised classroom environment already exists

(Goodson and Mangan, 1995). The suggestion seems to be that when the subject culture is pupil centred, the introduction of ICT into subject teaching is likely to be seen as less problematic. On the other hand, in subjects with a more teacher centred culture, ICT may be viewed as a threat to traditional classroom processes of teaching and learning (Selwyn, 1999). However, we think that it is unwise to assume that teaching based on the use of ICT is inevitably pupil centred or individualised.

One of the difficulties which has always been associated with individualised approaches is that although it sounds superficially attractive to allow pupils to work at their own level and at their own pace, in reality some pupils persist in choosing a low level and a pace which varies between very slow and stopped. Current developments in the Key Skills of literacy and numeracy reject earlier trends towards individualised approaches to learning in favour of teaching approaches that place the teacher in a leading role. These approaches are not 'traditional' in the sense of emphasising mechanical skills and techniques. Rather they emphasise interaction, involvement and the articulation of ideas by pupils. The role of the teacher is to support the structured development of key concepts, to maintain the pace and set targets.

The best lessons which we observed in the ITCD project (Kennewell *et al.*, 2000) had a high level of teacher input and support for learning, incorporating many of the ideas of interactive teaching expressed above, no matter what the subject context. It is clear that for some teachers this would represent a significant change in their current pedagogy.

The introduction of ICT into subject teaching includes a number of separate elements: the development of technical skill, the use of new materials, the use of new teaching approaches and possible changes in pedagogical beliefs. Where there is a mismatch between subject aims and those of ICT, and a demand for pedagogical change, subject teachers often express resentment at being expected to teach ICT. However, ICT capability, like other Key Skills, demands application in authentic tasks. If technology is the sole focus of the task the activity is inauthentic. Such applications of ICT tend to be transient and are quickly dropped from the subject curriculum under the pressure to achieve examination success.

If the introduction of ICT is to make an impact within subject teaching, the first step must be to convince subject teachers of its value in terms of their own needs. For teachers of other subjects, the introduction of ICT must be practicable and must improve pupil learning. Practicality implies easy access to facilitate short term planning and familiarity with the software to promote personal confidence – implying regular use. This probably implies departmental ownership of a local facility. Improved pupil learning will almost certainly be judged by improved examination results in the longer term, but may be satisfied by improved pupil motivation in the short term.

The introduction of ICT into subject teaching should make it possible for pupils to learn more effectively than they did before. However, before this improved performance can be achieved, subject teachers must adjust their goals and strategies in the light of the possibilities offered by ICT. In some cases it may also be necessary to reconceptualise their subject in the light of changing technology. However, many of these issues become apparent only after teachers have begun to introduce ICT to their subject and become more familiar with its potential. Unfortunately, teachers are only likely to persist with the introduction of ICT into their subject if they see evidence of success in their own terms in the initial stages of implementation (Fullan, 1991).

Subject teachers thus require a set of activities which can reasonably be expected to produce success. They also require support to help them manage technology with which they are unfamiliar. Both of these should be provided through collaboration with the ICT coordinator.

COLLABORATING WITH COLLEAGUES WHO TEACH OTHER SUBJECTS

Coordinating ICT across the curriculum

The role of the ICT coordinator includes monitoring and assessing the development of ICT capability across the curriculum, staff training, classroom support and system maintenance. Most significantly, coordinators are expected to work with the senior management of the school and with heads of subject departments to guide and plan the effective use of ICT across the curriculum and to ensure the appropriate exploitation of new technological developments (NCET, 1998). To fulfil such a role effectively would seem to demand high status within the school; however, most ICT coordinators feel that they lack status (Kennewell and Selwood, 1997).

Success often relies primarily on the personal qualities of the ICT coordinator, although clearly this should not be at the expense of managerial structures. Typically, an effective coordinator has an assertive yet approachable interpersonal style. Co-ordinators also need to understand the subject cultures and teaching styles of other staff. Furthermore, they need to be respected in the staff room for their teaching ability and need to demonstrate a personal teaching approach that provides a good model of how to manage an ICT-based classroom. These characteristics are more important than technical knowledge.

Few schools can afford to rely on ICT coordinators being charismatic superteachers, however. Most are likely to be normal competent teachers with the usual strengths and weaknesses of human beings. The most effective schools we found in the ITCD project had supported their coordinator by setting up managerial structures and procedures to facilitate two-way communication. These were backed up by clear messages from the senior management team that the development of an effective ICT policy was a priority for the school.

You may find that your school has set up an ICT committee that includes one teacher from each subject area. The role of the departmental representative is, first, to ensure that explicit references to ICT are included in the departmental schemes of work, and second to monitor and facilitate the performance of the agreed activities. This includes working with their colleagues to ensure that each teacher in their department has sufficient ICT capability to plan, prepare and teach the required sequence of lessons. Where teachers lack confidence in their own technical abilities, the ICT coordinator tries to provide appropriate support. You may be able to assist in providing such support.

Task 11.4 How is ICT coordination managed in your school?

Identify the managerial structures that are in place in your school to coordinate the development of pupils' ICT capability.

● What structures and procedures are there to plan for the professional development of staff in the use and application of ICT in their teaching?
● How are less confident staff supported when they attempt to teach a lesson using ICT?

Supporting teachers of other subjects in their lessons

Subject teachers who are beginning to consider using ICT in their classrooms usually report that they are most concerned about their lack of technical skill. Clearly, you should try to help with this aspect where necessary, but teachers often require more help in the area of pedagogy and the identification of learning opportunities with ICT.

In order to avoid continued reliance on ICT specialists, you should aim to foster technical independence among subject staff as quickly as possible. Clearly any staff training should aim to achieve this. However, if a school is able to support an ICT technician, part of the role should be to provide technical support in the classroom to boost the confidence of novices that they will be able to cope with unforeseen problems.

Teachers express a strong preference for school based training by their colleagues rather than external agencies, and organising this is usually part of the coordinator's role. However, in the early stages of their development, subject teachers will not be able to identify appropriate applications for themselves and will need support in identifying appropriate ways for ICT to enhance their subject teaching. ICT specialists who lack appropriate knowledge in other subjects often find this difficult, especially with older pupils.

Fortunately, National Curriculum subject orders indicate opportunities for ICT applications, and many ideas have been generated in response to the UK government's training scheme for ICT in subject teaching (TTA, 1998). It is important for heads of department to ensure that their schemes of work incorporate these activities as a minimum. Furthermore, their schemes should indicate clearly their subject aims for the activities and when they should be taught. When subject leaders incorporate the use of ICT in their own teaching, it is far more likely that their colleagues will do likewise. Thus targeting heads of department for support may be a good first strategy. However, the work of a junior member of staff who is keen can sometimes act as a catalyst of change. In fact, a good student teacher who is personally ICT capable, and who brings new ideas from college or university, can often move a department forwards. This is particularly true if the ICT coordinator is aware of the student teacher's potential and uses him or her as a focus of staff development.

The decision to introduce ICT into subject teaching ought to be a natural response to the needs of the pupils and the opportunities offered by the technology. However, for many teachers the introduction of ICT to their teaching represents a threat to their professional standing. Most teachers are already operating successfully according to their own standards and to the norms of their school. To ask them to change their pedagogy to accommodate ICT is to ask them to take a risk. Otherwise experienced teachers who are new to working with ICT become like novices in the new environment, often swinging from excessive strictness to permissiveness, focusing on class management and control issues and superficial features of the learning (Mevarech, 1997).

Your role in supporting professional development is to present the subject teacher with activities that are feasible using current teaching approaches and to provide support with technical concerns so that professional reputations are not exposed to unacceptable risk. However, it is also necessary for the activities to demonstrate sufficient advantages for learning according to the teacher's current aims and beliefs, so that they are inclined to persevere. You need to work collaboratively with the subject teacher to develop appropriate lesson ideas, which meet these criteria and then support their implementation in the classroom to remove worries about technical problems.

Some of the most successful lessons we saw in the ITCD project had been developed collaboratively between an ICT coordinator and a teacher of German. The lessons had been developed with a spirit of joint action research, with both teachers contributing their own distinct expertise. The German teacher devised the language aims for the lesson and the ICT teacher worked on the pupils' ICT portfolios.

The lessons were based on the task of producing an advertising leaflet for the Rhineland in German. The spell checking facility was not used in this lesson, as practising dictionary skills was one of the aims. The text had been produced on paper, but the pupils used the computers for drafting and redrafting. Genuine advertising material was available and pupils scanned in appropriate pictures using frames. Not all the pupils knew how to do this and a system of 'peer teachers' was utilised very effectively. They were trained to help the less ICT capable pupils without doing things for them. They explained how to do things and did not take over keyboards themselves. The ethos was one of collaborative learning: those who knew how to do something explained to those who did not, whether pupil or teacher, German or ICT.

In the early stages, both teachers taught the lessons as a team, but as the German teacher grew in confidence, the ICT coordinator gradually withdrew, dropping in only occasionally to offer moral support. The style of question that the ICT coordinator had typically posed to pupils to help them to generalise their ICT knowledge was gradually incorporated into the repertoire of the German teacher.

The German teacher focused on developing written communication in the target language and saw the use of ICT as an important aspect of communication in any language. His aims were associated with written communication in the German language and the use of dictionaries. He encouraged pupils to apply familiar techniques and to focus on the content and structure of the language. However, although he did not deliberately set out to teach ICT, his ongoing questioning focused on their ideas and decisions, helping them to develop higher order skills, and through effective use of plenary sessions he helped them to generalise the ICT knowledge which was used.

> **Task 11.5 What are the key features of successful subject support for ICT?**
>
> Look back over the description of the German lessons. What are the key features which made them a success for (1) the German teacher, (2) the ICT teacher, (3) the pupils? Try to express them in general terms that would apply to other subject applications.

We identified four key features that led to the lessons being judged successful by the German teacher, the ICT teacher and the pupils. They are associated with relations between the two teachers, the classroom ethos, the authentic nature of the task and the emphasis on higher order skills and processes to encourage knowledge transfer.

Research has long shown that supportive collaborative relations between teachers are necessary for effective school based curriculum development (Hargreaves, 1994). Their approach was based on collaborative action research, so they reflected together on their experiences and were able to generalise their experiences. The learning process was supported further by the ethos of the classroom that encouraged effective peer tutoring. The task itself was authentic in terms of both its subject specific aims, the use of ICT in support of those aims and the real life source materials provided.

Finally, the use of plenary sessions to encourage reflection on the ICT learning that had occurred helped pupils to generalise the ICT knowledge that had been applied, to encourage the development of transferable knowledge. The plenary sessions also provided opportunities for formative assessment and target setting, which encourages progression in ICT capability. You may recall from Chapter 7 that such formative assessment is highly significant in raising standards.

SUMMARY

Curriculum models for developing ICT capability may be placed on a continuum from discrete to fully cross-curricular. Although cross-curricular models were originally seen as the ideal form, all models have their own distinct advantages and disadvantages, and we consider it most important that the model chosen suits the size of the school and the outlook of the staff. In all cases, however, it is necessary for ICT skills to be applied in a range of contexts if pupils are to learn to generalise and transfer their knowledge.

ICT teaching should focus on higher order skills and processes rather than low level techniques. In order to teach for transfer it is necessary to encourage children to reflect on and talk about their work. Pupil articulation of the key ideas should be a significant element in any effective teaching strategy. The plenary session can be a particularly significant point in the lesson when pupils can articulate the learning that has occurred.

Children should experience the authentic use of ICT in a wide range of contexts. However, teachers of other subjects will be willing to modify their pedagogy to incorporate ICT only if the activities concerned are practical and provide success according to their current beliefs about their subject. In the early stages teachers who lack technical expertise will require support in their classrooms. Such support is most effective when the relation between teachers is collaborative and collegial. Collaborative action research is a helpful model for such curriculum development.

FURTHER READING

Leask, M. (ed.) (2001) *Issues in Teaching using ICT*, London: RoutledgeFalmer. Provides deeper examination of many of the issues involved in the use of ICT in teaching and learning.

Leask, M. and Pachler, N. (eds) (1999) *Learning to Teach using ICT in the Secondary School*, London: RoutledgeFalmer. This book is in the same series as the present one, but focuses on using ICT in other subjects.

12 Professional Development

Neil Stanley and John Parkinson

Professional development is a key issue in current thinking on school improvement. The UK government has promised better quality continuing professional development (CPD) for all teachers and plans to introduce programmes to support teachers during their early years in the profession (DfEE, 2001).

During your period of initial teacher education you will start to develop the skills required for lifelong learning about teaching. There are three key strands that you will need to develop:

- improving and extending your subject knowledge of ICT (covered in Chapter 3);
- improving your knowledge of learning and teaching;
- learning how to work effectively in a team of teachers for the benefit of all learners and the school.

Being enthusiastically engaged in professional development will help you to maintain an interest in the teaching of ICT and ensure that your knowledge is kept up to date. The General Teaching Councils for England and Wales came into existence in 2000 with a specific remit to promote teachers' professional development through approaches such as:

- producing a professional code for teachers;
- providing small amounts of money for teachers to go on courses or to carry out in-school investigations into improving teaching.

Once you become a qualified teacher you will be required to become a member of one of the councils and will be obliged to comply with the code. Your continued enthusiasm for your subject will be reflected in the way you teach and in the success of your learners.

OBJECTIVES

By the end of this chapter, you should be able to:

- develop professional relationships with your HE tutor, school based tutor, head of department and other colleagues;
- evaluate your effectiveness in teaching and set personal targets;
- keep up with technological developments and professional issues through reading, direct and electronic discussion and web research;
- contribute to the work of the department, including developing and revising effective resources and coherent Schemes of Work to promote continuity of experience and progression of learning;
- provide INSET for the school and show awareness of a whole school approach to ICT capability;
- manage, plan and develop school ICT resources to provide support for improved teaching and learning.

RELATIONSHIPS

Developing the right sort of relations with both teaching colleagues and pupils is not always as easy as it may at first appear. An important aspect of being a teacher is being a member of a team, contributing to the work of the team, sharing the same goals and responsibilities. It goes without saying that you should be reliable and act in a responsible way when you are involved with young people. While in school you need to conduct yourself in a manner that you would expect of a teacher. You become a role model for a large number of young people. If you take little pride in your appearance, why should they? If you arrive late for lessons, they may do the same. If you do not mark their homework on time, why should they bother to hand it in on time?

Effective schools depend on all teachers contributing their share of development work. Just as you should not expect to be spoonfed whilst undertaking your own academic studies, you should not expect everything to be specified for you in school. It is up to you to instigate some of the activity you choose to undertake. In particular, you are in the position of having current educational (and possibly real world) subject experience and you may well know or have done things that the team in a school have not had the opportunity to undertake. For example, one of the things that you may be asked to do is to prepare modules of work on new or upgraded systems. (You will be seen to have time to experiment and need the practice.) You may even be asked to contribute to the development of new resources as a result of your previous experience in a work or study context. When you do this, make sure you clearly understand what you have to do, consult the relevant documents (for example, school policies, literature on teaching particular techniques, the National Curriculum) and check from time to time with your mentor that you are on the right track. Be prepared for criticism from your mentor, who will be able to comment on your work in the light of his/her experience of working with pupils over a long period of time.

As well as being a member of the ICT team you will need to relate to all the other subject teams in the school. You will need to understand how ICT is used in each of the different curriculum areas and how this use matches the work done in ICT lessons. In this respect you may need to develop high level diplomacy skills to deal with such tricky situations as:

- teachers making unreasonable demands (for example, on your time, on the use of the ICT facilities);
- teachers using software and activities that are inappropriate for pupils' conceptual level;
- teachers' lack of knowledge of or misconceptions about ICT.

You also need to build that special teacher–pupil relationship with the young people in your care. This can be quite difficult for some young student teachers, who find themselves becoming over-friendly with the pupils. You need to have some distance between yourself and those whom you teach. If you find that the pupils go to the same clubs or pubs that you do, then you should change your habits and go somewhere else. You may be flattered by the attention given to you by some youngsters, but you must resist the temptation! Over-friendly relations with your teaching colleagues are also to be avoided whilst you are a trainee in a school.

An important aspect of ICT is the level of extracurricular work involved. As a student teacher you will be expected to help out with lunchtime and after-school computer sessions. This gives you an opportunity to help individual pupils develop their knowledge and understanding of techniques and skills. It should also take some of the strain off the usually overburdened ICT coordinator. You should be enthusiastic about volunteering but do not be afraid to say if people are taking advantage of your enthusiasm. You will also need to work with technicians, classroom assistants and other learning support teachers. It is good practice to inform and involve these colleagues in what you are doing in a particular session.

It is worth bearing in mind that overconfidence can often be read as arrogance; likewise, timidity can be read as indifference. It is important to try to gauge the right level of enthusiasm and the contribution you should make. See Capel *et al.* (2001: unit 1.2) for further guidance on professional relations.

Task 12.1 Extracurricular activities

For your current placement make a note of all the extracurricular activity that the ICT team are involved in.

- How do these extracurricular activities help pupils to improve their knowledge of ICT?
- How could you encourage those who do not avail themselves of the extra sessions to attend?

THE TEACHER AS LEARNER

You can learn about teaching by:

- thinking about your own experiences as a learner;
- observing experienced teachers at work (see Parkinson, 1994: 53–6 for some additional guidance on lesson observation);
- reading about approaches to teaching and how pupils learn;
- attending lectures/seminars/pre-service and in-service courses;
- discussing your lessons with mentors and tutors;
- reflecting on your own teaching performance.

One advantage of being a trainee is that you have an opportunity to spend some of your time in school observing others teach. As an ICT trainee observing in an IT room it will be very easy to feel obliged to spend most of your time helping pupils, but in the long term it is more important to take the opportunity to be an observer.

All teachers (in all subject areas) can offer useful observation opportunities. For example, watching how a PE teacher deals with a group of boys who have been causing you difficulties may suggest possible strategies. Observing an English teacher who is experienced in the use of group work for discussion may also be valuable. Try also to choose a subject to observe that will raise similar issues to those you are having difficulties with. Aspects of the D&T curriculum (see Chapter 2) could also raise parallel issues to working in ICT, especially transitions between formal and practical activity, and being able to share your support out fairly among the group when using technology.

It is essential that your observation opportunities are focused. Common courtesy to colleagues is important:

- Always ask permission before joining a class.
- Always act politely and respectfully.
- Always try to discuss the focus of your observation with the teacher prior to the start of the class.
- If asked to comment afterwards always do so in a non-critical way.

- Do not discuss that teacher's lesson behind their back.
- Write the observation up for your records in as anonymous a way as possible.

You may well face a difficulty if you see pupil misbehaviour that has not been noticed by the class teacher. To tell the pupil(s) off yourself might undermine the class teacher, but to ignore it may undermine your future authority. You will need to discuss this possibility and what you should do with any teacher whose classes you observe.

Your observations may focus on:

- the arrival and departure of pupils;
- the management of transitions;
- teacher talk and explanation;
- teacher questioning;
- the effectiveness of the teaching strategy employed;
- critical incidents;
- teacher use of space and resources;
- other aspects that you could use to improve your own practice and strategies.

Task 12.2. Observing experienced teachers

ICT classes need to move from introduction to task to plenary stage and this normally involves the physical movement of the pupils. Undertake an observation that focuses on arrival–transition–departure.
  You should address and make notes on the following:

- How are the pupils greeted?
- How are they calmed for the introduction?
- How are any late arrivals managed?
- How is the transition to computer-based work managed?
- How is the transition from computer-based work managed?
- How are the pupils allowed to depart?

Can you identify the management strategies that the teacher used? One aspect that you should quickly realise is the need to minimise the number of transitions in a lesson and the problems they can instigate. Another observation might focus on the strategy used to deliver some formal IT subject knowledge. In this case note and reflect on:

- The resources used by the teacher: video, OHP, ICT-based, etc.
- The structure of the delivery: teacher-led, pupil-discovered, etc.
- The nature of talk in the classroom.

Afterwards try to think why it was approached that way, whether there are other strategies that could use the available resources. Did the strategy used permit all the learners to maximise their potential learning?

Table 12.1 Stages in the reflective process

Impressionistic   One or two instances stick in your mind and they colour your interpretation of the whole lesson. *Simon arrives late to your class. He is on report. He fails to engage with the work and needs to be dealt with through normal discipline procedures. The rest of the group were on-task and made good progress. Apart from Simon (outside your control) it was a good lesson.*

Beginning to focus   You look at the achievements of different groups of pupils. You focus on one or two specific issues. *Cathy and Amanda, bright Year 8 students, worked on the set project very well whilst Peter and Ian, bright and in the same class, failed to respond to the challenge. What are the factors here? Is the task gender biased?*

Reflective practitioner   You look at a range of evidence and are able to make sound judgements about how to improve. *The lesson went well – how can I fine tune what I did to improve my performance? Can I pass more control to the learners? Is there an alternate delivery strategy that might be better?*

A great deal has been written about reflection in teaching (such as Pollard and Triggs, 1997; Schön, 1991) concerned with what it is and how to do it. A reflective teacher is someone who thinks about what goes on in the classroom, makes an appraisal of the situation and then uses the information to improve. On one level this may simply be taking into account something that happened during the lesson and remembering to do it differently next time. On a deeper level it involves a rigorous analysis of what has gone on during the lesson by asking the question 'Why?'

It is very difficult to observe your own lesson closely. Your mentors have the advantage of not having to teach whilst they observe. Think about what they look for when they observe you. They may have a checklist or may negotiate a focus with you beforehand. As you are trying to observe whilst you teach you must plan the issues you are going to address – although other, more urgent, unplanned-for ones may take over during the lesson.

It is normal for trainee teachers to try to focus on themselves, their own perform-ance and classroom management. Observing yourself is almost impossible (unless you are videoed or have big mirrors on the wall). It is much easier to focus on pupil learning, perhaps initially identifying 'typical' learners or groups of learners that you can make observational records on. You must focus on specific variables. Were they on task? How far did they get with the activity set? How much peer and teacher support did they request? The sort of reflection that you carry out will develop as your experience grows.

Task 12.3 Effective learning

How would you judge whether the lesson had been effective?

- Were the pupils enjoying what they were doing? Did they seem to be motivated and keen to get on with the work you set? When you moved around the class, during a group activity, were pupils talking about the work?
- How well did pupils respond to your oral questions? How keen were they to let you know that they understood the work (bearing in mind that some older pupils may be reluctant to answer questions in front of their peers)? What sort of questions did pupils ask you?
- If included, what was the quality of their written work? Was it complete, neat and correct?
- How well did pupils perform in any written tests?

Early in your teaching experience

Consider how you are going to reflect on one or two aspects of your teaching, for example questioning where the points you may wish to consider could be:

- your distribution of questions around the class;
- your use of a variety of questions;
- your responses to pupils' answers;
- the quality of pupils' responses.

Consider how you would collect evidence for these points. It is good practice to script your questions in advance and to have a good idea of whom in the class you might ask first.

Later on in your teaching experience

Get an overview of the quality of a lesson by completing a self-evaluation form and then look at one or two areas in more detail. A self-evaluation form might cover the following areas, with space for you to give your level of satisfaction with your performance:

- subject knowledge;
- timing and pace;

- planning and preparation;
- assessment of pupils' understanding;
- availability of resources;
- monitoring of pupils' progress;
- starting the lesson;
- control and discipline;
- use of technology (interactive whiteboard, etc.);
- the plenary and the ending of the lesson;
- your communication skills;
- quality of the pupils' learning;
- management of activities;
- your enthusiasm and interaction;
- the pupils' enthusiasm and interest.

Towards the end of your teaching experience

Evaluate the quality of the pupils' learning through a study of their oral and written contributions to lessons. Are they able to recall information you gave them correctly? Are they able to go beyond that and use information in a variety of ways? Is there any indication that they have found out additional information for themselves? Have the pupils been able to monitor their own learning? How might your assessment strategy stimulate pupil ownership of learning?

You will find it helpful to think of each lesson as a learning opportunity for yourself. To make this effective you will need to analyse carefully what you do and consider how you can modify your teaching and aspects of the learning environment to improve pupils' learning. You should consider:

- the lesson plan you prepared and the extent to which it was implemented in the classroom;
- your performance during the lesson and the changes you had to make;
- your evaluation of the lesson in terms of pupils' learning.

Remember, it may not be the format of your input that is the underlying issue. Wet and windy days, following on from PE or games, Friday afternoons – all have an influence. Some say the moon has too! This process is a form of action research and a tool commonly used in CPD work.

You need to be focusing on the learning rather than the common student teacher failing of solely focusing on your performance. So for a start you need well defined learning objectives for your lessons and clear, measurable assessment activities. You need to record evidence of success (or failure) as proof for your professional development portfolio or similar. There are three levels of evaluation you need to consider:

- *Immediate*, where evidence of a misconception is detected during a session and you can see a way of curing the problem straight away. This is a change in your current lesson plan and needs to be noted.
- *For this cycle*, where something has not worked and you need to correct it for next lesson. This is a change in the plans for your unit of work and needs to be noted.
- *For the next teaching cycle*, where you realise that you could have done something in a more effective way. This needs to be noted promptly or you will not remember next time.

It is important that you learn to stand back from yourself and take any mentor criticism as supportive and developmental. In most cases as you develop as a teacher you will be able to predict the comments that will be made by an external observer. You will find that you have the opportunity to learn quite fast during your period of school experience when you are teaching the same topic to different classes in the same year group.

It is essential that you critically assess the events that happen within your classroom. As a student this should be in a very formal structured way, but as you mature you will be able to use your previous experience to develop shorthand ways of undertaking this analysis.

Education and specifically ICT education is always subject to change – new software and operating systems at one level, through to the introduction of Key Skills and the KS3 National Strategy for ICT. You must be prepared for this and the ensuing academic debate such changes inspire.

TAKING RESPONSIBILITY

It will not be many months before you are a qualified teacher working with your own classes and you need to take responsibility for your own performance as a provider of learning. At the end of your initial teacher education course you will complete a career entry profile and will identify targets for your future learning.

Throughout your placements you will have been set or have negotiated targets to do with your teaching. It may be helpful to take the SMART approach to your own targets:

- *Specific*. Keep targets small and well defined.
- *Measurable*. If it cannot be measured it cannot show an improvement.
- *Achievable*. It must be in your power to solve or sort.
- *Realistic*. Can it be done with your current resources (knowledge, time, hardware)?
- *Timely*. It should be possible to do now and within a defined time period.

Task 12.4 SMART targets

Look at a target you have recently been set and complete a grid like the one below for it.

Target	
How will you measure success?	
Are there aspects that will need help from others?	
What resources do I need and have I access to them all?	
Deadline	

Your Career Entry Profile (CEP), completed as you finish your studies, will list four areas of strength and four areas in need of development. These targets will have been negotiated with your mentors and tutors. The CEP copy you get will go into your first appointment with you and will form the basis of your induction year training programme.

Examples of development needs could include:

- additional experience of PSHE and citizenship work;
- experience of summative assessment Key Stage 3;
- guidance on marking GCSE project work;
- further opportunities to work with SEN pupils, IEPs and the SENCO;
- network management training.

They are intended to be developmental rather than highly critical. You have passed the criteria to become a teacher, and your identification of needs should enable your employing school to structure the support they can give to you.

PROFESSIONAL COMMUNICATION

Although ICT department teams are getting larger in many schools you may still find yourself working in a team of one or two subject specialists. You need to ensure that you do not become isolated.

An idea would be to try to set up a discussion list or conference for your colleagues on your ITE course so that you can remain in contact when you start teaching and continue as a self-help group. There are several Internet companies that offer such a service at no cost (but with some advertising included).

Task 12.5 Continuing professional development

Talk to members of the ICT department or team in your placement school. When did they last have an opportunity of professional development? How was it funded? How do they keep their skills and ideas current?

One method of getting this support is to maintain membership of professional bodies and subject associations. Besides the production of useful magazines and journals, many of these have an up-to-date web presence (with access to teacher created resources) and some will offer access to mail lists where you can ask for help and share ideas. Most offer annual conferences and some are now branching into online electronic conferencing as well.

Task 12.6 Subject associations and other support

BCS British Computer Society www.bcs.org.uk (look for 'schools')
ACITT Association for ICT in Education www.acitt.org.uk
CEG Computer Education Group www.ceg.org.uk
BECTA British Education and Communications Technology Agency www.becta.org.uk

Visit the websites of some of these. Try to decide how useful they are. Other sites are run by individuals or small groups. Take a look at www.theteacher.freeserve.co.uk and www.icteachers.co.uk.

Your local LEA will have an advisory team and you will normally need to look in your authority's 'bulletin' to find the events and courses they are offering. Attending these events will help you build up a local network of contacts.

The popular nature of IT means that ICT specialists have access to many monthly computer magazines. Titles such as *Personal Computer World* and *PC Advisor* often contain useful material that can spark off an idea for an activity. The software on the cover disk can also provide opportunities for extending your own skills and stretching those of some of your learners.

At a more academic level many of the journal publishers publish full text versions of their journals on the web. Indeed, many conference proceedings are often published this way, giving you an opportunity to access leading edge ideas. A web search using the key terms you are interested in will frequently lead to useful results. (See books like Cooke, 1999, for helpful guidance on successful web searching.) Some journals are available only on (often expensive) subscription, so you may need to visit a university library to gain access. Useful titles include:

- *Computers and Education*
- *Journal of Computer Assisted Learning* (JCAL)
- *Journal for IT in Teacher Education* (JITTE – soon to become *Technology, Pedagogy and Education*)
- *Association for Learning Technology Journal* (ALT-J)

In addition many other academic education journals will contain useful articles. For example, e-learning is a pervasive theme across most subject areas.

Task 12.7 Finding out

Use the Internet to locate: the current thinking on the 'digital divide' (the gap between those with and without computer or Internet access at home) and how schools can compensate for this; the ideas and current practice in the use of the school intranet as a method of communicating with parents. Summarise your findings.

You also need to keep aware of any new classroom resources that become available. Many book publishers have representatives who visit schools and you should make sure you take advantage of this. Publishers also send out catalogues and you can obtain inspection copies of anything that you feel may be useful.

PROFESSIONAL DEVELOPMENT FOR OTHERS

Another aspect of the work of an ICT teacher in a secondary school is that of providing INSET. This is a unique aspect of the subject. Sometimes it will be as simple as casual 'corridor conversations' explaining how to carry out certain functions. This type of *ad hoc* support is vital to the efficient running of the ICT system and may be all that some teachers require. However, it is often appropriate to provide planned support to a teacher or department to enable them to use ICT resources as part of their teaching.

Planning for the teaching of peers should be no less rigorous than planning for the teaching of pupils. With colleagues the curriculum is normally defined by the audience and it will be necessary to negotiate and clarify exactly what they hope to achieve. Even so, the needs may change during the process. The same critical reflection should also take place after each session and it is good practice to get some sort of formal feedback from the learners too.

The stages of the process become:

- Have a preliminary discussion of needs with learners (all, individually).
- Refine those ideas into a manageable unit and define a context.
- Revisit the learners with your plans for approval.
- Refine planning and develop resources.
- Carry out the sessions with reflection and feedback after each.
- Carry out a final holistic summative evaluation.

Although you will normally be helping enthusiastic learners, sometimes it will be necessary to support the more reluctant ICT user. The key here is to start small with some aspect of ICT that they can readily see will make their life easier (even if this is beyond the initial negotiated curriculum).

There may well be an expectation that you will work with other subject teachers to implement some of the school's ICT strategy. It is common for subject areas to have responsibility for certain aspects of the ICT curriculum although the implementation of the KS 3 strategy for ICT in English schools may reduce much of this.

> **Task 12.8 Supporting ICT in other subjects**
>
> Consider your experience of working with other subjects to deliver ICT as part of their teaching. What were the main issues that you needed to address? Did you have to provide 'technical' support? Were the ICT learning outcomes overt and were pupils' achievements mapped against them? If you have had no such experience, talk this over with a colleague who has.

SUMMARY

Much of your professional development as an IT teacher will be self-supported. You will also be seen as a support resource for others. You will need to build space for this into your life (and hopefully work load). Maintaining links with other colleagues and professional associations as well as involvement in online conferences and mail lists will be important strategies for you to follow. As you become involved in exam work good opportunities for personal development will be offered by the examination boards.

FURTHER READING

Baumann, A., Bloomfield, A. and Baughton, L. (1997) *Becoming a Secondary School Teacher*, London: Hodder & Stoughton. Takes an approach to development as a teacher based on the processes of reflection and action research.

Capel, S., Leask, M. and Turner, T. (1996) *Starting to Teach in the Secondary School*, London: Routledge. A companion volume to *Learning to Teach in the Secondary School* which deals with issues faced during the transition from initial teacher education to the full role of a teacher.

Appendix
Minimum competences related to subject-specific knowledge and understanding for trainees to teach ICT

From a scheme by Teresa Farran, Liverpool John Moores University

The trainee must have the required knowledge and appropriate understanding to be able to teach and assess each of these aspects within the National Curriculum for Information Technology at Key Stage 3, for GCSE at Key Stage 4 PoS and for non-advanced post-16 courses.

Ref.	Competence	Range

1 Systems analysis and solving a problem using IT

Ref.	Competence	Range
1.1	Understand the purposes for which IT systems are used. Describe processing activities, and IT methods used to implement them	Manipulation, sorting, selecting, calculation, interrogation, repetition, merging volumes of data, accuracy
1.2	Describe and establish the user information needed to initiate a feasibility study to solve a given problem	Purpose, description of present system, expectations, constraints

1.3	Explain and perform the stages of systems analysis to solve a given problem	Feasibility analysis, problem statement, investigation, recording, reporting. Produce relevant algorithms
1.4	Describe and produce analysis documentation to solve a given problem	Systems flow charts, data flow diagrams, DFDs, process specification, testing, user guide, evaluation report
1.5	Describe and produce the elements of a system specification as a solution to a given problem	Input specification, output specification, process specifications, resources, constraints

2   Knowledge of applications of IT

2.1	Investigate and analyse industrial IT systems	Considering the limitations of IT systems, difficulties, advantages. Process control, robotics, environmental control, traffic control
2.2	Investigate and analyse commercial IT systems	Consider the limitations of IT systems, difficulties, advantages. For instance an MIS: library/school, EPOS, EFT, stock control, payroll
2.3	Simulations	Difficulties, advantages, appropriate situations
2.4	Artificial intelligence and expert systems	Purpose, nature, use and significance

3 Legal aspects and social effects of IT

3.1	Investigate the safety, data integrity and security requirements of a data handling agency	Data validation and verification, software and data misuse, data protection legislation, codes of practice, disaster planning, data security and integrity, malpractice, copyright, back-ups
3.2	Investigate the legal and security issues related to the use of a WAN and the Internet	Malpractice, data security and integrity, viruses, system security, audit requirements
3.3	Investigate the health and safety issues related to working with IT equipment	Eye strain, radiation, stress, ergonomic hazards

| 3.4 | Investigate the effects on society of the growth of IT systems | In business, manufacturing, industry, commerce, the home and education, employment issues, equal opportunities, patterns of work |

4 Structuring and finding information: databases, hypertext

4.1	Understand and create a relational database as a solution to a given problem	Data consistency/redundancy / independence, file organisation, DBMS, primary and secondary keys, storage structures, data input forms, queries and reports
4.2	Interrogate a database using complex queries	Complex combinations of logical operations – AND, OR, XOR, NOT. Sorting, searching. Interpreting information
4.3	Undertake file maintenance activities on an established database	Amending, deleting, appending, data entry
4.4	Describe and evaluate the use of the WWW within the setting of an educational experience	Research, interrogate the web, download files, save images, access educational sites
4.5	Perform systematic search methods to obtain accurate and relevant information from a range of sources. Consider the limits and constraints of IT tools and sources	Simple and complex searches. CD-ROMs, web search engines
4.6	Using an authoring package create a simple website which displays awareness of the structure of HTML	Images, tags, links, files, HTML

5 Developing and presenting ideas: graphics, word-processing, DTP, presentations

| 5.1 | Process commercial documents | Templates, full range of business documents in a corporate style, use software tools, accuracy and security checks |
| 5.2 | Process presentational and technical graphic designs | Graphic type, purpose, context, content, dimensions, image and page attributes |

5.3   Use IT for a presentation activity   Produce and evaluate a slide show, web page, for a specific educational purpose

5.4   Combine the use of several application packages to produce a whole solution to a given problem and evaluate the effectiveness of this solution   Word processor, spreadsheet, database, DTP, web authoring

6   Communications and networking including the use of the Internet in education

6.1   Awareness of distributed systems and the benefits and use (where appropriate) of network services   E-mail, conferencing, bulletin boards, file transfer, direct interaction, technical services

6.2   Describe and connect the system components required for data transfer   DTE, connectors, software, cabling. Data transmission methods

6.3   Describe the types and topologies of networks and data flow control methods   LAN, WAN (public and private), ring, star, bus, mesh, reservation, contention

6.4   Describe standards for electronic communications, protocol parameters and modes of electronic communication   Data representation, transmission rates, flow control, data bits, start/stop bits, parity, terminal modes, transmission modes

7   Control and modelling including spreadsheets, automated procedures

7.1   Investigate and explain the purposes of different computer models   Simulation, prediction, gaming, 3D representation

7.2   Design, construct and evaluate the accuracy and effectiveness of a spreadsheet computer model by use of 'what if' scenarios. Explore the model with a number of variables in order to detect patterns and relationships   Input, calculations, graphs, constraints, variables, cost, speed, accuracy, flexibility. Quantitative and qualitative data. Absolute and relative referencing, built-in and user defined functions and automated interface

7.3   Investigate the production of automated procedures   Plan, develop, test and modify. Macros in word processing, spreadsheets, databases. Links in HTML

7.4	Design, implement, test and evaluate a logo computer program for a given specification	Process, output, ease of use, learning opportunities
7.5	Develop a control system according to a specification, explain the use of feedback and evaluate its effectiveness	Use of different sensors, processors, output devices, schematic diagram, feedback loop, efficiency, accuracy, alternatives

8   Technical competence to manage IT equipment and networks effectively within a schools context

8.1	Understand the purpose and significance in terms of performance of the various hardware components in an IT system	Processor, cache, RAM, ROM, hard drive, floppy drive, input devices
8.2	Describe the categories of software and their purposes	Operating systems, utilities, GUIs, programming languages translators, generic packages, subject-specific applications, application generators
8.3	Set up a specified system for use. Troubleshoot any common problems encountered	Connect hardware components together, configure software, install software, replace components, upgrade
8.4	Manage the use of a network	Install new users, undertake file management activities, modify the access rights of others

References

ACAC (1996) *Consistency in Teacher Assessment: Exemplification of Standards*, Cardiff: ACAC

Babbage, K. J. (1998) *High Impact Teaching: Overcoming Student Apathy*, Lancaster PA: Technomic.

Barton, R. (1997) 'How do computers affect graphical interpretation?' *School Science Review* 79, 55–60

Baumann, A., Bloomfield, A. and Baughton, L. (1997) *Becoming a Secondary School Teacher* London, Hodder & Stoughton

Ben-Ari, M. (2001) 'Constructivism in Computer Science education', *Journal of Computers in Mathematics and Science Teaching* 20, 45–73

Birnbaum, I. (1989) *IT and the National Curriculum: some fundamental issues*, Doncaster: Resource

Birnbaum, I. (1990) 'The assessment of IT capability', *Journal of Computer Assisted Learning* 6, 88–97

Black, P. and Wiliam, D. (1998) *Inside the Black Box*, http://www.pdkintl.org/kappan/kbla9810.htm (25 October 2001)

Bourne, R., Davitt, J. and Wright, J. (1995) *Differentiation: taking IT forward*, Coventry: NCET

Bradley, R. (1999) *Understanding Computer Science for Advanced Level*, London: Nelson Thornes

British Computer Society Schools Committee Working Party (eds) (2002) *A Glossary of Computing Terms*, tenth edition, Harlow: Addison-Wesley

Brophy (1981) 'Teacher praise: a functional analysis', *Review of Educational Research* 51 (1), 5–32

Brown, J. S., Collins, A. and Duguid, P. (1995) 'Situated cognition and the culture of learning', in P. Murphy, M. Selinger, J. Bourne and M. Briggs (eds) *Subject Learning in the Primary Curriculum*, London: Routledge/Oxford University Press

Butler, R. (1987) 'Task-involving and ego-involving properties of evaluation: effects of different feedback conditions on motivational perceptions, interest and performance', *British Journal of Educational Psychology* 79 (4), 474–82

Butler, R. (1988) 'Enhancing and undermining intrinsic motivation: the effects of task-involving and ego-involving evaluation on interest and performance', *British Journal of Educational Psychology* 58, 1–14

Capel, S., Leask, M. and Turner, T. (1996) *Starting to Teach in the Secondary School*, London: Routledge

Capel, S., Leask, M. and Turner, T. (2001) *Learning to Teach in the Secondary School*, London: Routledge

CCW (1990) *Information Technology in the National Curriculum: Non-statutory Guidance for Schools*, Cardiff: Curriculum Council for Wales

Christopher, D. (2000) *Computing Projects in Visual Basic*, Ipswich: Payne-Gallway

Coley, A. M., Gale, M. T. and Harris, T. A. (1994) 'Effects of gender role identity and experience on computer attitude components', *Journal of Educational Computing Research* 10 (2), 129–37

Cooke, A. (1999) *A Guide to finding Quality Information on the Internet*, London: Library Association

Culley, L. (1988) 'Girls, boys and computers', *Educational Studies* 14 (1), 3–8

Deadman, G. (1997) 'An analysis of reflective writing within a hypermedia framework', *Journal of Computer Assisted Learning* 13, 16–25

DES/WO (1990) *Technology in the National Curriculum*, London: Department of Education and Science/Welsh Office

DfEE (1998) *Survey of Information and Communications Technology in Schools 1998*, London: Department for Education and Employment

DfEE (1999) *Information and Communication Technology: the National Curriculum for England*, London: DfEE

DfEE (2001) *Learning and Teaching: a Strategy for Professional Development*, London: DfEE

DfES (2001a) *Key Skills*, http://www.nc.uk.net/LACcs_keyskill.html (1 December 2001)

DfES (2001b) *Key Stage 3 Scheme of Work for ICT*, http://www.standards.dfee.gov.uk/schemes/ict2_pdf/ (1 December 2001)

DfES/BECTA (2001a) *ImpacT2: Emerging Findings from the Evaluation of the Impact of ICT on Pupil Attainment*, London: DfES

DfES/BECTA (2001b) *Using ICT to enhance Home–School links*, London: DfES

Downes, T. (1997) 'The computer as a toy and tool in the home: implications for teacher education', in D. Passey and S. Samways (eds) *Information Technology: Supporting Change through Teacher Education*, London: Chapman & Hall

Doyle, S. (2001) *Information Systems for You*, third edition, London: Nelson Thornes

Estyn (2000) *The Annual Report of H. M. Chief Inspector, 1998–99*, Cardiff: Estyn

Estyn (2002) *The Annual Report of H. M. Chief Inspector, 2000–01*, Cardiff: Estyn

Evans, P. (2001) *GCSE Information and Communication Technology*, second edition, Ipswich: Payne-Gallway

Facer, K., Furlong, J., Sutherland, R. and Furlong, R. (2000) 'Home is where the hardware is: young people, the domestic environment and "access" to new technologies', in I. Hutchby and J. Moran-Ellis (eds) *Children, Technology and Culture*, London: Falmer

Freeman, R. and Lewis, R. (1998) *Planning and Implementing Assessment*, London: Kogan Page

Fullan, M. (1991) *The New Meaning of Educational Change*, London: Cassell

Galton, M., Gray, J. and Rudduck, J. (1999) *The Impact of School Transitions and Transfers on Pupil Progress and Attainment*, London: HMSO

Goldstein, G. (1997) *Information Technology in English Schools: a Commentary on Inspection Findings, 1995–96*, London: Office for Standards in Education

Good T. L. and Grouws D. A. (1975) *Process–Product Relationships in Fourth Grade Mathematics Classrooms*, report No. NE-G-00-0-0123 for the National Institute of Education, Columbia MO: University of Missouri

Goodson, I. F., and Mangan, J. M. (1995) 'Subject cultures and the introduction of classroom computers', *British Journal of Educational Research* 21 (5), 613–28

Hammond, M. and Mumtaz, S. (2001) 'How trainee teachers of IT approach teaching their subject', *Journal of Computer Assisted Learning* 17, 166–76

Hargreaves, A. (1994) *Changing Teachers, Changing Times: Teachers' Work and Culture in the Postmodern Age*, London: Cassell

Heathcote, P. M. (1999a) *A-level ICT*, second edition, Ipswich: Payne-Gallway

Heathcote, P. M. (1999b) *Successful IT Projects in Excel*, Ipswich: Payne-Gallway

Howe, J. (1983). 'Towards a pupil centered classroom', in D. Walker, J. Nisbet and M. Hoyle (eds) *Computers in Education*, London: Kogan Page

Kennewell, S. (2001) 'Using affordances and constraints to evaluate the use of ICT in teaching and learning', *Journal of Information Technology and Teacher Education* 10, 101–16

Kennewell, S. and Selwood, I. (1997) 'The professional development needs of secondary school IT co-ordinators', *Journal of Information Technology in Teacher Education* 6 (3), 339–56

Kennewell, S., Parkinson, J. and Tanner, H. (2000) *Developing the ICT Capable School*, London: RoutledgeFalmer

Kerry, T. (1998) *Questioning and Explaining in Classrooms*, London: Hodder & Stoughton

Kyriacou, C. (1997) *Effective Teaching in Schools*, second edition, Cheltenham: Stanley Thornes

Lambert, D. (1994) *Differentiated Learning*, London: Institute of Education

Lave, J. (1988) *Cognition in Practice*, Cambridge: Cambridge University Press

Lave, J. and Wenger, E. (1991) *Situated Learning: Legitimate Peripheral Participation*, Cambridge: Cambridge University Press

Leask, M. (ed.) (2001) *Issues in Teaching using ICT*, London: RoutledgeFalmer

Leask, M. and Meadows, J. (2000) *Teaching and Learning with ICT in the Primary School*, London: Routledge

Leask, M. and Pachler, N. (1999) *Learning to Teach using ICT in the Secondary School*, London: RoutledgeFalmer

Lovegrove, N. and Wilshire, M. (1997) *The Future of Information Technology in UK Schools*, London: McKinsey

Mevarech, Z. (1997) 'The U curve process that trainee teachers experience in integrating computers into the curriculum', in D. Passey and B. Samways (eds) *Information Technology: Supporting Change through Teacher Education* (pp. 46–51), London: Chapman & Hall

Muijs, D. and Reynolds, D. (2001) *Effective Teaching: Evidence and Practice*, London: Paul Chapman

Mumtaz, S. (2001) 'Children's enjoyment and perception of computer use in the home and the school', *Computers and Education* 36, 347–62.

NCC (1990) *Non-statutory Guidance: Information Technology Capability*, York: National Curriculum Council

NCET (1996) *Delivering Capability in IT*, Coventry: National Council for Educational Technology

NCET (1998) *IT Coordination in Secondary Schools*, Coventry: National Council for Educational Technology

Newton, D. (2000) *Teaching for Understanding*, London: RoutledgeFalmer

Ofsted (1995) *Information Technology: a Review of Inspection Findings, 1993–94*, London: Office for Standards in Education

Ofsted (1999) *Standards in the Secondary Curriculum, 1997–98: Information Technology*, London: Ofsted

Ofsted (2001a) *Good Teaching: Effective Departments*, London: Ofsted

Ofsted (2001b) *Subject Reports, 1999–2000: Secondary Information Technology*, London: Ofsted

Ofsted (2002) *HMCI Annual Report, 2000–01*, London: Ofsted

Owen-Jackson, G. (ed.) (2000) *Learning to Teach Design and Technology in the Secondary School: a Companion to School Experience*, London: RoutledgeFalmer

Pachler, N. (1999) 'Linking school with home use', in M. Leask and N. Pachler (eds) *Learning to Teach using ICT in the Secondary School*, London: RoutledgeFalmer

Papert, S. (1980) *Mindstorms: Children, Computers and Powerful Ideas*, Brighton: Harvester

Papert, S. (1996) *The Connected Family: Bridging the Digital Generation Gap*, Atlanta GA: Longstreet Press

Parkinson, J. (1994) *The Effective Teaching of Secondary Science*, London: Longman

Pollard, A. and Triggs, P. (1997) *Reflective Teaching in Secondary Education: a Handbook for Schools and Colleges*, London: Cassell

QCA (1998) *Primary Schemes of Work: IT*, London: Qualifications and Curriculum Authority

QCA (1999) *Information Technology in the National Curriculum*, London: Qualifications and Curriculum Authority

QCA (2001a) *Assessment for Learning*, http://www.qca.org.uk/ca/5-14/afl/ (1 December 2001)

QCA (2001b) *Using Assessment to raise Achievement in Mathematics*, http://www.qca.org.uk/ca/5-14/afl/afl_maths.pdf (1 December 2001)

Russell, T. (2001) *Teaching and Using ICT in Secondary Schools*, London: David Fulton

Salomon, G. and Globerson, T. (1987) 'Skill may not be enough: mindfulness in learning and transfer', *International Journal of Educational Research* 11 (6), 623–37

Schagen, S. and Kerr, D. (1999) *Bridging the Gap? The National Curriculum and Progression from Primary to Secondary School*, Slough: NFER

Schön, D. (1991) *The Reflective Practitioner: how Professionals think in Action*, Aldershot: Arena

Selinger, M. (2001) 'Learning information and communications technology skills and the subject context of learning', *Journal of Information Technology and Teacher Education* 10, 143–56

Selwyn, N. (1997) 'The effect of using a computer at home on students' use of IT', *Research in Education* 58, 79–81

Selwyn, N. (1999) 'Differences in educational computer use: the influence of subject cultures', *Curriculum Journal* 10 (1), 29–48

Smith, A. (1998) *Accelerated Learning in Practice*, London: Network

Smith, H. (1999) *Opportunities for Information and Communication Technology in the Primary School*, Stoke on Trent: Trentham

Smith, M. (1991) 'Curriculum models for the effective delivery of information technology capability in secondary schools', *Computer Education* 69, 2–5

Smith, M. (1995) 'The IT audit', in B. Tagg (ed.) *Developing a Whole-school IT Policy*, London: Pitman

Stevenson, D. (1997) *Information and Communications Technology: an Independent Inquiry*, London: Independent ICT in Schools Commission

Sutherland, R. (1992) 'Thinking algebraically: pupil models developed in Logo and a spreadsheet environment', in E. Lemut (ed.) *Cognitive Models and Intelligent Learning Environments for Learning Programming* (pp. 276–95), Berlin: Springer

Sutherland, R., Facer, K., Furlong, R. and Furlong, J. (2000) 'A new environment for education? The computer in the home' *Computers and Education* 34, 195–212

Tanner, H. F. R. (1991) 'The information technology curriculum and Mathematics', *Computer Education* 69, 7–11

Tanner, H. F. R. (1992) 'Teacher assessment of mathematics in the National Curriculum at Key Stage 3', *Welsh Journal of Education* 3 (2), 27–34

Tanner, H. F. R. and Jones, S. A. (1994) 'Using peer and self-assessment to develop modelling skills with students aged 11 to 16: a socio-constructive view', *Educational Studies in Mathematics* 27, 413–31

Torrance, H. and Prior, J. (1998) *Investigating Formative Assessment: Teaching Learning and Assessment in the Classroom*, Buckingham: Open University Press

TTA (1998) *The Use of ICT in Subject Teaching: Expected Outcomes for Teachers*, London: Teacher Training Agency and Department of Education

Wardle, H. (1998) 'The way forward: IT secondary/primary liaison', *Computer Education* 90, 8–12

Wellington, J. (2001) 'Exploring the secret garden: the growing importance of ICT in the home', *British Journal of Educational Technology* 32 (2), 233–44

Wiliam D. (1999) 'Formative assessment in mathematics' 2 'Feedback', *Equals* 5 (3), 8–13

Wiliam D. (2000) 'Formative assessment in mathematics' 3 'The learner's role', *Equals* 6 (1), 19–22

Wilson, S., Shulman, L. and Richert, A. (1987) '"150 different ways" of knowing: representations of knowledge in teaching', in J. Calderhead (ed.) *Exploring Teachers' Thinking*, London: Cassell

WJEC (2000) *GCSE 2002: Information and Communication Technology*, Cardiff: Welsh Joint Education Committee

Wragg, E. and Brown, G. (1993) *Questioning*, London: Routledge

Index